**For the inside of the book:**

Big Business, Big Responsibilities makes a valuable contribution to both the debate and practice of responsible corporate leadership in an increasingly complex global operating environment. Written by three highly-regarded practitioners who are working at heart of the corporate sustainability agenda, the book provides a succinct overview of global challenges and operational barriers to change... Optimistic, yet grounded in the day-to-day realities of running a business, the authors offer a leadership agenda for the 21st Century Corporation and for the consumers, regulators, activists, executives, and above all employees, who are helping to drive this agenda forward. **Jane Nelson, Director, Corporate Responsibility Initiative, Harvard Kennedy School.**

I have believed for some time that big business need not be the sustainability villain, and that big business can bring about big outcomes. The examples in this book paint an encouraging picture of how far we have come. The book's themes of shared responsibilities, collaboration, trust, regulation and opportunity-not-risk are important messages for the future. **Janis Kong OBE, non-executive director Kingfisher plc and Portmeirion Holdings, board member of Visit Britain.**

This engaging book shows you how, and why, many large companies are leading the way on sustainability. Wales, Gorman and Hope have produced an entertaining and informative read that challenges both business and NGOs to raise their game on partnerships and collaboration. **Toby Webb, Founder and Managing Director, Ethical Corporation.**

The narrative of the Global Network Initiative – how three information technology companies came together with NGOs and other stakeholders to forge protections for human rights – is illustrative of the broader themes this book highlights: addressing corporate citizenship questions remains complex and unfinished work, but the way business approaches these questions is changing in important ways. **Chuck Cosson, Senior Policy Counsel, Microsoft.**

# Big Business, Big Responsibilities

## From Villains to Visionaries: How Companies are Tackling the World's Greatest Challenges

Andy Wales

Matthew Gorman

Dunstan Hope

palgrave
macmillan
ocn 502031109

First published 2010 by
PALGRAVE MACMILLAN

Palgrave Macmillan in the UK is an imprint of Macmillan Publishers Limited, registered in England, company number 785998, of Houndmills, Basingstoke, Hampshire RG21 6XS.

Palgrave Macmillan in the US is a division of St Martin's Press LLC, 175 Fifth Avenue, New York, NY 10010.

Palgrave Macmillan is the global academic imprint of the above companies and has companies and representatives throughout the world.

Palgrave® and Macmillan® are registered trademarks in the United States, the United Kingdom, Europe and other countries

ISBN 978-0-230-24395-8

This book is printed on paper suitable for recycling and made from fully managed and sustained forest sources. Logging, pulping and manufacturing processes are expected to conform to the environmental regulations of the country of origin.

A catalogue record for this book is available from the British Library.

A catalogue record for this book is available from the Library of Congress.

10  9  8  7  6  5  4  3  2  1
19  18  17  16  15  14  13  12  11  10

Printed and bound in Great Britain by
CPI Antony Rowe, Chippenham and Eastbourne

# Contents

## ACKNOWLEDGEMENTS

We would like to thank all of the committed 'everyday champions' (too many to mention) making business more sustainable that we've had the privilege of working with over the past eleven years. Your energy is inspiring and this book would not exist without you. And we would like to thank Jamie Allison, Amy Gorman and Jenny Wales for being hugely patient and supportive, and Jemima Kingsley for the encouragement.

The views expressed in this book represent those of the authors and not necessarily the organizations by which they are employed.

# WHY WE HAVE WRITTEN THIS BOOK

The three authors first met in 1998 as young students drawn together as part an intriguing experiment in education: the Forum for the Future 'Masters Degree in Leadership for Sustainable Development'. Based around work placements rather than classroom teaching, the aim of the course was – and remains – to create a generation of sustainability leaders creating change in various sectors of society: business, government, non-governmental organizations (NGOs), media and finance.

We had been attracted to the course for similar reasons. All three of us were seeking careers that enabled us to live the values that we believed in; all three of us wanted to do this not in the fringes of the economy but in its mainstream. We wanted to experience big business and discover how sustainability would fare when merged with the desire to make money.

Eleven years have passed and with that the experience and insights to test our original intentions. For Andy, four years were spent with the sustainability pioneers at textiles business Interface, three more years at the environmental services company Severn Trent and since 2007 he has worked at the global brewer SABMiller. For Matt, an internship with global consultancy Environmental Resources Management was followed by four years with Forum for the Future itself and then a move to BAA, the UK's leading airport operator. For Dunstan, five years in the sustainability team at British Telecommunications was followed by a move across the Atlantic to lead the Information and Communications Technology practice at Business for Social Responsibility (BSR) in San Francisco.

During this time we've had the privilege and opportunity to help tackle some of the world's toughest social and environmental problems. We've experienced up close business efforts on challenges as diverse as climate change, HIV/Aids and internet freedom. We've led board room discussions, advised a variety of CEOs and negotiated agreements between companies, governments and civil society organizations. We've devised and executed global business strategies, reviewed and improved company operations and made the case to investors. We've been a part of the burgeoning corporate responsibility agenda that has been transformed from a niche peculiarity when we first met to the mainstream profession that it is becoming today. But throughout this time we've tried to stay true to the original goal we set ourselves when embarking on these careers in the first place: to bring our values to the workplace while improving, not detracting from, the commercial success of our employers and clients.

So with more than 30 years between us in working to bring sustainability to life inside business, where do we stand on the responsibility of big business? Have we sold out, captured by the glamour of global corporations? Or have we become disillusioned, unable to create the change we were seeking?

The answer is that we stand in remarkably similar positions to where we started. Has big business changed for the better? Yes. Is the change going far enough? Not yet. And most importantly, what can we do about it? Continue to work with business to ensure that it creates, not destroys, value for society.

Throughout this book we tell stories and provide insights based on our real experiences working in the private sector over the past decade. We do so not as academics seeking to prove or disprove theories, or as commentators looking for the latest angle with which to tell a story. Rather, we have written this book to provide a perspective from a place that all too often remains silent in the corporate responsibility debate – those seeking to drive sustainability from inside the corporate world.

This is, at its heart, an optimistic book. We argue that companies succeed best in societies that succeed, and that businesses have a strong interest in supporting economic and social development and environmental protection. We have seen, and believe in, the potential of business to lead change and progress. But we know also that this potential is severely limited if it is undertaken in isolation from others. It is only through collaboration, shared learning and consensus building between business, government and civil society that we will attain the systemic change required to achieve sustainable development.

## Why do so many people think big business is the villain?

We are entering a period in which big global companies will come under ever greater scrutiny. The recent tumultuous economic events, the time it will take public finances to fully recover, and the questions being asked about how to prevent a catastrophic economic collapse happening again will all combine to make the coming decade a testing time for business. This will include any situation where businesses (and the people working for them) can be perceived as gaining unfairly at the expense of the rest of society, whether that is executive pay, tax policies, or use of scarce resources such as energy, food crops or water.

However, despite the sharper focus which the economic downturn has provided, the perceived value of big business to society in the public consciousness has been low for some time. The scandals of Enron and Worldcom in the last decade eroded trust in business, but even before then deep skepticism existed concerning how large companies operate, how they are owned and how they distribute the profits they earn. Big business has consistently come near the bottom in the 'most trusted institution' rankings of various global surveys, in sharp contrast with non-governmental organizations (NGOs), who usually come top.

We believe there are seven myths that together explain society's skeptical attitude towards business. These myths are all rooted in some form of truth, but have become exaggerated to the extent that they paint a dangerously misleading picture of big business and its role in society.

We also believe that these seven myths stand in contrast to five emerging realities that are increasingly driving big businesses to become more responsible. There are many good reasons why business has frequently been cast as the villain in the past, but these are becoming outdated, to be replaced by new realities that will increasingly place business in the role of the visionary in the creation of a sustainable future.

Throughout this book we provide examples of progressive companies which understand these new realities and are acting on them to create competitive advantage. However that is not to say that all big businesses are ready to be visionary. The extent to which companies integrate these new realities into their strategies will be one of the defining features of corporate success in the coming decades and those businesses which ignore them will find success more difficult to obtain.

These seven myths and five realities are themes that we will return to throughout this book.

## Seven myths: 'why big business is bad'

### Myth 1. All big companies abuse the planet and people

Since the 1970s campaigners have successfully increased society's awareness of our overuse of environmental resources and our abuse of the planet's ability to absorb pollution such as carbon dioxide. Similarly, campaigners have focused on social issues such as poverty, international development and how the wealth created by trade in basic commodities such as coffee, sugar and tea is distributed inequitably. After initially focusing predominantly on governments and encouraging them to solve problems with new laws and regulations, campaigners turned their efforts to the big businesses who directly use the resources, create the pollution or engage in trade.

Campaigners realized that companies were perhaps an easier target than governments, especially those with highly valued brands to protect. They used well communicated examples of child labor in Asian supply chains, discrimination against unions in Latin America and oil pollution in west Africa to build public support for higher standards of environmental protection and social welfare. The evidence they uncovered can be haunting: there are well documented and terrible cases of child labor, environmental damage and unethical business practices which have been deservedly exposed.

However, this awareness raising was (by necessity) based on a relatively small number of case studies of environmental abuse or unacceptable behavior towards people by big business. The effect of this awareness has been to build up a widespread and deep suspicion of the activities and motives of all big business: there is now a significant collective doubt concerning the way that business treats people and the environment – in all places, and at all times – when no one is looking. Perhaps even more important is the assumption that such malpractice is always intentional, that if there is a piece of environmental or social damage, then business made a deliberate choice to cause it.

The scale of the outrage and the understandable drive to expose business malpractice can lead us to under-explore the question of why malpractice takes place and, as we describe elsewhere in this book, underestimate the significant contribution business can make to solving real sustainability problems.

## Myth 2. Only profit motivates

The word that underpins many people's suspicion of big business is 'profit' and the assumption that good cannot come from a selfish profit motive.

Indeed, profit is a powerful driver within business, and is an important, but not the only, measure of competitive success. A senior executive's goals will usually, but not exclusively, focus on short-term profit, but that is not all that motivates them. Almost everyone wants to leave some form of legacy in business, whether that is building one of the world's biggest companies in a certain sector, or being known as the company that always innovates a new product first, or operating the most efficiently, or the recognition of becoming a business which is known for its contribution to broader society: different senior managers have different motivations. Many of the mergers and acquisitions that take place between big companies destroy value, not create it, yet such transactions continue to be encouraged. Why? Because the struggle for greatness is as much a part of the corporate psyche as hard cold profit numbers.

Beyond senior management motivation is even more diverse. Big business is full of caring, motivated people who enjoy working, making something, completing a process, doing a good job, working in teams with their colleagues. Scientific curiosity in research departments; communicators in marketing departments; due process lovers in audit teams: business contains a lot of great people doing great jobs for reasons that include but are not limited to money.

## Myth 3. Rich shareholders have all the power

Alongside the myth relating to profit this has been the myth of the 'shareholder', often depicted in campaigning circles as the anonymous wealthy person quaffing champagne in a private members' club, who is the sole beneficiary of the success of global business. Yet we are all shareholders: when our pension values decline and the costs of insurance policies increase because of a failure of economic confidence, it shows us all who the real losers are when big finance goes wrong. But there is a second layer of this myth, the perception that shareholders operate effective control of companies.

In economic theory this is called the principle-agent problem: managers acting as agents of the real owners of a company may have different motivations than if they themselves were the real owners. They have access to more detailed information on the company they are running than the owners, and this creates an imbalance of power. Long-term incentive schemes such as share options were developed as solutions to this problem, to align the motivation of managers with that of owners. However the agency problem for most public companies is amplified by the fact that there are two sets of agents between the activities of the company and the shareholders who actually own the shares: the company's managers and the managers of the investment fund.

This leads to a doubling of the detachment of control from those whose values should really be shaping the way that a company operates: the teachers, policemen, doctors, nurses and company employees themselves who between their pension funds, insurance policies and savings accounts actually own the stock.

So, far from being rich anonymous beneficiaries of company profits, most shareholders are actually normal people with little sense of where their pensions or savings are invested, benefiting from management practices and company behavior they may, or may not, condone.

## Myth 4. Business doesn't do any good

It is intriguing how a consumer or even an employee can simultaneously believe in the generic view that 'big business is bad' while quite happily consuming a product or service from a major global brand, or feeling quite contented in their employment. What's remarkable is that the amazing things that business does, such as innovation to create mobile phones and iPods – which enable joy, connection between people and real social value – are often seen as morally neutral. Because that's what business is expected to do: create things which people need and want.

There is some interesting psychology at play, which has been illustrated most vividly in the speed at which companies that were initially underdogs, such as Google or Facebook, can quickly become businesses whose previously 'good' intentions are widely doubted once they operate on a much larger scale and bump up against some of the difficult issues of our global society.

## Myth 5. Business runs the global show

There is a common statistic quoted that of the top 100 economies in the world, 29 are multinational businesses.[1] The fact that Exxon's economic value added is comparable to the value added of economies such as Pakistan or Chile is used as evidence to support the view that such businesses are so big, so wealthy, so powerful, that they have an unhealthy influence in global affairs.

It is true that when competing to host an investment in their region, local governments, and sometimes national governments, do make generous concessions to attract businesses and to create jobs, multiplier effects and increase long-term tax income. These measures may include temporary corporate tax reductions, low priced land, or low rates of income tax to attract corporate headquarters.

However, the perception that due to their sheer size business can influence policy as much as they are thought to is misleading. Governments are still very much in the prime role of making decisions and shaping the operating environment for business. The financial crisis of 2008–09 brought this into sharp relief because governments were the only institutions able to fund bail outs for banks, auto makers and other companies on the scale that was necessary. However, even before the financial crisis, you could have taken a look at political dynamics in Latin America, with its various anti-capitalist movements, or the way that the Chinese government shapes its domestic business environment, and concluded that even major global businesses do not have the power some suspect them of.

## Myth 6. Business never wants regulation

There is a general perception that business is always anti-regulation because it improves accountability and transparency and businesses don't like that. Yet one of the biggest changes in recent years has been in the tone of business engagement with new areas of regulation around environmental and social issues. Far from being opponents of regulation, a number of global businesses have become advocates for sensible early regulation to deal with issues such as climate change. Being proactive allows business to shape regulation in a way that solves the problem, such as reducing greenhouse gas emissions, but in a way that promotes economic growth, through mechanisms such as greenhouse gas cap and trade schemes. Effective regulation also creates level playing fields where leading businesses can be recognized for the early work they have undertaken, such as increasing recycling rates or reducing water pollution, whilst other laggards then have to catch up.

Increasingly business leaders talk openly about market failures, where externalities such as the cost of direct environmental pollution are not included in the price of a good or service. Another example is the use of scarce resources such as water, which may be under-priced compared to the real value they provide to society. The scale of such environmental impact is becoming so critical that business leaders are now prepared to speak out publicly, such as the recent statements by the chairman of Nestlé that the price of water used by farmers is too low.[2] The implication is that the farmers from whom his company buys their crops might have to pay more for the water they use, which presumably will have some knock on effect for Nestlé's input costs.

As long as regulation is efficient to implement, tackles an issue which business genuinely has control over, and applies equally to a particular industry without competitive disadvantage, then business may well be more positive about regulation than many believe.

## Myth 7. BIG is always bad

There is a whole stream of thought and behavior which says that 'local' is best, regardless of the wider consequences. This is represented by a diverse set of groups, most visibly brought together at demonstrations such as the Seattle World Trade Organization meeting in 1999. They fear or oppose globalization for a variety of reasons: the perceived cultural domination of the 'west' through global restaurant chains, music and TV channels; the 'unfair' global trade rules that they feel disadvantage poorer countries; and the way that global trends can occur with such energy that they can overtake small local communities who feel powerless in their onslaught.

Take the emergence of decent coffee shops, one of the major changes to shopping streets in the UK over the last 15 years. There are plenty of people who believe that the arrival in their neighborhood of a Starbucks cafe represents corporate domination. But before the advent of Starbucks, in many UK shopping streets you could only buy poor quality coffee in a not particularly attractive environment. This of course is why Starbucks has become such a success and the formula it pioneered in Seattle became attractive to consumers in many markets. Moreover, Starbucks has been able to use its size to very positive effect by developing new ethical standards for coffee sourcing, certainly better than many of their competitors who supply coffee for people to buy in supermarkets. There is a remarkable side effect of being so successful that whilst being welcomed with open arms by consumers, there is also an innate suspicion that a company must be doing things that are wrong.

Big should not instinctively be thought of as 'bad'. Of course we do need balance – a way of allowing big and small business to co-exist side by side, as often they are targeting different groups of consumers anyway. That is why well designed planning regulation is important to protect the nature of local neighborhoods.

### Introducing five emerging realities: 'why big business needs to be responsible'

This book steps beyond these seven myths to assess the con-tributions that big businesses are making to protect the planet, improve human welfare and protect freedoms. The authors have all worked with both businesses and NGOs throughout their careers and in many ways have a philosophical home closer to that of a campaign group rather than a typical multinational business. Yet we feel that the major contribution that business is making – and the greater contribution it can make – to tackle the challenges that society faces is significantly under-valued.

We believe that in recent years five new realities have emerged which mean that a major global business is now more likely to be leading calls for environmental protection rather than lagging behind them; to be promoting human rights than to trampling on them; and to be working with NGOs rather than against them. These are realities that we will return to through-out this book.

### Emerging Reality 1. Shared risks mean shared responsibilities

One of the most compelling arguments for companies under-taking action to protect the environment or promote social wellbeing is 'enlightened self-interest'. This philosophy has been developed in recent years to explain why a business might consider issues more broadly than just its immediate operational needs and short-term profitability. It has been applied in particular to why companies undertake activities in their local communities, realizing that they interact with their employees, their customers and often their regulators when they promote community activities. The 'enlightened self-interest' concept has also been used to explain why it is in a company's interest to promote good ecological management such as reducing energy use and pollution in order to lower costs and protect its informal 'social license to operate'.

However the enlightened self-interest approach has its limits. At its extreme it essentially states that a company will only care for a broader social or environmental issue if it can see and understand a clear and specific business benefit for the individual company. It is well suited to a well managed and stable economy: a situation where social services are well catered for and environmental regulation is clear and well enforced. In this context a company knows where it stands and it can make a greater contribution to social or environmental causes whilst knowing that government will do the 'heavy lifting'.

In contrast, we believe that on many issues companies are moving beyond a philosophy of enlightened self-interest to recognize that they are but one institution that faces shared risks and therefore shared responsibilities. One of the most important concepts in environmentalism is the 'tragedy of the commons'. In this dilemma, individuals acting rationally will continue to utilize a common resource for their own benefit to the point at which that resource is exhausted, with potentially catastrophic consequences for all users.

We argue that in fact it is the largest global companies – especially those that depend on scarce land or water resources such as food and beverage companies – that will first see and respond to new 'tragedies of the commons' in the coming decades. Some of the world's largest companies are leading projects to understand environmental resource scarcity and ensure that these resources are managed successfully to support generations to come. It is hard to make a case that it will always be in an individual company's best interests do this in all cases, given the uncertainty that remains regarding how scarce resources should be allocated, which is why this emerging reality represents a new philosophy of 'shared resources and shared risks'.

Good examples of this work include the Climate Group, an alliance of companies, local governments and academic institutions to promote action on climate change, and the 2030 Water Resources Group, a set of companies working with the International Finance Corporation and consultants McKinsey & Company to scope out the necessary investments to cope with the water scarcity projected by 2030 in many parts of the world.

### Emerging Reality 2. Today's challenges are best addressed through collaboration

Major companies are global organizations full of talented and skilled professionals, from engineers to salespeople, and from financiers to marketers. Yet the scale of sustainable development challenges we face today means that even these big global organizations do not have the breadth or depth of skills needed to deal with the challenges they will face. This is why partnerships are so important, because no institution can aim to manage the challenges of climate change, human rights or water scarcity alone.

Organizations such as the Worldwide Fund for Nature (WWF), that have traditionally developed philanthropic relationships with companies, are now being seen as vital partners who can help companies understand the sourcing risks they face from failure of eco-systems. Oxfam, which has historically focused on providing assistance to the poor and lobbying government to improve international aid, is now working with companies to help them understand how to maximize the development benefits of their activities.

Governments are also recognizing the value of partnerships by putting money into the private sector to support development. The Africa Enterprise Challenge Fund, established by the UK government's Department for International Development (DFID) amongst others, provides matched funding and loans to for-profit companies that want to expand their positive development impact.

This approach to partnerships is relatively new and companies, NGOs and governments are learning the opportunities and challenges of working together. There is interest in such approaches beyond a group of leading companies and it is possible that these partnerships will lead to greater and more significant links between these institutions, particularly businesses and NGOs.

## Emerging Reality 3. Being trusted has never been so important

It is almost a maxim now that global businesses need to have a clear and trusted reputation. This is not just for marketing purposes, but more it is connected to the deeply held belief, from the shop floor to the management suite, that what a business does day in day out is a good and valued thing for society. When companies are exposed as having abused human rights or attacked for undermining environmental standards, nowhere is it more keenly felt than internally. Surveys of recent university graduates regularly cite the perception of the social responsibility of a company as a major reason for choosing a particular business to work for and this remains an important issue once people get into their careers.

Companies also understand the value of a trusted reputation externally. If a company wants to grow in its operations globally then it needs to be trusted by governments, business partners and investors that it understands and respects the social and cultural priorities of that market This is much more critical now that the internet enables such rapid communication between disparate groups, now that video filmed on a mobile phone can be uploaded and shared globally in seconds. Major global companies are attuned to this and have put in place the controls needed to ensure that they understand and manage their environmental, social and economic impacts and that their subsidiaries and suppliers also have the same steps in place.

### Emerging Reality 4. Changes in public policy to address sustainability challenges will increasingly shape the business operating environment

Over the past ten years working within business we've witnessed the media interest in challenges such as climate change, human rights and water scarcity ebb and flow. But the reality is that these challenges are not going away. As we describe in Chapter 1, climate change is real and the impacts of water scarcity are increasingly being felt. And with this reality will come increasing intervention from governments wielding the three policy levers of tax, public expenditure and regulation to penalize, incentivize or instruct behavior change from business.

Action from government to address these global challenges is beginning to re-shape the regulatory and market context within which business operates and this trend is likely to accelerate as momentum for action grows within governments. However, the exact form of this intervention is still being shaped and leading businesses are beginning to recognize that it is far better to engage constructively in the co-creation of policy approaches that achieve sustainability outcomes consistent with business success, than to shout from the sidelines and be subject to poorly crafted legislation.

### Emerging Reality 5. The successful companies of tomorrow are treating sustainability as an opportunity for innovation, not as a risk to be mitigated

A decade ago addressing social and environmental challenges was frequently viewed by big business as solely an exercise in risk management. Here was a new set of threats, impacts and unknowns that needed to be identified, avoided, mitigated and deflected. Business was to carry on as normal, provided the right risk mitigation strategies were put in place; solutions to sustainability problems would be found elsewhere.

The contrast between this risk mitigation approach and the innovative approach taken by the leading businesses of today is stark. As we describe later in this book, an increasing number of businesses view these global sustainability challenges not just as risks to be mitigated but also as opportunities to drive innovation. The successful companies of tomorrow will not be those that carry on with business as usual, but those who view solutions to these global challenges as drivers of innovation and opportunities to develop the successful products of tomorrow. As Alcatel-Lucent's CEO Ben Verwaayen bluntly told his audience at BSR's annual conference in 2009, 'green is no longer a hobby… it's not just a lifestyle issue… green is a new source of creativity that will give everybody in every industry an opportunity to rethink the way we operate… a driver for innovation and new business models'.[3]

## Reality check

These five realities shape the operating environment of companies now and will do so into the coming decades. For different industries some of these emerging realities will be far more important that the others, but no business will be untouched by these changes. Whilst many big businesses do understand these realities and are responding rapidly, not all companies are in this progressive position: far from it. We must remember that business is of course not a unified group.

There are some companies whose only focus is to find, exploit or process oil reserves, for example, that have little interest in tougher carbon legislation to solve the climate crisis. However there are a number of very large businesses in that industry, most notably BP and Shell, who recognize that the oil industry must take a different approach and who have already been engaging with governments around the world for over a decade to seek to manage the climate crisis.

The big businesses who understand these five realities exist in all industries and are an increasingly vocal group. They exert influence over other companies through their leadership of industry bodies, through ensuring that their suppliers act progressively and through changing society's expectations of what being a responsible big business means. The pace at which the rest of business around the world follows the lead set by the group of leading big businesses will be critical in shaping our collective response to our shared sustainability challenges.

## Navigating this book

This book describes our experience of why and how business is stepping up to address global sustainability challenges in four separate sections.

First, we describe the scale of the social, environmental and ethical problems facing the world today, challenges that are increasingly shaping the landscape in which business operates. We set out why and how leading companies are responding to these challenges, and why this is increasingly done in collaboration with government and civil society. But knowing just how much still needs to be done, we also describe why reforms that are good for everyone can still be defeated by vested interests and how, despite the goodwill of many in big business, sensible changes can still be thwarted.

Second, we examine the connection between businesses and consumers. We consider how businesses can help consumers reduce their own environmental footprints and how companies and governments are even restricting consumer options ('choice editing') in the name of sustainability. We also describe how in both the virtual and real worlds, businesses can often find themselves in coalition with consumers in support of more proactive or responsible actions by governments.

Third, we address the question of who is driving this change. We describe how in certain emerging markets with weak civil society it is governments that are playing a strong role in shaping the actions of companies – but at the same time are bracing themselves for new waves of civil activism. By contrast, we describe how in more developed western markets an intriguing inter-play between CEOs and increasingly engaged employees ('everyday champions') is enabling innovation for sustainability and the development of more responsible approaches by big businesses.

Fourth, and finally, we set out our vision for a more responsible and sustainable future. We look back a generation to reflect on just how much business has been transformed in this time and consider what is within society's grasp in the coming decades.

# A challenging world with some unexpected heroes

## CHAPTER 1

# The scale of the challenge for change

## Why businesses must integrate environmental protection, social wellbeing and economic development into their business models to thrive

The global financial crisis that began in 2008 had at its roots a critical failure of central assumptions that underpinned many business models. One of these assumptions was the easy and continued access to cheap debt, which facilitated both the ballooning of sub-prime consumer debt and ambitious corporate finance deals. From UK bank RBS's expensive purchase of ABN Amro to Lehman Brothers' bullish approach to mortgages, the system depended on cheap debt to grease the wheels of continual growth.

The assumption that business will have continual access to cheap resources extends well beyond these financial instruments and into the environmental realm. Here a similar dynamic is at play, with environmental resources obtained and used by business at an unrealistically cheap price. Water is a good example: manufacturing, energy generation and agriculture all depend on an assumption of cheap and reliable access to clean water, yet the United Nations projects that by 2025 more than half of the world's population will live in areas of significant water shortages. Despite these trends, water remains under-priced and overexploited in many parts of the world that will desperately need more water in the coming years to feed their populations, grow their industries and improve their quality of life. We need a significant change in water efficiency around the world.

Carbon is another example. The stronger carbon emissions caps that are likely to emerge in the coming decades will radically alter some industries, including energy and metals, putting to an end their previous access to cheap energy. Businesses, non-governmental organizations (NGOs) and even governments are only just beginning to understand the extent of the changes we will see to big business as a result of environmental limits and the end of access to cheap environmental resources. Now is the time to review our current assumptions.

Nor is this necessary re-think restricted to environmental issues. For a long time there has been a polemical debate within the international community regarding whether international development is best assisted by overseas aid or by foreign direct investment (FDI). The two were seen as poles apart. The business community often saw overseas aid as at best a distraction from the real business of stimulating economic growth and at worst a honey pot for corrupt individuals in developing country governments. Meanwhile the overseas aid community had major doubts about the real development value of foreign investment and especially the enticements created to attract it such as free trade zones, tax breaks, and weaker labor laws. Yet in recent years it has become clear that neither foreign aid nor FDI will suffice on their own – nor will they succeed if they remain disconnected. Rather, much more positive opportunities can be created by using private investment, in partnership with the skills and financing of government aid agencies and the relationships and community understanding that NGOs can bring.

The changing environmental, social and economic contexts within which businesses operate inevitably lead to new ways of reaching customers, different sourcing strategies and ultimately a redefinition of business models. Those businesses which invest in understanding the changing world, adapting their businesses to it, and actively shaping the way that society responds to big issues such as climate change, water scarcity and poverty, will not only grow their profitability, but will also deliver a vast social dividend. This chapter considers the scale of the changes that are needed to protect the environment, reduce poverty and ensure that economies are more resilient.

## Shared risks mean shared responsibilities: challenges for the whole of society, including business

The Millennium Development Goals (MDGs), established in 2000, set a range of global social, environmental and economic targets to dramatically reduce poverty, improve gender parity and ensure more equitable access to education and healthcare. They include halving, between 1990 and 2015, the proportion of people in the world who suffer from hunger; halting and beginning to reverse, by 2015, the spread of HIV/AIDS; and halving, by 2015, the proportion of people without access to safe drinking water or sanitation.

There has been significant progress against some of these goals in certain parts of the world. In East Asia, especially China, the proportion of children who are underweight has more than halved between 1990 and 2006. It is likely that on a global level we will meet the target to reduce by half the proportion of people without access to clean drinking water. Again this is due in large part to progress in Asia. But equally there remain many outstanding targets, especially in sub-Saharan Africa. Every day nearly 7,500 people are infected with HIV and 5,500 die from AIDS, mostly in Africa.[1]

Much of the progress towards achieving the MDGs has actually been met not through development aid, but through the power of economic growth. China averaged 10% annual GDP growth between 2000 and 2008, whilst sub-Saharan Africa averaged nearly 5.9%, compared to an advanced economy average of 2.2%.[2] This growth is primarily driven by business, both national and multinational, in response to both domestic consumer demand and international trade.

The impact that one major business can have in an economy is startling. Work by Professor Ethan Kapstein at INSEAD business school uses government data to calculate the impact of specific value chains on economies. Kapstein's work for consumer products group Unilever revealed that in South Africa it contributes just under 1% of employment through its value chain.[3] His work for brewer SABMiller in Uganda revealed that for each job created at their subsidiary Nile Breweries, 100 jobs were supported in the wider economy.[4] Clearly the power of a consumer buying a product, whether a bar of soap or a bottle of beer, has major implications for employment, wealth generation and the public services that are funded through taxation of that wealth.

However, contributing to short-term GDP growth alone is not enough. Long-term growth is underpinned by improvements in education and skills, healthcare, gender empowerment and environmental protection. For many businesses it is the emerging and developing world where long-term growth lies, but to secure that growth businesses need to be committed to the broader development cause. This is not a philanthropic gesture but a long-term business case: a realization that business success is tied to the success of the country as a whole.

One way businesses can contribute is to recognize their position in the value chain as an opportunity to encourage development. This could be through extending their health programs for their own employees, such as HIV/AIDS prevention, to farmers, small suppliers and distributors of their products, as SABMiller has done. When it comes to improving business training, companies can view their supplier relationships not just as financial transactions, but as the opportunity to share skills to support the capability and sustainability of that supplier, not just for their business purposes for but the benefit of the broader market. If a business does not do this then growth may be limited, especially where governments lack capacity to deliver these services themselves.

### Shared risks mean shared responsibilities: We're hitting the environmental limits

Wealth generated through business generally comes with an environmental cost in the form of the resources used to create, package and transport these products and, if they are not recycled, the land used to bury the waste once they are done with. Our economy is oil dependent and climate change, rather than running out of oil, is likely to be the biggest driver for business change. The Intergovernmental Panel on Climate Change's (IPPC) 2007 report, the output of the largest collaboration and consensus process yet undertaken by scientists at a global level, concludes that there is a 90% certainty that climate change is occurring due to man made emissions. Businesses are involved in producing a significant proportion of these greenhouse gas emissions. Industry's direct emissions are only 19% of the global total, but it is the products made by businesses that are used for transportation (13%) and public and private energy supply (26%), and businesses are also major users of forestry products (17%).[5]

The IPPC projects a temperature increase of around 1.8–4 degrees Celsius this century based on business as usual. They also suggest that a temperature change of over two degrees is more likely to lead to dangerous climatic change, with significant increases in water scarcity, more intense weather events such as floods, significant loss of biodiversity (30% of species) and falling crop yields.

These impacts are far from peripheral for businesses. Agricultural land, transport infrastructure, energy availability, employee health and even consumer preferences are all going to be influenced by climate change and businesses need to understand this to survive this century. Sir Nicholas Stern, previously chief economist at the World Bank, led a major research project which concluded that without intervention the impact of climate change on global GDP would be a reduction of around 5–20% by 2050, whilst reducing emissions to prevent this would cost a mere 1% of GDP by 2050. Clearly this latter option is better for business in the long term.

However there will be short-term costs to adapt to a low carbon economy. Consulting firm McKinsey & Company, working with the Carbon Trust, a UK government agency tasked with encouraging low carbon business, has estimated the impact to 2020 for six major industrial sectors, from aluminium manufacture to consumer electronics, of measures to reduce greenhouse gas emissions. Their analysis suggests that for aluminium and automotive sectors up to 60% of annual cash flows are at risk, whilst for the brewing industry it is up to 15% and for consumer electronics below 10%.[6]

This climatic challenge may be the most urgent problem, and one that continues to be the focus of significant debate and discussion amongst national leaders, but other environmental issues are also critical. The world is living in a water bubble that is likely to burst, even without the challenge of climate change. Global demand for food, especially meat, as the population grows and gets wealthier in countries such as India and China, will lead to a significant increase in water use for irrigation. Agriculture already takes 70% of the world's freshwater use each year, yet groundwater is being over-abstracted in many places. Industry also needs water to grow, with 30% of freshwater in the United States being used by the power industry. At the same time domestic water use is increasing as people buy power showers, high pressure car hoses and dishwashers.

## Where does the wealth go? And are people treated properly?

There are also big questions regarding the equitable distribution of the wealth created by economic growth. Whilst soft drinks or beer are usually local products, manufactured locally for local consumption, there are other consumer goods which depend on global trade, whether agricultural goods such as coffee and cocoa beans from Africa, textiles from India or Pakistan or toys and consumer electronics from China. Often campaign groups highlight that only a very small proportion of the ultimate sale price goes to the growers or producers of the raw materials, with much greater proportions going to the trading 'middle men' and the processing and marketing companies.

This concern accounts for the rise of Fairtrade, a certification scheme that ensures that developing world producers of goods such as coffee, chocolate and sugar are paid reliable prices above the market average, that social conditions such as schooling for children are met and that labor rights are respected. Since the mid 1990s this movement has been growing in Europe and the United States, with sales of $1.6 billion in 2007, a 47% increase since 2006. Despite the recent downturn Fairtrade has continued to grow, with UK Fairtrade spending increasing by 44% to over £712m in 2008.[7] Figures for the year 2009 and beyond should show a further increase as mainstream brands such as Cadbury's Dairy Milk and Nestlé's Kit Kat switch to Fairtrade status, though overall these numbers remain a small portion of the overall marketplace.

There is also the issue of working conditions. In the 1990s there were a number of stories that hit the media regarding the quality of the working environment and labor rights in Asian supply chains for major clothing companies. Child and forced labor, poor health and safety conditions, pay below living wages, and bullying and harassment have all been documented and exposed. As a result a whole industry has bloomed with supply chain auditors undertaking audits across Asia to assess compliance with labor standards, to the point where suppliers complain of audit fatigue. Yet stories continue of those local suppliers who game the system, bully staff to return the 'correct' answers when asked by auditors and therefore the value of these audits has been called into question.

## The tipping point: when some businesses chose to lead

The clarion call on the environmental and social challenges identified above has generally been issued first by the campaign groups rather than business. They have played a critically important role for society in seizing new environmental science or evidence of social oppression and publicizing it to ensure that voters, employees and consumers are more aware of the impact that companies have. There are clearly trade-offs between the way we have been creating wealth and its environmental and social consequences, but until the advent of powerful NGOs in the last 30 years, business tended not to see its place as being aware of these trade-offs or responsible for resolving them. Whilst much of the original research comes from academics, the NGOs amplify their findings through targeted, creative and culturally resonant messaging. The success of the NGO campaign movement has been to ensure that businesses become aware of their 'externalities', whilst raising public expectation that they should take responsibility for them. In parallel a less effective campaign stream has been getting governments to force businesses to take account of these externalities through regulation.

The tipping point for business leadership on environmental issues became visible around 2002, at the World Summit on Sustainable Development in Johannesburg (WSSD). It was the ten year follow up from the Rio Earth Summit in 1992, the seminal summit from which much global environmental policy has since developed.

From the public perspective that summit was a rather low key affair, and very little came out of it. But while the tipping point wasn't particularly visible outside of the world of those who work on these issues within business, it was critical nonetheless. The preparations for that summit, with President Bush in the White House, very deliberately kept the topic of climate change out of the official discussion program for the summit. You would have expected that global businesses would have been happy with that: as major global polluters, you could argue that they stood to lose from a stronger global regime around carbon emissions. Yet some businesses, such as the UK-based oil major BP, felt differently enough to get on a stage with Greenpeace International in a packed side room of the summit and together call on governments to stop ignoring the real perils of climate change and bring it into the summit's discussions.

Their calls were ignored, but for the first time there was a visible alignment of businesses and NGOs together leading the debate and calling for governments to catch up. Behind the scenes many major US-based businesses were aghast that their colleagues in the corporate world would do such a thing and a split began to become visible between the businesses that really 'got it' – who understood that their long-term business success would only occur if society succeeded in dealing with the challenge of climate change – and those businesses that only thought short term.

The ground for this important event was laid earlier that year, when at the preparations for the WSSD in Montreux in spring 2002, one oil CEO sat in a room of 15 other CEOs from the energy, mining and chemicals sectors and challenged them that business had to begin to lead: it couldn't just react defensively to the emerging science on climate change, the global concern regarding poverty and health challenges such as HIV/AIDS. Business could and should do much more.

Since then the group of businesses calling for stronger action on climate change has grown dramatically, and those holding back the pack has dwindled. Most important has been the role that major US corporations have played, with increasing numbers of companies understanding what environmental and development campaigners have been telling them for decades: these concerns are real.

One of the most important organizations in changing the outlook of business in this way has been the World Economic Forum (WEF). Founded by Professor Klaus Schwab in 1970, the WEF brings together senior leaders from across government, business, NGOs, inter-governmental organizations, and academia to discuss the common problems facing the world. It's the place at which, for example, CEOs of pharmaceutical companies, health ministers, leading scientists and NGOs focused on disease eradication can come together and discuss how malaria, HIV/AIDS and other infectious diseases are being tackled and how they can work together better. Throughout the year at regional summits around the world, in addition to the annual meeting in January each year at Davos, Switzerland, these conversations take place not just on health but on climate change, innovation, development, peace, ethics and many other topics. The WEF also brings into these conversations a diverse range of people who will shape the world of the future, such as the Young Global Leaders, a community of 600 people from around the world who are leading change in their own fields, and a group of leading social entrepreneurs, who have a very different approach to running businesses.

The WEF offers a place for leaders to step outside of their organizations for a few days and think of the world in a new way, to listen to others who have a very different worldview, and to consider how the world's greatest challenges can be tackled together. Creating a place of such open conversations has taken time and patience and over the decades the approach of business has changed. On some issues, such as global water scarcity, it is the business leaders who are putting the issue on the agenda at Davos in a way that would not have been expected even five years ago. Primarily this is because the business case for engaging in these issues is changing.

There are some business leaders who care about these issues at a deep moral level: Ray Anderson, the well known chairman of Interface Inc, the commercial carpet company, was an early convert to the 'moral case' for business leadership in sustainability. He developed a new strategy for his company based on resource efficiency and closed loop manufacturing and set a goal for the business to be fully sustainable by 2020 – a stark contrast for a previously 'take-make-waste' petrochemical-based industry. Interface has worked hard down that road and its path hasn't always been easy, but it has made significant progress. Over time this vision and leadership from Interface has challenged the whole of their industry – customers, competitors and suppliers – to the point where commercial textiles as an industry is ahead of many other similar industries.

But for most business leaders it's not about the moral case. They can see an alignment of their business needs – to reduce costs, to protect their use of scarce resources, to grab new market opportunities, to improve reputation, to connect with new 'ethically minded' young employees – and the needs of the environment and society. This alignment has taken these issues mainstream within the business community, and a regular topic for board conversations at companies around the world: a situation uncommon even 20 years ago. They understand that to be a successful business in today's world means having a much broader view of the world and being prepared to think more creatively about how their business can grow whilst making a greater contribution to meeting the world's needs.

## The pace of change makes addressing sustainability challenges all the more complicated

One of the greatest sources for improved quality of life in recent years has been the pace of innovation. The internet, mobile phones, and portable digital music have all changed the way that consumers in both the developed and developing worlds live, work and socially interact, especially for younger consumers. In particular the advent of social networking sites has enabled global real time communities to be established, whilst search engines provide access to knowledge and opinion from around the world at a speed unthinkable even ten years ago.

Yet this pace of change also brings major challenges. Some of these challenges are relatively straightforward, relating to the increased environmental impact of digital lifestyles. Whilst some companies are investing in more efficient home appliances to reduce our emissions, others are rapidly developing new products which may well use more power. Plasma flat screen TVs may look amazing but use a lot more power, and home air conditioning may well become standard in the UK in the coming decades, a country that is traditionally thought of as rather chilly. The advance of technology always needs to take account of the environmental reality we live in.

More difficult though are the implications for the management of personal information and communications in the digital age. The United Nations Universal Declaration of Human Rights (UDHR) was adopted in 1948 and, while it has stood the test of time remarkably, is beginning to be tested in today's digital age. Take Article 12, which states that 'no one shall be subjected to arbitrary interference with his privacy, family, home or correspondence, nor to attacks upon his honour and reputation', or Article 19, which states that 'everyone has the right to freedom of opinion and expression [including the] freedom to hold opinions without interference and to seek, receive and impart information and ideas through any media and regardless of frontiers'. In the age of the internet, with massive growth in user generated content and an explosion of personal information moving from one legal jurisdiction to another, interpreting these human rights today raises all sorts of ethically difficult questions for companies hosting the information. As we describe in Chapter 6, companies are facing responsibilities on an entirely new scale when challenged with increasing demands from law enforcement agencies around the world to restrict access to content or to hand over personal information.

## Conclusion

The role of business in meeting today's consumer needs is critical, yet it is only in recent years that businesses have woken up to the environmental impact of their products and services. Equally, more and more businesses are understanding that to be successful in the future they need to be contributing to the wellbeing and development of the emerging and developing markets they are growing into, whether through education, skills or healthcare.

However business needs to go further. There is a much greater interest amongst governments, civil society leaders and consumers concerning what business can contribute to tackling the environmental and social challenges we face. Equally, staff within businesses are motivated by understanding that the way they do their jobs can make a real difference. However, as the next chapter describes, there is already much more going on in big business than many people – both within business and outside of it – might think.

## CHAPTER 2

# Changing course: how big business began to lead

Big business has historically been the *bête noire* of green and community pressure groups. That isn't surprising – there's a long roll-call of well documented cases of environmental damage and social injustice linked to industry, from the chemical leak at Bhopal in India in the early 80s, through the huge oil spill in the Prince William sound in Alaska at the end of that decade, to poor working conditions in the supply chains of some of the world's biggest retailers. And with NGOs successfully highlighting examples of corporate malpractice, the image of big business abusing both people and the planet in the name of profit has gained credence over recent decades.

But with the wake-up call of NGO campaigns ringing in their ears, big business is changing. Where once corporations were considered by many to be the villains, today a growing number of leading companies are integrating sustainability into their core business in increasingly sophisticated ways. What started out as simple brand protection in response to pressure group campaigns has become, for a growing number of companies, a proactive search for opportunities to improve social well-being and achieve corporate financial success at the same time. Tackling sustainability concerns is increasingly recognized by leading businesses as a driver of competitive advantage, and is being integrated into mainstream decision-making – from product development to marketing. And with that integration is unleashed a whole new world of pro-sustainability innovation, experimentation and energy.

It might seem surprising to some that big business is changing course. But we believe that leading companies are increasingly aware of the five 'emerging realities' we set out in the introduction. These companies understand that they will be negatively impacted by the scale of environmental and social challenges we face and so share in the responsibility of addressing them. In other words, they have come to realize that the challenges of climate change, human rights, poverty and water scarcity are not just real challenges for society – they are real challenges for big business too. But it is more than simply securing long-term access to scarce resources. In a world where consumers can feel overwhelmed by the environmental and social problems they are bombarded with through the media, there's a genuine competitive advantage for companies in differentiating their products and services and becoming the brand that consumers trust to 'do the right thing'. And there is a recognition by leading businesses that the scale of the sustainability challenge will require new ways of doing business and new products and services. As well as presenting a risk, social and environmental issues represent a real opportunity for innovation.

We believe that these drivers are increasingly powerful ones for big business. As a result, progress in the last decade on the big sustainability challenges we face – climate change, global development, resource depletion and human rights – has increasingly been achieved with big businesses, not despite them. There is a whole host of examples of changing corporate behavior, from different companies, sectors, countries and continents, which taken together mark a real shift in the way big business is doing business.

In this chapter we highlight some of those examples of changing corporate behavior. As we set out in this book, the move from 'villains to visionaries' isn't universal, and it certainly doesn't mean that business couldn't do more. But we believe that it points to a world in which, with the right public policy framework in place, big business can play a significant part in solving the world's toughest sustainability challenges.

The chapter divides the response by big business to social and environmental challenges into three phases of increasing sophistication:

1. Companies responding to pressure from campaign groups
2. Companies moving from defensive 'brand protection' to pro-active integration of sustainability into core business strategy
3. Transformative change by companies on the biggest sustainability issues in their industry.

## Step one on the road to change: pressure from NGO campaigns

How and why business tackles environmental, social and community issues varies from company to company and sector to sector, but in many cases pressure from campaign groups has been both an early and a powerful part of the mix. Non-governmental organizations (NGOs) commanded the most public trust of the four types of institution surveyed in the 2009 trust barometer produced by leading PR agency Edelman[1] – beating business, government and the media in every region bar Asia Pacific. And they know how to use that trust to mobilize public and political support around a cause – whether it's human rights in the oil industry or deforestation in the timber industry.

The largest NGOs are adept communicators with slick media operations and large memberships to back them. Greenpeace has been particularly vocal on the role of business in solving environmental problems, for example, while the Royal Society for the Protection of Birds (RSPB) is UK's largest environmental group with over one million members, more than all the UK's main political parties combined. And it's not just about large groups – there are civil society groups focusing on almost every conceivable social and environmental issue in almost every sector, from bananas to tourism. With NGOs, size isn't proportional to media clout – small, single-issue campaign groups can and do make the headlines too.

The roll-call of companies that have been the focus of NGO campaigns is a long one. Shell is one of the most oft-quoted, targeted in the mid 1990s for its plans to dispose of the Brent Spar oil platform in the North Sea and for the impacts of its operations in west Africa. Nike's another – it became a poster-child for supply chain labor concerns in the 90s, with labor and student groups in the US boycotting its products. Pick any industrial sector and you're likely to find a company that's been singled out.

How influential are these campaigns, both in the company in question but also its sector? From our perspective inside the corporate sector there is no doubt that campaigners drive change in big business, and it's not difficult to see why. Big companies usually have high profile brands recognized and trusted by consumers and with significant value tied up in them. If those brands become associated with ecological damage or human rights abuses, they become tarnished, the brand value suffers and it can take time to recover. Far from being the source of poor ethical standards, a high profile brand can be a powerful source of corporate accountability.

The significance of a high profile brand to corporate accountability was witnessed by one author during a visit to a consumer goods factory in China's Guangdong Province on behalf of a well-known consumer products company. The factory conditions were extremely poor, with unguarded cutting machinery, blocked emergency exits, filthy canteen facilities, evidence of child labor, and cramped living accommodation. The factory manager refused to allow the auditors to interview the workers, afraid of what they might reveal about life at the factory. But asked by the author why the factory could risk losing business from this customer (the brand, knowing how poor the factory was, later withdrew its business) the factory manager was unapologetic: around 75% of his business came from supplying no-brand products to customers in Eastern Europe and the Middle East who didn't care about working conditions. By contrast the high profile brands were much more difficult to supply to because they cared so much about the working conditions – so rather than improve his own ways he decided to leave that business to the higher quality factories.

This case provides an illustration that companies with high profile global brands have an incentive to respond constructively to criticism from NGOs that others do not. For Shell, the response was a cultural shift in how the company worked with its many different stakeholders, including NGOs – engaging them early in dialogue about issues in which they have expertise in order to address their concerns on issues such as climate change and human rights. For Nike, it led to a far-reaching program to improve labor conditions in their manufacturing supply chain and an initiative to build environmental criteria into the design of its products. In 2005 Nike became the first company in its industry to publish the names of all of the factories around the world that it sources from.

Pressure group campaigns are only one driver of corporate change of course. In some parts of the world, civil society groups are much less influential, and not all global companies have the brand profile that makes them a valuable target for campaigns. But there's no doubt that pressure groups have been an important force in driving business to tackle their social and environmental responsibilities.

## Step two on the road to change: from brand protection to core business strategy

Big business has plenty of self-interest motivation to protect its brand and has acted promptly to do so. But more impressive is how and why a growing number of large companies have increasingly integrated sustainability considerations into the heart of their activities and used it to transform their products and services – and entire market places – in a pro-sustainability direction.

The changes made by leading retailers in the US and the UK over the last decade provide a striking illustration of this change within one sector. Partly as a result of high-profile pressure groups campaigns on everything from nuclear power to GMOs, consumers are increasingly aware of green and ethical issues. While not everyone will scrutinize the ingredients list of everything they buy, or scrupulously select only Fairtrade or organic products, more and more consumers want some reassurance that the companies they're buying from are doing the right thing. In a recent survey, 75% or more of consumers in ten countries (including the US, China and a selection of European economies) thought it was 'important' or 'very important' that companies have high green and ethical standards and provide information on their environmental impacts.[2] And demand for green products is still rising despite the economic downturn, with 34% of consumers saying they systematically look out for and often purchase green products.[3] This means there's competitive advantage for retailers in differentiating their products on sustainability, allowing them to increase loyalty among existing customers and to attract new ones.

Marks & Spencer (M&S) is one of Britain's best known retail brands, with over 21 million UK customers, and is the country's largest clothes retailer. Its recent research supports evidence of a growing competitive advantage in addressing sustainability. The company conducted research on its customers' attitudes to green issues, and found four identifiable groups.[4] Ten percent of customers are classed as 'Green Crusaders' – a well informed and passionate group, already taking action on green issues themselves and looking to business to take a lead as well. A further 35% are increasingly aware of the need to address sustainability, and willing to play their role 'If it's easy'. The largest group – 36% – were classified as 'What's the point?'. They're concerned, but don't believe they can make a difference. However they may be willing to make changes if others match their efforts. The remaining 19% of the company's customers – the 'Not my problem' group – are not interested in these issues.

That suggests four out of five of M&S's customers are aware of the need to tackle sustainability issues and are potentially responsive to how the company markets its products on ethical grounds – though for a large proportion of that group the company has to make it easy for them, and show it's playing its part too.

In 2007, M&S launched Plan A,[5] which set out 100 commitments on the most important social, environmental and ethical challenges facing the business. The company's sustainability commitments have become a core part of its marketing, with stores communicating very visibly to consumers on the issues and on M&S's response. Given its scale and ambition, Plan A has become something of a flagship initiative, watched closely by others in the retail sector and by many beyond. For Stuart Rose, the CEO, the case for integrating sustainability into the company's core business strategy is clear: '[Our customers] value the difference between us and other retailers, they understand the commitment we've made and they trust us to stick to it....Leading on sustainability issues not only differentiates our business and drives sales, but also makes us more efficient'.[6] The company had originally planned to invest £200m over five years in Plan A, but after two years the initiative had become cost positive mainly through operational savings from climate change and waste initiatives.

The world of retail is renowned for its competitive nature, and M&S isn't the only company in the UK supermarket sector to have set out its stall clearly on sustainability. The last decade has seen each of the UK's major retailers develop their approach to sustainability to help differentiate themselves in the market place and tap into growing consumer awareness. That competitive spirit can be an important driver of change. Greenpeace first produced a league table ranking the UK supermarkets on their seafood policies.[7] Nearly 90% of the UK's fish sales are made through supermarkets, so the approach that they take is important. M&S and Waitrose came top, a recognition of their 'detailed and well implemented sustainable seafood policies'. Asda was ranked bottom in the table. Roll forward four years and Asda now has a target for all of its fresh and frozen fish to be certified by the Marine Stewardship Council (MSC) by 2011.

These changes haven't been confined to the UK retail sector. Walmart has been one of the companies that NGOs most love to hate. It grew rapidly through expanding its 'big box' model across the US, then through acquiring overseas brands such as Asda in the UK. Its business model has been built on a low cost base, including staff costs, which led to very public debates with unions and NGOs regarding workers' rights and benefits. Labor conditions have been under scrutiny in its extensive developing world supply chains too, as have the environmental impacts of its big suburban and out-of-town stores and low-price products.

However, from the mid 2000s, Walmart began a turnaround, investing heavily in understanding its key environmental impacts in particular, and has moved quickly to become a respected leadership company in this area. In 2005, the company set three challenging long-term goals:[8] to be supplied 100% by renewable energy; to create zero waste; and to sell products that sustain natural resources and the environment. There's a strong cost driver for the company's sustainability strategy – reducing energy use and waste will save the company costs too. But the company has also positioned itself as the brand consumers can trust to do the right thing. In doing so it isn't just responding to changing sustainability awareness among its global consumers, it is leading and increasing that awareness too.

Walmart is a business with truly global scale. In addition to the US, it operates stores in South America, Europe, China and India – 7,800 in total, employing two million people around the world and serving customers 200 million times weekly. It also has more than 100,000 suppliers worldwide, so when it decides to change what it buys – requiring its suppliers to meet certain labor standards, or stocking more energy efficient light bulbs for example – it matters.

The sheer scale of Walmart's transformation potential was made evident in its huge China Sustainability Summit, held in Beijing in October 2008. Over 1,000 local suppliers joined with Chinese officials and NGOs to discuss a series of aggressive goals and expectations to build a more sustainable supply chain. In addition to re-enforcing the basic – but all too frequently unfulfilled expectation – that labor and environmental laws and regulations should be adhered to, Walmart announced a goal for 20% energy efficiency improvement by 2012 in the top 200 factories it sources from in China and communicated that it would prefer suppliers who share Walmart's ambition of driving sustainability practices throughout their businesses.

Walmart's evolving strategy doesn't mean that it has transformed its performance overnight and its goals are not yet sufficient to fully address the sheer scale of the sustainability challenge that we all face. But by seeking to transform the products that it sells in its stores and drive improvement through its supply chain it has begun to demonstrate that it has a significant role to play in helping to solve some of the global challenges that we now face.

## Step three on the road to change: tackling your biggest impacts

In the early days of the corporate response to NGO pressure the trend seemed to be to tackle the full range of issues being raised by stakeholders, no matter what their significance to the company. Afraid of missing something of importance, companies attempted to cover all issues rather than focus on the most significant. The result was corporate responsibility approaches with two significant shortcomings:

- First, with effort spread over a wide range of issues, companies seemed unable to address any single issue with sufficient focus or resource to make a positive impression given the scale of the sustainability challenge.
- Second, with issues of relative unimportance to the core operations or financial success of the business being given attention, agents of change within the business seemed unable to push sustainability into the mainstream functions of the business – product design, investment, marketing and the like – from where real change could be enacted.

Over the past decade it's become more and more clear that the true test of whether a company is serious about its responsibilities to society is whether it is grappling with the sustainability challenges that are the most significant to its business and to society at large. And a mark of just how far sustainability has been integrated into the strategy of some of the world's largest companies is the sophistication by which companies are seeking to achieve just this.

In a process known within the corporate responsibility profession as 'materiality', leading companies such as Shell, BP, GE, Vodafone and Hitachi are ranking issues across two dimensions: significance to the business (such as impact on revenues, cost and brand) and significance to stakeholders (such as impact on human rights, climate change or poverty reduction) and focusing their sustainability strategies on those issues ranking most highly on both. While addressing sustainability was once characterized by responding to pressure applied from the outside, now it is about the strategic identification of the areas where a company can maximize its positive impact.

Four examples of companies re-orientating their business strategies to prioritize key sustainability challenges are provided by BP (influencing climate change policy), GSK (access to medicines), Vodafone (access to communications technology), and P&G (access to clean drinking water).

## Climate change – a defining challenge for the energy sector

For energy companies climate change is the defining sustainability challenge, and a company's response to it is the test of how seriously it is integrating sustainability. It's easy to forget how significantly the business response to climate has shifted over the last decade. In the late 1990s, BP became the first major oil company to acknowledge the emerging scientific consensus over climate change. 'We must now focus on what can and what should be done, not because we can be certain climate change is happening, but because the possibility can't be ignored' John Browne, Chief Executive, told the audience at a landmark speech at Stanford University in 1997. 'If we are all to take responsibility for the future of our planet, then it falls to us to begin to take precautionary action now'.[9] In the same year BP also announced its withdrawal from the 'Global Climate Coalition' an industry group that had spent the 1990s challenging the emerging science of climate change.

The importance of taking a public position such as this cannot be underestimated. With companies very much aware of what their competitors are doing, a big player in an industry setting out its stall to openly tackle a major issue effectively challenges its peers to do exactly the same. Roll forward to 2009 and companies pulling out of lobby groups are almost two-a-penny. The US Chamber of Commerce has seen a number of high-profile departures by its members – including Nike (leaving the Board) and Apple – as a result of its stance on climate change. But in the 1990s BP's approach, and that of a handful of other companies, did represent a leadership position that helped to move forward the debate on climate change.

BP's transformation from 'oil & gas' to 'energy' company is often mocked. Critics note that despite the transformation only 5% of the company's capital investment is in alternative energy.[10] BP points out that the figure still represents a significant investment compared to its peers, and that public policy frameworks still need to do more to make lower carbon energy sources competitive with conventional sources. Whatever the rights and wrongs of BP's own investment in renewables, the point on the role of public policy is a fundamental one. Leading companies increasingly recognize that when it comes to a market failure on the scale of global climate change they can't solve it alone – only government policy will be able to drive the emissions cuts and investment needed. The challenge for companies is to engage with governments to support, rather than fight, the policies that will be needed. Leading companies are increasingly collaborating with NGOs and governments in initiatives that do just that, as we discuss further in Chapter 3.

## Meeting the needs of the developing world

We live in an era of unprecedented wealth and technological progress. But the benefits of that wealth are not spread equitably, and for all the progress in international development, a gulf between rich and poor remains in many parts of the world. A range of human development measures – from childhood mortality rates to death from preventable diseases to educational attainment – testify to the mountain still to climb.

Big business has an important role to play in meeting this challenge. Complex, global supply chains often extend back to developing countries where goods are produced for the world marketplace – from coffee in Colombia to consumer electronics in China. Big businesses also invest directly in the developing world – where each job created in a global business can create between 30–100 jobs in the wider economy.[11] And it's no longer a case of companies from the big economies of the north – the US, Europe or Japan – setting up subsidiaries around the world. Increasingly this is about companies in China, India and the other big emerging economies investing at home and acquiring overseas.

The potential role of big business is acknowledged by the international development agency Oxfam, which describes how 'the private sector plays a central role in development, having an impact on or contributing to poverty reduction in many different ways'.[12] At one level, that may seem a statement of the obvious – economic growth driven by business is fundamental to development. By doing what it does as a matter of course – providing goods, services, credit and employment – business can and will contribute to development. But increasingly businesses are focusing on how they can maximize that contribution and raise quality of life for those consumers at the 'base of the pyramid' (the two billion in the world who live on less than a dollar a day) by providing goods and services much more deliberately tailored to their specific needs.

The pharmaceutical industry has been one of those most in the spotlight for its contribution to development. Big drug companies have been singled out by pressure groups for the high prices of medicines in the world's poorest countries and for focusing the development of new drugs on rich world ailments. Take Glaxo-SmithKline (GSK), the world's largest drug company. At the start of the last decade the company was the target of a campaign by Oxfam for the high prices that it charged. That campaign focused in particular on the cost of medicines to treat HIV/AIDS in South Africa, where 20% of the adult population live with the disease. Yet in 2009 GSK CEO Andrew Witty announced that it was 'time for a new mindset in our industry and a new contract with society'. In developing countries, he added, 'we must transform GSK into a local company addressing local healthcare needs'[13] and identified several areas where the company would do things differently and incorporate development concerns more centrally into its strategy. Those included:

- Explore a more flexible approach to intellectual property rights to incentivize research into 16 neglected tropical diseases.

- Reduce prices for patented medicines in the 50 poorest countries in the world so that they're no higher than 25% of the developed world prices, and lower if possible.
- Reinvest 20% of the company's profits from selling medicines in those countries to strengthening healthcare infrastructure.

The move was welcomed by Oxfam, which congratulated GSK for 'breaking industry ranks' and 'taking a major step toward helping poor people in developing countries to get better access to medicines',[14] although it still wanted to see more and faster progress on a number of issues. It's still too early to judge the impact that GSK's moves will have on the sector as a whole. But GSK has clearly taken steps to reorient its strategy to help to maximize the contribution that it can make to disease in the developing world. And when the world's largest drug company starts to make the commitments that GSK has done, it does represent a major step and one that sends a strong signal to the rest of the sector.

Telecommunications is another sector with real potential to contribute to development. Access to mobile phones has grown hugely in the last decade – with 4.1 billion subscribers at the end of 2008, compared to just one billion in 2002.[15] 'Mobile phone technology has the capacity to leapfrog more traditional forms of communication and bring much of Africa into the 21st century' according to Anne O'Mahoney, Kenya Country Director for development agency Concern Worldwide.[16]

Vodafone, one of the world's leading mobile communications companies, has been conducting research on the socio-economic impact of mobile technology since 2004, to understand where it can best contribute to development. It has developed a number of products and services for specific developing world markets that allow it to enhance its contribution to economic development, while also developing new revenue streams. One of the company's products, for example, is a mobile money transfer service, now available in Kenya, Tanzania and Afghanistan.[17] This enables people without a bank account to transfer money via a mobile phone. In Kenya the service is known as 'M-Pesa' – Swahili for M-Money – and now has over 6.5 million users. It uses are widespread, including salary payments, international money transfers and also delivery of humanitarian aid. In the upheaval after the 2008 elections in Kenya, M-Pesa was used by Concern Worldwide to deliver cash transfers to isolated communities to allow them to purchase essential food and supplies. Similarly, Vodafone is now exploring the potential of 'mHealth' where mobile phones are used to assist healthcare delivery in much of the developing world. Applications include supporting diagnosis and treatment and the collection of health data in the most remote and resource-poor rural areas. And as we describe in Chapter 8 China Mobile is having an increasingly significant impact on rural development in China.

Clean drinking water is another big sustainability challenge, with over a billion people lacking access to clean water and more than 4,000 children dying every day as a result. Leading consumer products group P&G developed a low-cost water purification system called PUR to help address this challenge, aimed at low-income consumers in the developing world. One sachet of PUR cleans and sterilizes 10 litres of water to WHO drinking water standards, even from heavily contaminated sources. But the journey from product development to market hasn't been a straightforward one, and PUR provides an interesting insight into the complexities of reaching the 'base of the pyramid'.

'It's not just about making consumer products cheaper,' Peter White, Director of Global Sustainability at P&G says. 'You've got to come up with products that actually meet the specific needs at the bottom of the pyramid....You have to actually go and find out, and so we send researchers to find out how people live – how they do their washing, their cleaning (and) what are their problems.'[18] P&G identified the need for a low-cost, simple to use water purification product. But after three years of commercial tests, PUR was struggling to make it as a commercial proposition.[19] Since 2003, P&G has instead worked in partnership through non-profit organizations, selling PUR to them at cost price. Those groups use social marketing techniques to build and sustain the introduction of the PUR technology. This includes education on the local level about the importance of clean drinking water and how to use the PUR sachets.[20] End result: not a commercial product reaching the bottom of the pyramid, but a new business model that allows the benefits of the technology to be used in tackling a key development challenge around the world.

## Conclusion

We live in an era of unprecedented wealth and technological progress, but also an era of unprecedented challenges. Economic progress around the world is impressive, but its benefits haven't been spread evenly. We are also hitting environmental limits on a number of fronts, with population growth bringing both of these issues into stark relief.

Leading businesses increasingly recognize that they share the risks posed by social and environmental issues and so need to share the responsibility for solving them if they are to survive and prosper in this changing landscape. Importantly, companies are increasingly moving from viewing sustainability as a risk to be managed to viewing it as an opportunity to pursue.

Although action by big business to address sustainability often started in a defensive bid to protect corporate reputation, companies are increasingly recognizing the value of sustainability as part of their core strategy: something that will help them manage risks, develop innovative products, build customer loyalty and generate new revenue streams. This sends a strong signal to government and civil society that today's leading companies are ready and capable of being positive, active and constructive partners in the search for sustainability solutions.

This optimistic conclusion doesn't mean that the whole business community has transformed overnight. It is a cohort of leadership companies that has been forging the trail, and even among them there's a way to go. But we believe that where big businesses were once considered by many to be the villains of the piece, today they are increasingly integrating sustainability concerns into their core strategy, and with the right policy framework in place, big business can play a significant part in solving the world's toughest sustainability challenges.

## CHAPTER 3

# The new collaboration zone

**A transformation in how business, NGOs and governments are working together**

It's Autumn 2009 and the Copenhagen climate summit, an important milestone in the international talks to agree on a global deal to cut carbon emissions, is rapidly approaching. UN Secretary General, Ban Ki-Moon, has warned world leaders that failure to agree on a treaty at the December summit would be morally inexcusable: 'The fate of future generations, and the hopes and livelihoods of billions today, rest, literally, with you',[1] he told them at a pre-summit gathering at UN Headquarters in New York.

At the same New York meeting, Mr Ban received a high-profile statement from a group of organizations calling for an 'ambitious, robust and equitable global deal on climate change'. In a 'Copenhagen Communique' they stressed the need to 'respond credibly to the scale and urgency of the crises facing the world' and supported a global cap on carbon emissions, with cuts of between 50 and 85% by 2050.[2] The Communique called for world leaders to put in place a range of policies to deliver those cuts, including an international carbon market; a massive roll-out of clean technologies in the developing world; and an emergency funding package to halt tropical deforestation. 'Delay is not an option', the statement concluded bluntly.

Powerful rhetoric, and nothing out of the ordinary for an environmental pressure group looking to mobilize public support and influence political opinion ahead of a major summit.

Except that this statement was issued by more than 700 major global companies, representing industrial interests in every sector – from energy to IT, transport to retail, finance to consumers goods – and on every continent. The group included some of the world's best known companies and brands – Coca Cola, BP, General Electric, Vodafone and Gap. These companies had come together through the Corporate Leaders Group on Climate Change, an initiative run by not-for-profit Cambridge Programme for Sustainability Leadership which works with business, government and civil society to address critical global challenges.

The Corporate Leaders Group doesn't fit the stereotypical narrative of relationships across business, government and civil society. In that narrative businesses are lobbyists for the status quo, often working through anonymous industry associations which default to the lowest common denominator position, putting the brakes on progressive policies. Governments, reliant on those businesses as engines of wealth creation and national competitiveness, are unwilling to stand up to them and to regulate for higher social and environmental standards. And civil society pressure groups are the only trusted guardians of truth and justice – exposing corporate wrong-doing and campaigning for regulation to put it right.

But in reality there has been a significant shift in the last two decades in how businesses, NGOs and governments work together in what one might call a new 'collaboration zone'. These groups are often portrayed as being in conflict, yet in reality there is continual dialogue and collaboration between big companies, groups such as WWF, Greenpeace and Oxfam, and policy-makers. The last ten to 15 years have seen real growth in this 'collaboration zone'. Initiatives that were once innovative experiments – campaigners collaborating with food retailers to develop ethical product standards, or oil and gas companies working to promote stronger governance in some of the world's poorest countries – have moved into the mainstream. Taken together, these examples mark a sea change in the way leading businesses are working with others to address some of the most pressing global challenges.

One of the important shifts in the relationships between business and NGOs occurred in the mid 1990s, when a number of former campaigners decided to play a more proactive role in advising business on why emerging environmental and social issues were so important for their business success. By changing the language from one of confrontation to one of collaboration, these individuals and the organizations they founded began a different conversation with business, and many were surprised at the willing engagement they found.

One of the pioneering organizations was Forum for the Future, the UK-based sustainable development NGO which works with business, government and academics to develop common solutions. Founded by Jonathon Porritt, Sara Parkin and Paul Ekins in 1996, the organization has assisted many leading UK and global businesses in reviewing their business strategies in the light of the expected environmental and social changes of the coming decades. Similarly Business for Social Responsibility (BSR) is a non-profit organization founded in 1992 that now works with more than 250 member companies to develop sustainable business through advice, research, and cross-sector collaboration. With staff in Asia, Europe, and North America, BSR works with industries as diverse as pharmaceuticals, energy, communications technology, agriculture, financial services and consumer products. The organization has helped create some of the most innovative partnerships that exist between business and NGOs today.

This doesn't mean of course that all businesses have embraced this change. Neither does it mean that the days of NGO campaigns drawing attention to poor practice by companies are over – such practice still exists and it won't disappear overnight. But it's important to understand why leading businesses have pushed the frontiers of collaboration, and why big businesses aspiring to succeed in the 21st century would be well advised to do the same. In this chapter we take a look at how some of the world's leading companies are increasingly collaborating with NGOs to drive change in two main ways: first, by developing new and practical solutions to complex sustainability problems, and second by calling for substantial changes in government policy.

## Practical solutions to real and complex problems: how businesses & NGOs are stepping up where governments are falling short

Business participation in collaborative initiatives to address sustainability challenges is not just about how businesses can help create the political space for governments to introduce more ambitious policies; in many cases they're also about business working with NGOs to identify and implement practical solutions to real sustainability problems. Often known as 'multi-stakeholder initiatives', this new breed of collaborative action typically involves companies teaming up with the very NGOs that have previously been critical of companies – and often remain so – but who also have the expertise and knowledge to help define the practical solutions. Crucially, NGOs also have the ability to act as 'critical friends', helping to hold corporate feet to the fire and make sure any initiative is a credible one in the eyes of the public.

One of those initiatives is the Forest Stewardship Council (FSC), which has transformed from an innovative idea in the early 1990s to being the leading sustainable forestry organization in the world today. Deforestation was one of the poster-child issues that drove the late 1980s resurgence in the environmental movement, along with Chernobyl nuclear disaster and the Exxon Valdeez oil spill in Alaska. Dramatic images of tropical forests being felled, and dire warnings about the species being lost as a result, helped drive up the profile and influence membership of environmental groups. And the notion of the corporation as the villain was an easy case to make when major home improvement retailers were unable to state from where in the world their wood came from, let alone whether its source was a sustainably managed forest.

The FSC was established in 1993 in response to this rise in public concern. The purpose of the FSC was simple – establish clear standards for what constituted sustainable forestry and provide consumers and retailers with assurance that the wood they were purchasing was bought from responsible sources. Its subsequent experience demonstrates very well both the potential and the limitations of multi-stakeholder initiatives:

- The potential: multi-stakeholder initiatives can establish clear, credible and robust standards where previously there were none, and tend to spark collaboration between organizations from different sectors that can achieve more together than they can alone. Companies learn from experts about the scale, nature and realities of the sustainability problem; other stakeholders are able to learn from companies about how revised business models can drive change and bring pilot projects to scale.
- The limitations: without broader policy, regulatory or systemic change, multi-stakeholder initiatives are limited in the ultimate impact of the solutions they provide, and lessons learned need to be integrated into the setting and execution of government policy if they are to be truly effective.

Developed by a coalition of progressive timber companies, timber users and environmental and human rights organizations, the FSC focused on promoting responsible forest management rather than boycotting poor practices. Its growth has been impressive. A consumer in the early 1990s would have struggled in the stationery or the home improvement store to be any the wiser as to where their paper or wood came from; but in 2008, with many large retailers now stocking FSC-labelled products, sales have reached over $20 billion and more than 100 million hectares in 79 countries are certified to the label's standards.[3]

The FSC has taken a lead in showing how cross-sector collaboration can be successfully institutionalized and has set a strong foundation for further growth. Its multi-stakeholder approach has ensured that its standards hold credibility with the public, with FSC members representing the whole spectrum of those interested in sustainable forestry: environmental and social groups, the timber trade and the forestry profession, indigenous people's organizations, corporations and community forestry groups. And it has a strong governance system to represent the diversity of those interests, with a General Assembly including environmental, social and commercial interests from both the developed and developing world.

However, for all the impressive statistics, there's still a long way to go. Although it's grown a lot, over 15 years after coming into being the FSC's standards only cover 5% of the world's productive forests. Every year an area half the size of the UK is still cleared of natural forests around the world with significant impacts for the 60 million people living there and the many species of plants and animals which are dependent on the forests.[4] The implication is clear: despite its growth, a multi-stakeholder, consumer-focused labelling scheme is only part of the solution to an issue as complex as deforestation – a robust international climate treaty will have a vital role, for example, in providing the right rewards to countries to keep forests standing rather than cut them down.

A similar illustration of the potential and limitations of multi-stakeholder initiatives to provide solutions to the world's sustainability problems is provided by the Marine Stewardship Council (MSC). Marine eco-systems and fish stocks are now up there with forests in the dubious 'top ten' of threatened natural resources, and the statistics that illustrate the scale of the challenge are similarly eye-catching. Marine environments are vital for livelihoods and economies around the world. But the world's oceans are under increasing pressure – according to the UN, a quarter of the world's fish stocks are overexploited or depleted and a further half are fully exploited.[5] This has real implications for the 200 million people whose employment depends on fishing, and the one billion people, largely in the developing world, who depend primarily on fish as a source of protein.[6] And while consumers are increasingly aware that there is a problem, it's not always easy to know what they should change about their weekly shop to help solve it. Should they stop eating fish altogether? Or just some species? And how, without acquiring a PhD in fisheries management, are they meant to know what's sustainable?

For companies and conservationists, overfishing represents a shared problem. Those two groups, often portrayed in the media as being at loggerheads, have joined forces to develop a common solution, through the MSC. The idea initially emerged in the mid 1990s from discussions between the Worldwide Fund for Nature (WWF)– one of the world's biggest environmental groups – and Unilever – one of the world's biggest food companies. Similar to the FSC for forests, at the heart of the MSC was the idea that a credible scheme would help recognize where fisheries were being managed responsibly, and a label for products would help consumers choose sustainably caught fish.

Like the FSC, the growth of the MSC has been a success: over 100 fisheries worldwide are now engaged in the MSC program, with more than 2000 MSC labelled products on sale in 40 countries around the world.[7] And there are signs of momentum building. Walmart, the world's largest retailer has set a target that 100% of their fresh and frozen fish in the US market should be MSC certified by 2011.[8] The kind of approach that a company as big as Walmart takes is watched closely by its competitors. But the same caveats apply as for the FSC as a multi-stakeholder labelling scheme by itself won't solve the issue and there's still a way to go. The MSC's standards still only apply to 7% of the world's fisheries.[9]

So there are two striking facts in the twin cases of both the FSC and the MSC. First, that it's been business and NGOs who have been leading the charge rather than governments. There are existing government policies and regulations around both forest management and fisheries, but leading companies and pressure groups saw the need for consensus-based standards and a clear product label that would work for consumers and rather than pushing for governments to put a scheme in place, they set out to do it themselves. Second, that while the change resulting from these ambitious initiatives has been significant, it is not yet of the scale required to take us to sustainability.

### Multi-Stakeholder Initiatives are effective ways to establish new and credible norms and standards

The Forest and Marine Stewardship Councils are far from unique and there are myriad examples of companies working with NGOs, in formal or less formal ways, to develop credible solutions to environmental and social problems. One aspect of these partnerships that has perhaps proved most fruitful has been their ability to create credible standards around which companies, governments and NGOs can all align.

The whole field of 'carbon reporting' by companies provides one such example of effective multi-stakeholder standard setting. Over the past decade or more, businesses have been under increasing pressure to publish figures on their greenhouse gas emissions so that wider society can benefit from a clear picture of the scale of the impacts and insights into whether a company's $CO_2$ emissions are increasing or decreasing. But understanding how to achieve this in a credible and comparable manner is complex. How does a company decide which emissions it 'owns' and should report, and which emissions are 'owned' by others in the value chain and so should be reported by them? How do companies avoid double-counting? And how do different companies reliably provide figures that can easily be compared with those published by other companies?

The answer has been the 'Greenhouse Gas (GHG) Protocol', now the most widely used international accounting tool for government and business to understand, quantify, and manage greenhouse gas emissions. It provides the accounting framework for nearly every GHG standard and program in the world, including hundreds of GHG inventories prepared by individual companies. And as of 2009, 63% of the Fortune 500 companies were using the GHG Protocol.[10]

Again this global standard emerged from an NGO-business partnership rather than government intervention. In this case, the collaboration involved the World Resources Institute (a respected environmental think-tank in the United States) and the World Business Council for Sustainable Development (a coalition of 200 international companies from more than 35 countries and 20 major industrial sectors). Steered by a group with members from other environmental groups (including WWF, the Pew Center on Global Climate Change and the Energy Research Institute) and from industry (among them Norsk Hydro, Tokyo Electric, Shell), the Protocol was first published in 2001.

The debate about how businesses should tackle green and development issues can become a polarized one. At one end of the spectrum is the view that it is in companies' 'enlightened self-interest', and that voluntary action by companies will generate far-reaching change. At the other, the argument that without regulation by government nothing significant will change, and that any company that tells you otherwise is just greenwashing. As this case demonstrates, the reality is not so black and white, with a whole mosaic of different activities taking place right along that spectrum. And this interplay between voluntary activity by companies and government intervention is a vital one for business to understand and manage.

So partnerships between business and NGOs help establish clear, credible and robust standards but are on their own insufficient to provide the full solution to a particular sustainability challenge. Rather, in most cases, government intervention is needed to maximize the impact of the multi-stakeholder initiatives and realize their true potential. The GHG protocol is a good example here: it started out in life as a voluntary initiative, but is now the single recognized international carbon accounting system and forms the basis for the International Standards Organization's guidance for the reporting of GHG emissions by organizations. However, there's an important role for government in taking the standard further: it seems likely to be only a matter of time before governments make $CO_2$ emissions reporting mandatory for all public companies or for private companies over a certain size.

## Companies and NGOs alone cannot solve the catch 22 of climate policy

Leading companies are increasingly recognizing some of the inherent limitations that multi-stakeholder partnerships have, and the need for governments to put in place the right policy frameworks, and are actively engaging with NGOs and governments to help them do that. The changing approach that leading companies have taken to engaging on climate change policy in the last decade is a striking illustration of this trend.

Roll back to 1997, the year of the landmark global climate conference at Kyoto, and business positioning ahead of the summit was more in line with the traditional stereotype of business engagement with public policy. Much to the ire of environmentalists, the 'Global Climate Coalition' (GCC), backed by some of America's biggest companies, was a major presence in the media in the run-up to the talks, particularly in the US. The coalition had been active throughout the 90s, seeking to 'present the views of industry in the global warming debate'.[11] As the UN's expert scientific panel continued to investigate the causes and potential impacts of global warming, the GCC had sought to highlight the continuing uncertainties in the science, pointing to these as a reason for governments to avoid introducing new policies. In the run-up to Kyoto, the group also made much of the cost that international policies might impose on American consumers.

There were signs of change in the late 1990s, with a number of companies reconsidering their membership of the GCC. Leading UK-based energy company BP withdrew in 1997, when CEO John Browne expressed his view that 'the time to consider the policy dimensions of climate change is not when the link between greenhouse gases and climate change is conclusively proven, but when the possibility cannot be discounted and is taken seriously by the society of which we are part'.[12]

However the Corporate Leaders Group on Climate Change (see the introduction to this chapter), and similar initiatives such as the US Climate Action Partnership and BICEP (Business for Innovative Climate and Energy Policy), represent a significant shift in the attitude of business since the end of the last decade. It is a striking change: where once there was an apparently unified business voice against strong action on climate change, today there is a growing – though by no means unanimous – business voice calling for an urgent transformation in policy frameworks and economic incentives to address the climate challenge.

The foundation of the Corporate Leaders Group on Climate Change was based on a simple premise – that businesses and government have been caught in a catch 22 in tackling climate change:[13]

- Governments have felt that their scope to introduce long-term policies, frameworks and financial incentives for emissions reduction are limited because they fear that lobbying by the business community will stand in their way

- Companies have been unable to bring initial investments in low carbon solutions up to the scale required because of lack of long-term policy frameworks and financial incentives to support them.

The idea of a catch 22 in the government-to-business relationship may be a simple premise, but it's an important one for big business. In many cases there will be a clear financial case for companies to improve their performance on climate change: energy efficiency means lower emissions but also lower costs. But these incremental improvements just won't meet the sheer scale of the challenge and the incentives for an individual company to take the action required won't stack up so clearly – a business setting out to make stringent carbon reductions could just find itself undercut by competitors who don't have the same scruples.

There's nothing new in this classic territory of market failure, where government policies are brought to bear to address the so-called 'external costs' that businesses wouldn't otherwise pick up the tab for. What is new though is how companies are starting to confront this: recognizing where there's a strong business case for them to take action, but also where the business case for sustainability runs out and where public policy needs to take its place; working with governments to develop and promote robust policies, with the level playing field that they put in place; and welcoming the challenge and scrutiny that not-for-profits can bring. In the 21$^{st}$ century, the companies that succeed will be those that push the boundaries of collaboration, embracing new ways of working that promote sustainability.

The Corporate Leaders Group has been explicit about its role in helping to break that catch 22 in climate change policy, creating the political space for governments to introduce more ambitious climate policies. For the companies involved there is a strong financial case for this kind of engagement. They have recognized that with an issue as significant as global warming – in the words of Nick Stern, author of the influential review on the economics of climate change the 'greatest market failure in history' – regulation will be an essential part of the solution. They will only succeed as companies in the long term if that market failure is corrected, and that can only be done by government. But as companies they can play a vital role in creating the space for government to act, and in helping to define the kind of policies that will be both environmentally credible and economically efficient. And there's a strong case for companies to help create a level playing field: 'Ensuring', as the group put it, 'that it's in the commercial interest of all companies to become engaged, not just those which are already committed to the goal of tackling climate change'.[14]

What's interesting too is that in many cases it is business that's been leading change, often moving ahead of government. As Craig Bennett, Co-Director of the Corporate Leaders Group, highlighted at the launch of the Copenhagen Communique, 'It has been extraordinary to see the level of support that has come in from the international business community…if it is possible for such a variety of companies to agree on the basic shape of an ambitious, robust and equitable global deal on climate change – surely it should now be possible for the world's governments to do the same?'.[15] And asked why he had signed up to the communiqué, Sir Richard Branson, founder of Virgin, echoed those sentiments: 'As a business leader I can only achieve my ambition if my actions are underpinned by the foundation of political intent and robust law. The bolder the political ambition the bolder I can be. This double act will filter down to citizens and encourage citizens to make their important contribution. I together with those other 6 billion citizens have high expectations that our leaders have the courage to make the decisions only they can make.'[16]

## Changing the system?

With an issue as fundamental to our future as climate change, the fact that big business was seen lobbying for an ambitious international treaty at Copenhagen is an important development. But what happens when companies are doing business in parts of the world where laws aren't as robust, or aren't as robustly enforced – as is the case for labor, health and safety law in many countries? Traditionally the choice for companies has been seen as quite a binary one: take advantage of the reduced operating costs that those lower environmental or social standards imply, searching the globe for cheaper locations to source goods in a race to the bottom; or raise the bar for a tough corporate standard for how to do business, even though it may mean losing margins to competitors. But here too the absence of action by local governments has led to the formation of multi-stakeholder initiatives – such as the Ethical Trading Initiative (ETI) in the UK and the Fair Labor Association (FLA) in the US – where companies have been able to collaborate with NGOs and trade unions to establish standards and approaches that, by bringing many major brands into the system, doesn't harm the competitiveness of any individual brand.

The ETI, for example, is underpinned by a code of practice based on the conventions of the International Labour Organization (ILO) and covers issues like wages, hours of work, health and safety and the right to join free trade unions. Significantly, the content of the code and the manner of its subsequent implementation was agreed by ETI's founding corporate, trade union and NGO members, each of whom are on an equal footing. And with combined revenues of over £107 billion,[17] the ETI's members include supermarkets, fashion retailers and department stores, as well as major suppliers to retailers of food and drink, flowers, clothing, and home improvement products.

The size and profile of the FLA and ETI mean that they too have the potential to drive significant change in their industries and it is certainly the case that business has a far more systematic, informed and impactful approach to increasing labor, health and safety conditions in the supply chain than it did just a decade ago. However, like the FSC and MSC, the scope for change brought by these initiatives will remain limited if it is not accompanied by greater intervention by government. It is for this reason that multi-stakeholder initiatives in the labor, health and safety field are, quite rightly, increasingly focused on changing public policy frameworks to foster greater enforcement of regulations by local officials and improved public-private dialogue.[18]

The ETI and the FLA aren't unique. Apparently impenetrable acronyms abound that represent a wealth of activity in the collaboration zone. The Extractive Industries Transparency Initiative (EITI) promotes disclosure and better governance of the funds that oil and gas companies provide to resource rich developing countries, and includes many of the world's major oil and gas companies among its members. The Business Leaders Initiative on Human Rights (BLIHR) was a collaboration of 16 of the world's leading brands which explored how best to implement the principles of the UN Universal Declaration of Human Rights in a business context. The Global Network Initiative (GNI) – described in more detail in Chapter 6 – is a group of internet companies, human rights and press freedom groups, investors and academics which has negotiated and created a collaborative approach to protect and advance freedom of expression and privacy on the internet.

These initiatives won't have it all right, but they do represent leading businesses taking the initiative, working with other companies in the same industry and relevant stakeholders to find solutions.

## What's in it for the NGOs?

In 2009 NGOs were rated the most trusted organizations in society.[19] And trust in corporations took a further blow that year – more than half of all respondents said they trusted business less than the year before. Given the degree of trust that the public has in NGOs to do what is right, why are many NGOs increasingly inside the tent working with business to find solutions, rather than outside it agitating for change?

The answer is that they are much more likely to achieve the policy objectives and social and environmental outcomes that they are seeking by working with business. Big business brings access to huge consumer markets, resources, and the ability to make a tangible difference to an issue when it changes course. Business can take solutions to global scale, and with companies increasingly looking to work with NGOs, the opportunity exists to scale up solutions on a whole host of issues.

For business, the *quid pro quo* is easier to understand: it's about trust and learning. Because campaign groups are the most trusted in society, working with them to advance policy change or entering into multi-stakeholder initiatives brings credibility. It means that businesses aren't just saying they're doing the right thing, but are seen to be doing the right thing, vetted by organizations that are viewed as independent and trustworthy. This may be seen by some as a cynical use of NGOs to 'greenwash' corporate activity. But it's also about learning: business people desperately need NGOs to help them hear what civil society wants and needs them to do.

Important and real as this move is for businesses to engage with NGOs, community groups and governments, it isn't, and shouldn't be, a headlong rush into a halcyon world of 'multi-stakeholder partnerships'. Although big business is changing, and is increasingly part of the solution rather than part of the problem, many companies still take a narrow view of their own interests, and industry associations are still often a voice for particular sectoral interests. The campaigning role that many NGOs play will remain critical in drawing public attention to environmental and social challenges and in scrutinizing companies.

A case in point is the decision by global human rights group Amnesty International not to be part of the GNI to protect freedom of expression and privacy online. In its view, while the GNI represented a degree of progress in addressing human rights concerns, they felt unable to endorse the GNI's Principles and Implementation Guidelines. That response shouldn't be seen as a failure by the Initiative, but as an important challenge to it to prove its value over time, with Amnesty International, and organizations like it, in the role of watchdog. This means too that where partnerships do exist, it's important that they are governed transparently, ensuring that they represent the interests of the different groups involved and retain their credibility.

## Conclusion

Collaboration aimed at achieving shared goals will be fundamental to tackling some of the big global challenges. There has been a real change in the last decade in how businesses, NGOs and governments are working together in what we've called the new 'collaboration zone', with examples from across the spectrum of industries and issues. There's also an increasing recognition by leading businesses that supporting progressive government intervention is an important part of the picture. This chapter has shown how forward-looking businesses are redefining how they work with pressure groups and policy-makers to lead change, and how all companies will need to work in the future if they are to be successful in the 21st century.

## CHAPTER 4

# Beware the power of the naysayers

The journey to advance corporate responsibility isn't smooth or uninterrupted. There are many obstacles to progress, and situations where individuals or organizations seek to stifle innovation arise all too frequently. This can be a frustrating experience, especially when it seems that a well thought out project or proposal to advance corporate responsibility is in danger of being defeated by ignorance, intransigence or just plain stubbornness. But these moments of frustration can turn into some of the most significant learning points in the transition to a more responsible approach to business, revealing as they do a great deal about what needs to be overcome if the vision of responsible business is to be achieved.

These barriers fall into four different categories, each a combination of the systemic – a fundamental feature of the overall system that acts as a barrier to long-term change – and the tactical – a collection of in-the-moment comments, manoeuvres and actions that act as a barrier to progress on a specific project or proposal.

## 1. 'My competitors aren't doing this, so why should I?'

When first entering into a conversation with a company about what type of strategy it should employ for sustainability it is tempting to jump to a few marquee ideas or headline innovations that instinct says would generate significant change for the better. But the immediate response from a company is frequently much more cautious: the first thing they often want to do is benchmark themselves against peers and competitors. This instinct is entirely natural; we all want to know how we are performing in comparison with our peers and competitors.

But what sometimes comes next is extraordinary. A predominant view is that capitalism is a race to be the first and to be the best, to beat the competition through innovation, superior products and leadership. So the natural outcome of this benchmarking, one would think, would be to use it to identify ways to beat the competition – to identify the areas where the company can go above and beyond its peers and employ sustainability for its competitive advantage.

You'd think so, but all too often the reverse is true. Frustratingly, the lack of action from competitors can, for some companies, become a compelling reason for inaction. Rather than looking at the poor performance of competitors and saying 'I can take this winning edge and use it to my advantage', all too often some companies conclude 'if they can get away with it, then so can I'.

It could well be of course that this head-in-the-sand approach is an indicator of deeper cultural problems at the company. If the company is benchmarking itself against competitors on areas like customer service or product quality and concluding that they only need to perform at the same mediocre level as competitors then the business really is in trouble. Maybe these companies just don't have the winning mentality required to succeed in the market place.

Fortunately there are plenty of exceptions to the depressing scenario just described. There are companies which look to the competition and say 'I can beat them and use it to my competitive advantage'. Interestingly, these companies are often ones that for one reason or another have found themselves poorly positioned in the market place and are embarked on a radical turn-around strategy. These are also the companies that have the potential to drive systemic change for the better.

One such example is the US-based telecoms company Sprint. For those not familiar with the US telecoms industry, Sprint's merger in 2005 with rival Nextel was widely criticized as a poor fit and the company had been losing customers at a worrying rate to rivals AT&T and Verizon. The company recruited a new

CEO, Dan Hesse, and has subsequently been turning itself around with some innovative plays in new products and services. Dan Hesse already had a history of commitment to the environment in his previous job as CEO of the smaller regional telecoms company EMBARQ, and intriguingly he made an innovative approach to sustainable product design one part of his turn-around strategy at Sprint.

Unlike other parts of the IT sector, standards for sustainable product design hadn't really reached the mobile phone industry. Energy Star labels were being successfully employed on TVs and computer manufacturers were increasingly seeking the bronze-silver-gold 'EPEAT' registration required of all computers bought by the US government. But despite concerns about hazardous materials and the increasing amount of energy consumed by electronics products, this approach to sustainable product design hadn't reached the mobile phone industry in any significant way. In a market characterized by rapid innovation and marquee 'must have' handsets it is perhaps surprising there was no stand-out green product, no equivalent of the Toyota Prius.

It would have been easy for the main phone companies to plod along with their existing portfolio of products, making incremental improvements until the regulators caught up. It would also have been easy for telecoms companies to produce a few token 'green models' that met certain green criteria but which weren't really intended as mainstream, competitive products in the market place.

But then came Sprint's 'Reclaim' phone, manufactured by Samsung.[1] A feature-rich phone with a slide-out keyboard designed for heavy texters, this product was full of the functionality required of high quality phones. But the Sprint Reclaim was heavily marketed too for its greenness: highest energy efficiency standards in the market place; use of bio-plastic materials; free of PVC and phthalates; and packaged in recycled materials. In short, the Sprint Reclaim phone was an attempt to set new standards for sustainable product design in the industry and to use this innovation for competitive advantage. Here is the case of a company that benchmarked the market place and chose leadership over mediocrity; it could have gone with the crowd, but decided not to.

A second example of a company looking at its competitors and going above and beyond is GE on the topic of ethics violations. As we have seen, one of the biggest challenges in the business community over the past decade has been trust and the fear that, left unchecked, business will tend towards corruption, malpractice and bad behavior. In response many business have taken action to improve risk management and business ethics processes, such as stronger codes of conduct, enhanced whistle blowing processes and more investment in training and awareness. But how much do we really know about the impact these investments are making? What types of integrity risk are most prevalent in business? What action is taken when violations are found? Are employees speaking up in companies more or less than before? We don't know the answer to these important questions because for the most part companies don't tell us. They look at their competitors and say 'they're getting away with not providing this information to the public; if they can get away with it, so can I'.

The stance taken by GE stands in sharp contrast to the rest of the pack. Rather than shying away from transparency, GE's approach has been to divulge all, and for the past five years the company has been publishing a revealing list of all of the integrity concerns raised during the year classified by type of incident (such as conflict of interest or privacy) and, more recently, by geography too.[2] The company also publishes the number of cases where disciplinary action was taken and provides examples. This is far more than is published by companies with a much more chequered history when it comes to ethics.

The GE report makes for fascinating reading, but what can one really tell from these numbers – after all, if the numbers go down, it could mean that there are fewer integrity concerns, or it could just as easily mean that employees are turning a blind eye and not speaking up about concerns. So why publish all this data? GE's answer is simple: the information is published to send a clear message across the business that poor ethics won't be tolerated. By revealing the bad news to the world, so the logic goes, they reduce the chances that bad will happen.

These two examples are very different in nature: one a product innovation to enhance competitiveness in the market place, the other a radical use of transparency to address real concerns around ethics and integrity. But what unites these two examples is the leadership they demonstrate in areas where other companies were ducking the challenge. These two companies could have benchmarked themselves against peers and competitors and found reasons to stand still, but they didn't, and corporate responsibility is better off for it.

Finally, this dynamic – 'my competitors aren't doing this, so why should I' – is displayed at the level of the country or region as well as the level of the company. Consider the case of climate change, where governments have been extraordinarily cautious about putting in place measures that, they fear, could cause home companies to shift their activities overseas to remain competitive. The EU emissions trading scheme is a prime example of this, with the EU creating a list of industries (such as steel, plastics manufacturing and food processing) that would be largely exempt from purchasing $CO_2$ permits for fear that their inclusion would lead to production being shifted to countries that don't have the same restrictions on greenhouse gas emissions. Moreover, in addition to this concern about jobs and competitiveness is the real fear that relocation to less-regulated markets by energy intensive industries would actually result in an increase of emissions, the so-called 'carbon leakage' effect.

The counter argument to this caution is that, by placing greater restrictions on business, governments could be doing their home companies a favor by helping them prepare for the inevitability of a carbon-constrained world and so innovate faster than their overseas competitors. The result of regulation would be innovation, and the net effect of innovation, so the argument goes, would be a net decrease in global emissions.

Attractive though this latter argument sounds, the risk of 'carbon leakage' in the absence of a global agreement on climate change is not a risk worth taking and points to the need for a government-mandated global approach to emissions reduction in which companies around the globe within a single sector are able to compete fairly in the pursuit of both energy savings and profits. As we will conclude later, while there are plenty of opportunities for leading companies (such as Sprint or GE) to break free of the barriers to corporate responsibility, this doesn't eliminate the need for government action to remove the barriers altogether.

## 2. 'In a business coalition, the lowest position always wins'

This dynamic – of heading for the mediocre or lowest common position, rather than one of leadership – can also exist when companies combine together in a coalition or when a collective response by companies to an issue is needed. The role of companies in addressing climate change provides the starkest example here, with a number of organizations, most notably the American Petroleum Institute, taking positions on climate change that are much less progressive than the position taken by many companies in its membership. Indeed, it is somewhat peculiar to note the overlap in company membership between the American Petroleum Institute, which continues to oppose many of the regulations put forward to address climate change, and the US Climate Action Partnership, which advocates for a strong cap and trade approach.[3]

An example of how the lowest position can win is provided by the sad demise of the Operating and Financial Review (OFR), which was intended to be an innovative component of a thorough overhaul of British company law that began in the late 1990s. During this period – known as the 'Company Law Review' – a considerable amount of consultation took place on how companies could be required to disclose more information about their social, ethical and environmental risks and opportunities. The sophistication of discussion during this time was considerable, and some of the best minds in British business were dedicated to developing and refining a set of proposals for a new annual 'Operating and Financial Review'. What resulted was a set of proposals around which a diverse set of organizations united and which represented a highly logical, well-thought through innovation of company law. Many companies began to create OFRs even before the requirement to do so was introduced, and the prospects for increased company disclosure on social, ethical and environmental matters – and therefore a more sophisticated discussion of the factors impacting the long-term prospects of business – looked promising.

But then in a single line in a single speech in November 2005 Gordon Brown put an astonishing end to years of hard work by abandoning the OFR proposals just months before companies were to begin publishing them. Labelling the reforms an example of 'gold plating' and an unnecessary and burdensome addition to company law, Gordon Brown stunned those who saw the changes as an uncontroversial advance in corporate responsibility. The common view at the time among commentators was that Gordon Brown had made this u-turn to score political points at a moment when relations with business were tense. But, unlike the way he framed the issue in the speech, Gordon Brown wasn't making a concession to the consensus or even dominant view of business that the proposed regulations were too much; rather, he was making a concession to the minority, lowest view of business. In one single moment many years of hard work and consensus building had been defeated by ignorance of the progress that had been made in the private sector towards a different way of doing business. Indeed, so widely accepted were the OFR proposals that, after some extensive lobbying by NGOs, most of the provisions were eventually enacted as part of requirements coming into force under European law.

However, this dynamic of heading towards the lowest position need not always win through. A good example here is provided by the Electronic Industry Citizenship Coalition (EICC).[4] In 2004 eight companies (Dell, HP and IBM, and five of their contract manufacturers, Celestica, Flextronics, Jabil, Sanmina-SCI and Solectron) brought together a number of different codes of conduct governing labor, environment, ethics and health and safety issues into one single code that has subsequently become the predominant supply chain code of conduct for the whole electronics industry. Here the companies followed an intriguing process. Rather than looking across the different company codes and on any one particular topic taking the lowest position, they did the reverse and took the highest position. As a result, this coalition approach was used to raise standards, not lower them.

Later on the group did find itself in a difficult position on a high profile issue – a potential addition to the code on the topic of collective bargaining – where there was significant disagreement among companies on the stance that the EICC should take. Prior to this discussion there was no provision in the EICC code for collective bargaining, in part because collective bargaining is rare in the electronics industry and many companies were reluctant to ask their suppliers to do something that they didn't themselves do. However, the EICC was under considerable pressure to insert a provision on collective bargaining from stakeholders who felt that collective bargaining and worker empowerment provide a fundamental foundation from which other improvements in labor conditions can be pursued. The resolution made by the EICC – to allow companies to add supplementary text on collective bargaining if they wished – didn't please everyone, but it did keep the coalition together and enable companies to take action forward without being constrained by a 'lower' provision.

### 3. 'No Good Deed goes Unpunished'

The third barrier frequently encountered is the apparent belief that, by making progress beyond the minimum required on corporate responsibility, companies are raising expectations about their future performance and as a result will have further to fall.

Over recent years it's become increasingly common to encounter companies who have decided not to undertake reforms or introduce new innovations out of fear that they will secure the attention of campaign groups and as a result be subject to more shareholder resolutions, campaigns and scrutiny. It's as if some companies believe that, by innovating or taking a leadership position on an issue of concern, they may as well be painting a giant target on their chest for campaign groups while shouting 'come shoot me now'.

The example of the Global Network Initiative (GNI) – a multi-stakeholder coalition promoting freedom of expression and privacy in the information and communications technology industry, covered in more depth in Chapter 6 – is a good one, where a large number of companies for whom the GNI's Principles and Implementation Guidelines are entirely relevant refused to participate in case it raised their profile on such controversial topics and associated them with companies having a difficult time in the press. As discussed in Chapter 6, the obsessive media focus on Google, Microsoft and Yahoo! perhaps made this position by companies out of the spotlight understandable. But it's not sustainable: the issues remain the same and will no doubt catch up with them in the long term.

Some of the fears raised can be ridiculous. There are companies who, even with a reasonably strong record on energy initiatives, have to date made the decision not to publish their $CO_2$ emissions because they fear that it will make their companies 'look bad'. This is despite the fact that 68% of the Global 500 companies have published $CO_2$ emissions numbers with apparently no negative consequences whatsoever.[5] It's as if these companies would rather suffer criticism for doing nothing than to receive credit for doing well.

But is it really the case that 'no good deeds go unpunished'? There is plenty of evidence that, quite the contrary, companies have been able to position themselves at the crest of a wave of consumer trends that have brought significant benefits by way of new products, revenues and reputation.

Going back more than 15 years, British home improvement retailer B&Q was under criticism for being complicit in the destruction of valuable forests. Somewhat embarrassingly, the company even had to admit back then that it didn't know where its wood came from. But rather than sit back, do nothing and hope that the issue would go way, B&Q decided to take the initiative to understand where its wood came from. Not only that, the company also decided to help shape new standards for sustainable forestry and help lead the founding of a multi-stakeholder approach to accredit wood sourced from locations using sustainable methods. The result is a product standard that is now very well known and used in the industry, the Forest Stewardship Council (FSC) label. By taking a lead in this way B&Q not only transformed the approach taken by an entire industry to a real sustainability challenge, but they also found themselves ahead of consumer trends rather than behind them and well positioned to benefit from significant marketing and reputational benefit. It's worth noting that these changes were not cosmetic or on the fringes of the 'real business' – rather, they transformed the content, source and marketing of core company products. By 2009, nearly 50% of the wood sold through King-fisher stores (Kingfisher is B&Q's parent company) comes from FSC accredited sources, and the company is committed to only buying from non-FSC accredited sources if the supplier is committed to achieving FSC accreditation in the future.[6]

Today it is possible to look at a wide range of other initiatives – the Marine Stewardship Council, originated by Unilever and WWF, Walmart's proposed sustainability index, Marks and Spencers' Plan A or GE's twin Ecomagination and Healthy-magination initiatives – to see similar approaches being employed by other companies to address their sustainability challenges. The lesson is that good deeds needn't always be punished, but can in fact bring with them a considerable amount of upside.

## 4. 'That's not the way we do things round here; our company is different'

There are many times when companies will seek to avoid taking a responsible approach with comments such as 'we're not like the other companies, we do things differently around here' or 'that's fine for other companies, but that's not the approach that we take'. The list of excuses based on the notion of exceptional-ism is surprisingly long: 'we're organized differently'; 'we're in different markets than the other companies'; 'our products and services are different, this issue isn't relevant for us'.

All too often these comments are made to suggest that respons-ibility lies not with the company in question but with other companies in other parts of the value chain. Too many com-panies think that they will be the exception, when in reality they are just like everyone else. They think they're different, but they're the same.

The Information and Communications Technology (ICT) indus-try is a good case in point here. Go back a decade or more and the conventional wisdom in the industry was that social and environmental challenges were at most fairly peripheral to the industry – 'we're a clean industry' went the motto, 'we're helping people make connections and are a force for good in the world'. And so unlike the apparel and footwear industries (famous for their sweatshops) the industry wasn't proactively taking a stance on improving labor conditions in manufacturing supply chains, and unlike the oil and gas sector, wasn't in any significant way addressing key human rights risks relevant to its products, services and markets. It also took significant effort by the European Union to shift the industry on the risks presented by toxic and hazardous materials in their products. Now the industry is addressing these issues, and as has been described elsewhere in this book, is doing so in an impressively proactive manner. But this wasn't always the case and many companies had to learn the hard way.

Watching companies avoid issues that are clearly relevant can be like watching a train crash in slow motion – you can see what is going to happen to the company eventually, but in the absence of immediate pressure the company becomes blind to what is inevitably going to come. Even today there is a question for the ICT industry that is only just now beginning to be picked up, the issue of the sale of equipment with surveillance, filtering or privacy-infringing capabilities to markets with poor human rights records, and the provision of consulting advice as a service alongside these products. For many inside the industry these questions have been around for years, but it's only recently – in part spurred on by the controversy over the role of communications technology in the 2009 Iranian elections – that attention is beginning to shift.

So why are some people in some companies apparently blind to what will inevitably come their way? Why is it that some seem unable to interpret and act upon the expectations that are so likely to be placed on them by governments, stakeholders and the public in years to come? There appear to be two main reasons.

First, because ignoring these signals is easier in the short term. Working inside companies that are often closed and insular, with their own internal rhetoric, language and culture, it is often all too easy to suffer from group-think and convince others of the same. In the absence of significant and immediate external pressure in the media or elsewhere, it is difficult for internal champions of change to win support for new approaches.

Second, because companies all too frequently let their corporate responsibility agendas be dictated by whatever is front of mind for the media and stakeholders at that particular moment in time. Companies seem particularly good at forgetting the limits of what the media and stakeholders know about their business – the products, services, markets and impacts – and seem to assume, falsely, that because an issue is not being raised right now it's not going to be raised in the future.

To address this shortcoming companies need to become more open to external opinions, ideas and perspectives. But in doing so companies need to learn not just to listen to the noise surrounding the topic of the day, but rather to enter into a longer-term conversation and exchange of perspectives with outside organizations most likely to bring insights, not just on what is relevant today, but on what is going to matter the most tomorrow. And achieving that will require mutual learning and openness: the company will need to listen to the insights provided by those external to it; but those external groups will also need to be open to learning in some depth about the companies' products, services and markets if their advice is to be truly impactful.

The companies who have done this best to date are those that have brought in outsiders to challenge their thinking not just once but over an extended period of time. The stakeholder advisory councils established by Shell, GE, Dow, BT and others have all made a lasting impact. Moreover, these conversations haven't taken place at the margins, but have been real exchanges with senior decision-makers in the companies. Under this spotlight companies and stakeholders frequently realize a paradox: every company is different, with its own unique products, services, markets and cultures that need to be understood if a long-term approach is to be created. Every company will necessarily have different priorities and risks and opportunities to be fully understood and pursued. But when it comes to the magnitude of the responsibility and the need to integrate aspects such as human rights and climate change into decision-making, all large companies are in fact the same.

Finally, the classic – the company that tries to convince itself that it doesn't need to change because it 'has a good story to tell'. If a dollar was paid into a savings account for every time that phrase was used, someone would be able to retire very handsomely by now. Indeed, there was once a well-known Fortune 500 company who, at the start of a project to publish their first corporate responsibility report, was provided with a list of important issues that they should consider covering in the report and including in their strategy. The response from the company was that they didn't need to cover some of these more difficult topics because they 'already had a good story to tell'. Days later an ethics scandal broke, the project was cancelled and the consultants hired to write the report never heard from the company again.

## Conclusion

This chapter has summarized four different barriers holding back progress to corporate responsibility. For each a case has been made that companies can, through leadership and innovation, overcome these barriers for the benefit of both society and their long-term business prospects. However, these four barriers can also be seen as inescapable and systemic features of the overall competitive landscape in which companies operate today. Leadership by visionary companies will take us some way towards the transition to sustainability that we would like to see, but the limits of this voluntary action and the need to address these systemic problems must also be recognized. This suggests that there is plenty of room for action by governments to level the playing field and provide a regulatory framework in which companies – and countries – can gain competitive advantage, rather than disadvantage, through pro-sustainability innovations.

# Smarter products and better protected consumers

## CHAPTER 5

# Looking beyond the label

If you had walked into a supermarket 15 years ago, you would have been hard pressed to find many products labelled according to their ethical credentials. Fairtrade goods were generally sold in small charity shops rather than the big chains, and organic fruit and vegetables were still very much in their infancy. The product labels that had taken off and caught the public's attention tended to be single-issue and focused on a specific product: free-range eggs, for example, responding to public concerns over battery-farming of chickens, or dolphin-friendly tuna, following an exposé of fishing practices. All in all, you had to be something of a green aficionado to seek out a more sustainable choice and to pay the premium price required. And you also had to be pretty dedicated to understand what a particular label was actually telling you about the good, the bad and the ugly in the ethical league.

Our shopping experience has been transformed since then. Sustainable products have entered the mainstream and big retailers have made a whole raft of commitments on what they will and won't sell. A decade ago, if you had told a committed green activist that all of Sainsbury's own brand coffee would be Fairtrade, or that Cadbury would have made the same commitment for the ubiquitous Dairy Milk bar, they would have thought were living on another planet. The fact that those and many similar changes have been made by iconic household brands shows the extent of the mainstreaming that has happened.

For all that change, you still have to be something of an aficionado to understand the difference between the plethora of labels that now exist. What labor conditions does Fairtrade actually guarantee? If you buy a Fairtrade product will it be organic too? In the new A to G energy efficient rating that all homes in the UK now have to produce before they can be sold, what does a 'D' rating actually mean, and what would you have to do if you wanted to improve it?

In this chapter we look at how companies are using different labels to inform consumers about the products they buy, assess what value they add for consumers and for companies, and ask what the future might look like as carbon footprints take off and join the ranks of green labels. But we also look beyond the labels to understand whether labelling on its own can drive change, or fully communicate to consumers the complexity of the environmental and social impacts of the products and services they buy.

## Active consumers have the power to act as agents of change

Public interest in the pressing environmental and social challenges we face is growing fast. Opinion surveys show rising awareness of the issues matched by an increasing demand for green products – with 34% of consumers in a recent Boston Consulting Group survey saying that they systematically look out for and often purchase green products.[1] Many commentators see this growing demand as a powerful force for change. Businesses are expert at identifying consumer trends and in responding to them, so if consumers are interested in sustainability, businesses will respond by stocking greener products and promoting their ethical credentials. The accepted argument is that this is a win-win for consumers, business, and government: consumers can make a sustainable choice more easily, with competition keeping prices in check too; businesses that get this right will see their market share grow; and governments can use the collective spending power of the green pound, dollar or yen to help deliver their environmental and social policy goals.

Recent research by Marks and Spencer (M&S), one of the UK's leading retailers, supports the evidence of growing consumer awareness. It suggest that four out of five of M&S's customers are aware of the need to tackle sustainability issues and are potentially responsive to how the company markets its products on ethical grounds – though for a large proportion of that group the company has to make it easy for them, and show it's playing its part too (see Chapter 2 for further information on this research).

M&S is one of the UK's higher-end retailers, so there is a question as to whether those results would be as strong across the whole market – the 34% figure quoted earlier as the percentage of consumers regularly seeking out green products may be closer to the mark. And there is of course the perennial issue that what people say about their ethical behavior when put on the spot in an opinion survey may not always translate to what they actually decide to do at the point of purchase. But the evidence does point to a growing body of consumers seeking to inform their purchasing decisions in part based on the environmental and social impact of the products.

How has the market responded to that demand and is the information on offer adding value to the consumer? There's certainly no shortage of labels providing information. The average customer doing their weekly shop at one of the UK's supermarkets would find a whole host of different standards displayed on products – from fruit and vegetables through to electrical goods. Food products could be Fairtrade, organic, free range, or certified by the Royal Society for the Protection of Animals (RSPCA)'s 'Freedom Foods' scheme. Fish could be rated by the Marine Stewardship Council (or MSC – see Chapter 3), or, in a twist on the acronym, the Marine Conservation Society (or MCS). Paper products can have various eco-labels attached to them, covering recycled content or whether they're certified to the Forest Stewardship Council (FSC) standard. All white goods – fridges, washing machines and the like – now also sport an A to G rating for energy efficiency, while carbon footprint labels are starting to appear too on a whole range of products such as orange juice and potato chips.

## Product labels: clarity or confusion?

Has this plethora of issue-specific sustainability standards served to provide the information that more aware shoppers are looking for? Or has it rather confused matters, with only the most dedicated of ethical consumers – those with the time and expertise to really look behind the label – making use of the facts and figures on display?

There is evidence that some of the high-profile labels have made it onto the radar of the shopping public in a significant way. The Fairtrade Mark is a case in point. Fairtrade products aim to promote more equitable terms of trade for farmers and workers in the developing world, providing better prices for products and helping to support more decent working conditions and local economic development. They first appeared in Europe in the late 1980s, in the form of coffee in the Netherlands. Several other European countries set up their own schemes, with the UK's 'Fairtrade Foundation' certifying chocolate, coffee and tea from 1994. However it was only in 1997 that the Fairtrade Labelling Organization was established to unite these various labelling initiatives under one umbrella and establish worldwide standards and certification.

Consumer awareness of the label in the UK has taken off over the last decade. In 2002, only 20% of the general public claimed recognition of Fairtrade labels, but by 2008 that figure had grown to 70%, with 64% of the population showing an understanding of the concept behind the Mark and linking it to a better deal for producers in the developing world.[2] In the same period, the Fairtrade market in the UK has grown from £63 million to £712 million, with sales of Fairtrade coffee representing more than 20% of the total UK market in 2008.[3]

Price clearly has a fundamental role to play for the vast majority of consumers. Part of the success of Fairtrade coffee is down to the fact that any price differential is seen by consumers as being within the price norm.[4] Organic food, conversely, has much smaller share of the UK market, at 1.3% in 2008,[5] albeit a rapid growth from a low base. While organics are widely available, they are still perceived primarily as a niche, luxury product, for consumers willing to pay a premium for perceived higher quality.[6] (That said, price isn't always the make or break factor that determines whether a more sustainable product makes it into the mainstream. Four out of ten eggs sold in UK shops are now either free range or barn eggs, with consumers apparently willing to pay a premium for the perceived benefits of freshness, taste and improved animal welfare.)[7]

However simply making information accessible to consumers does not always drive a change in purchasing patterns. Take the case of 'A-labelled' white goods – the most energy efficient fridges, dishwashers and washing machines on the market. The market share of these products in the UK rose to 75% plus by 2005, up from 0% in the late 1990s.[8] But according to the Sustainable Consumption Roundtable, a UK advisory body, labelling the products actually had a pretty limited effect from a consumer perspective, but it did enable a number of other changes.[9] These included a manufacturer agreement to raise the minimum standard for the goods, price incentives at a European level and so-called 'choice-editing' by retailers, with the least efficient models no longer being offered on the shop-floor. Again, price was important: A-labelled goods were offered at cost parity by familiar brands, meaning consumers were happy to adopt more efficient models.

What do these examples tell us about the role of labels in helping consumers make more sustainable choices?

First, information is increasingly widely-available, but it tends to be issue-specific, focused on developing world labor conditions for example, or animal welfare issues. By extension, moves to some sort of catch-all eco-labelling system are likely to be problematic. That was certainly the view of the UK Sustainable Consumption Roundtable which concluded that labels have driven change only when they are designed specifically for a small number of issues closely associated with a particular product and its value chain: forest labels and wooden garden goods for example, or energy efficiency ratings for white goods. Moves to an all encompassing labelling scheme have been limited to date, with the EU's Eco-label scheme still struggling to find appeal in the market place.

Second, labels do rely on consumers having a certain level of awareness and understanding to interpret them, though in many cases – for example Fairtrade – there's evidence that awareness is growing.

Third, price is not surprisingly an important factor in determining whether a product does go mainstream. Consumers are prepared to pay a premium in some cases, but as a rule, for a product to move beyond a relatively niche market it will need to be competitively priced.

Finally, and perhaps most importantly, labelling alone is rarely a sufficient force for driving a real shift in consumer behavior, something we turn to later in this chapter.

## How big is your footprint?

With climate change one of the defining challenges of our time, it's not surprising that 'carbon footprints' (a measure of the amount of carbon emitted by a person, product or organization over a defined period of time) are now coming into vogue. In an era of increasing carbon constraints, a 'carbon footprint' showing where carbon emissions come from in a company's value chain is a fundamental management tool. But can carbon footprints help consumers when they are used on individual goods and services? And do the same opportunities and limitations that apply for existing product labels apply in the case of carbon footprints?

As carbon gets priced into the market through government policies around the world, investors want to know the implications of climate change for 'value-at-risk' and 'value opportunity' in different sectors and companies. Recent research by consultants McKinsey & Company and the Carbon Trust concluded that there is 'considerable potential for companies which prepare well and positively position themselves for the climate challenge to outperform and create value'.[10] Perhaps unsurprisingly, the building insulation sector demonstrated the greatest opportunity, with up to 80% 'value creation opportunity'. The research also found significant opportunities in the automotive sector (up to 60%) and consumer electronics (35%). Conversely, the 'value-at-risk' for companies with strategies that are focused more on 'business as usual' were up to 65% in the automotive and aluminum sectors.

Maximizing the value creation opportunity from carbon and minimizing the risk relies on robust carbon footprint analysis to identify where the carbon comes from in a product value chain, and what the opportunities are to reduce it. As we saw in Chapter 3, a collaborative effort between leading environmental researchers and the world's biggest companies has already created a system for measuring a carbon footprint, one that has become established as *the* global standard.

The value of 'carbon footprinting' for an individual enterprise is demonstrated by the case of BAA, the UK's main airport company and owner of the world's busiest international air hub at London Heathrow. The aviation sector is in the spotlight for its contribution to climate change, and while the carbon emissions from flights are still a relatively small portion of total carbon dioxide emissions – 1.6% of the global total according to the UK Government in 2006[11] – they are growing at a time when other sectors have targets for big emissions cuts. Emissions from flights from the airport represent approximately 90–95% of the footprint of a passenger's journey from their home to their final destination. As an airport operator, BAA doesn't control those emissions directly, but as a big player in the sector it can use its influence to lead changes. It did this early in the last decade by developing a detailed policy proposal showing how aviation could be included in the fledgling European cap and trade system. The company was a strong supporter of European moves to integrate aviation in the scheme, which is now due to happen from 2012.

Although the 5–10% of emissions that aren't related to flights represents a smaller tonnage of carbon, this is where the company has greater influence or, in the case of energy use in buildings and airport infrastructure, direct control. Footprint analysis has focused the company's efforts on aircraft fuel use on the ground at airports. These are an important emissions source, and one where an airport operator can influence carbon emissions through how it runs the airports: minimizing taxi times, for example, or providing plug-in electrical power when planes are parked at terminals, to save them running their engines.

But while carbon footprints are an important management tool for companies, can they help consumers when they're used on individual goods and services? A number of UK companies have worked with the Carbon Trust – a body set up by the UK Government to drive emissions cuts in business – to develop a

'Carbon Reduction Label' for products. The label shows the total greenhouse gases from every stage of the product's life-cycle from production through transportation to preparation, use and disposal, and also indicates that the company is committed to reducing emissions. Among the household brands that now sport the carbon mark are Walkers crisps, Tesco's orange juice and Innocent smoothies.

For the companies involved, the Carbon Trust reports a number of benefits from using the product label, including uncovering the real drivers of carbon emissions through a product's life-cycle.[12] The biggest surprise for Innocent, for example, was the relative insignificance of 'food miles' – the transport of its raw materials – compared to the total footprint of a smoothie. Packaging and fruit growing were the most significant contributors, and the work has focused the company's efforts to reduce emissions on developing recycled packaging.

It is still early days in trying to understand the value of carbon labels to consumers. Only a small number of products use the labels and we're still a way off consumers being able to compare all the products in their weekly shop from a carbon perspective. It is also unclear whether consumers are yet carbon literate enough to interpret their impacts in grams and kilograms of $CO_2$. The '2 tonne' figure – the sustainable level of an individual's carbon budget if emissions were divided equally around the world – is much touted and is gaining some currency but it's very difficult for an individual to interpret that at the product level: is the fact that a can of Coke has a footprint of 170g good, bad or indifferent?

However the companies that are providing footprints for their products are likely to be at the vanguard of a major trend. In an ever more carbon constrained world, more consumers will want to know the carbon impacts of different products, and companies seeking a more engaged relationship with their consumers would be well advised to respond proactively.

There is already evidence that consumers want to play their part in addressing climate change, but feel they lack the information to do that. Recent market research by the Carbon Trust showed 73%

of UK consumers claiming that they are aware of environmental problems, but not solutions, while 79% didn't believe
that business is doing enough to give consumers the information
they need to make informed choices about the carbon content
of the products they buy.[13] Those percentages represent a pretty
clear challenge being laid by consumers at the door of businesses. The same research also highlights the value of a credible
carbon labelling system: 60% of consumers said that they didn't
think claims by manufacturers or retailers were credible, and 70%
that they would value an independent assessment of a company's
claims. Recent research from the UK's leading supermarket chain,
Tesco, is even more emphatic, indicating that 97% of consumers
'would actively seek to purchase products with a low carbon footprint if they were as cheap and convenient', while 35% would buy
lower-carbon products 'even with a cost/convenience trade-off'.[14]

And although carbon labelling is still in its infancy, it already
allows a degree of differentiation between products. Tesco, for
example, shows the different footprints of two sorts of orange
juice: fresh and long-life. The former has a higher footprint due
to the energy required to chill it. Likewise Coke sold in a can has
a footprint under half that of a glass bottle, a difference driven
by the weight of glass packaging.

What does this tell us about carbon footprints?

For companies, a robust carbon footprint is clearly a fundamental management tool, identifying both at a corporate and at a
product level where the biggest carbon risks and opportunities lie.

For consumers, there's evidence of a strong demand for more
carbon information to help them make their product choices.
We're still at a fledgling stage in terms of the individual shopper
being able to compare and contrast products in carbon terms,
but there are signs that that could shift rapidly.

Companies will have a key role in addressing the relative lack of
'carbon literacy' among consumers: helping them to interpret the
wave of facts and figures on grams of carbon per product that's
likely to be coming their way in future. As part of that awareness
raising role, companies will also need to position carbon footprints clearly alongside the raft of other sustainability issues

linked to products. While consumers are calling for greater carbon labelling, this does add another criteria on which a product can be assessed, adding to the complexity of choosing more sustainable goods. Tesco is researching this question through the 'Sustainable Consumption Initiative', to help it prioritize the products on which it should roll out carbon labels. The project seeks to assess potential conflicts with other sustainability objectives, with a view to focusing its labels on products which rank high on carbon opportunity and low on non-carbon risks.

Although it's still early days with carbon footprinting, the same conclusion that we drew for other product labels seems likely to apply here: consumer labelling of carbon impacts will help inform consumer choice and engagement in tackling climate change. However, taken alone, consumer labelling is unlikely to be a sufficient force for driving transformational shifts in consumer behavior and further proactive action from companies and governments to guide consumer behavior will be required.

## Big companies have the power to support consumers as agents of change

'Choice-editing' has a pretty big-brother ring to it, conjuring up images of faceless corporate or government technocrats determining what should or shouldn't be consumed by the average shopper. But it's an important part of the mix in promoting more sustainable purchasing patterns.

The logic is pretty simple: companies can drive consumer purchasing in a particular direction by only stocking products that meet certain social or environmental criteria. B&Q, the UK-based home improvement chain, was one of the early leaders here, with its approach to sourcing more sustainable timber. The company made the decision to purchase only timber products certified to 'Forest Stewardship Council' (FSC) standards. This means that shoppers can focus on the aesthetics and price of a door or shelf, safe in the knowledge that all the products in the store meet the same sustainability standards. The FSC standard is still a critical part of the process, but its real use is in the relationship between the retailer and its supply chain, when it's used by B&Q buyers to set the criteria for the products they purchase. Big UK retailer John Lewis took a similar approach with energy efficient products – taking a decision only to stock the most efficient A-rated goods in its stores, where a sufficient range was available.[15]

There's also evidence that leading retailers are looking to 'choice edit' for customers across all of their products – setting minimum standards and improving performance so that the shopper can purchase safe in the knowledge that the company's doing the right thing.

That's likely to be a welcome step for most consumers, as buying more sustainable goods can be a complex equation of weighing up different social or environmental issues. Most products have a variety of impacts attached to them, some positive, some negative. Farmed fish, for example can help address the overfishing of our oceans, but can also affect the marine environment through the discharge of nutrients, solid waste and medicines. Growing cotton for clothes can be an energy and pesticide intensive business, but can be an important source of income for developing countries.

Retailers are increasingly taking a lead in managing this complexity on behalf of their customer – grappling with these difficult trade-offs so that the consumer can choose the brand as a more sustainable one, rather than needing to make that choice for each product that they buy. M&S's Plan A initiative is one a striking examples here. Launched in 2007, it sets out 100 commitments to achieve within five years, to combat climate change, reduce waste, use sustainable raw materials, trade ethically, and help customers lead healthier lifestyles. The message from M&S is clear – choose us and you can shop safe in the knowledge that we have a plan in place to make our business a greener one, and address on your behalf the big impacts that our products have.

In some ways way it's easier for M&S, as it stocks almost exclusively own-label products, giving it a close control over its supply chain. But most big UK-based retailers are making strong moves in this space. And, as we saw in Chapter 2, the heavyweight global retailer Walmart is also stepping up its efforts: its commitment to sell only MSC certified fish in its US stores by 2011 is an example of choice-editing on a major scale.

Of course not all retailers will take a lead and 'choice edit', and not all goods are sold by big chains. That means that policies set by governments also have an important role in moving the market in a more sustainable direction. One of the highest-profile recent examples here has been the decision by a number of governments, including the European Union, Canada and Australia, to phase out traditional 'incandescent' light-bulbs in favor of more energy efficient versions. But governments have a range of policy tools at their disposal and their role is not just limited to phasing out certain products – for example, they can also use price signals to increase the cost of more polluting goods. A good case in point here is the recent introduction in the UK of a tax on new car purchases which is based on carbon dioxide emissions. This means that consumers buying less efficient cars face an additional 'showroom' tax in the first year that they own the car of up to nearly £1,000.

## Conclusion

There's real evidence of growing consumer awareness of environmental and social issues, and a growing demand for companies to respond by communicating information about how their products perform. Labels have been quite issue specific, focused on the most important impacts of a particular product: equitable trade with developing world suppliers, for example, or on carbon emissions. That trend is likely to continue, with all-encompassing eco-labels failing to take off to date.

Leading retailers are also increasingly looking to position their whole brand, rather than just specific products, as one that consumers can trust to 'do the right thing'. In effect, they're offering to do the heavy-lifting – rather than consumers needing to exhaustively select the most sustainable products in a store, those retailers are offering to edit the choices available so that consumers can shop safe in the knowledge that any product they purchase from that store has addressed its impacts.

It's also clear that government policy has a role to play in 'editing the choices' that are available to consumers in a more sustainable direction – with the recent moves to phase out high-energy 'incandescent' light bulbs in many markets a clear case in point.

## CHAPTER 6

# New responsibilities in the networked age

It's December 2008 – the 60th anniversary of the Universal Declaration of Human Rights – and in the grand surroundings of the Cathedral of Palais de Chaillot in Paris an eclectic mix of organizations have come together to discuss the role of business in human rights. After opening remarks from Mary Robinson, the former President of Ireland and UN Commissioner for Human Rights, speakers from Human Rights First, Microsoft, the Committee to Protect Journalists, Google, the Berkman Center at Harvard, Yahoo! and the Center for Democracy and Technology all lined up to give their views on how to protect and advance the human rights of freedom of expression and privacy in the online environment.

But unlike the adversarial exchanges on Capitol Hill earlier that same year – in which the then CEO of Yahoo, Jerry Yang, was dramatically accused of being a 'moral pygmy' – these speakers had come together to express their shared support for the launch of a new organization designed to protect the internationally recognized human rights of freedom of expression and privacy. Named the Global Network Initiative (GNI), this multistakeholder organization is designed as a collaborative approach to address the increasing government pressure to comply with laws and policies that sometimes conflict with human rights.

Three years in the making, the launch of the GNI highlights how the growing significance of the internet and the online environment raises tough new ethical dilemmas for business and brings with it new responsibilities. It also highlights how our collective

## The Global Network Initiative

All over the world companies in the Information & Communications Technology (ICT) sector face increasing government pressure to comply with domestic laws and policies in ways that may conflict with the internationally recognized human rights of freedom of expression and privacy.

Many will be familiar with the pressure that companies such as Google, Yahoo! and Microsoft face to filter search results, remove user generated content and respond to government demands for personally identifiable information in China. However, the reality is that such demands happen all over the world – from the Americas to Europe to the Middle East to Africa and Asia.[1] Indeed, every government is faced with the challenge of preserving national security and undertaking legitimate law enforcement activities while at the same time upholding the internationally recognized human rights of privacy (Article 12 of the Universal Declaration of Human Rights) and freedom of expression (Article 19 of the Universal Declaration of Human Rights).

The GNI is a multi-stakeholder group of companies, civil society organizations, investors and academics who embarked on a collaborative approach to framing how companies should respond to this challenge and protect these human rights in the jurisdictions where they are at greatest risk.

The GNI is founded upon three core agreements:

• **Principles,** which are based on internationally recognized laws and standards for human rights – including the Universal Declaration of Human Rights and the International Covenant on Civil and Political Rights – and describe the commitment of GNI members to collaborate to advance freedom of expression and privacy.

- **Implementation Guidelines,** which provide detailed guidance on how companies will put the Principles into practice – for example, how they should respond to requests by governments to restrict content or demands from law enforcement agencies for the disclosure of personally identifiable information.
- **A Governance, Accountability and Learning Framework,** which sets out a multi-stakeholder governance structure and system of company accountability to ensure the integrity of the GNI.

At the time of writing the GNI remained in start-up mode with three companies, nine civil society organizations, five investors and four academic representatives. Regardless of whether or not the GNI thrives as an organization over the coming years, its Principles and Implementation Guidelines represent the most significant attempt to define company responsibility on these issues and will likely live on as the expected norm in this field.

obsession with a small number of major brands and a few simple questions – the type that easily become front-page news – can dangerously draw our interest away from the responsibilities of a much wider range of companies that require urgent attention.

We live in a world increasingly dominated by ICT – the internet and the telecommunications networks and software that make it work increasingly influence our lives. Everyday tasks such as placing a phone call, banking online or making hotel reservations are all built upon extensive flows of information and supported by vast ICT infrastructures and have become a natural and unquestioned part of modern life.

But while the social responsibilities of companies have been increasingly well defined in other sectors of the economy – in mining, in manufacturing and in agriculture, for example – its meaning in the ICT world is still taking shape and is raising a whole series of new ethical dilemmas. It is possible to identify three features of the relationship between the internet and society that bring significant implications for companies in this new economy:

| Sphere | Internet and Society | Implication for Companies |
|---|---|---|
| The User | The role of the end user in advancing human rights is especially significant – this can mean everything from exposing human rights abuses to using the internet as a platform for political discourse. | Companies and users can often find themselves with a common cause – to uphold and defend rights to freedom of expression and privacy. |
| The Law | New technologies, products and services are introduced much faster than laws can be enacted to regulate them.

Moreover, the local laws and regulations that do exist often conflict with internationally recognized human rights of freedom of expression and privacy. | In the absence of regulation establishing minimum standards, the responsibility of corporations to be proactive becomes all the more significant.

In situations where the local law conflicts with human rights, companies may increasingly be expected to challenge the law and its implementation. |
| The Technology | New technology is complex to understand – the frequent and rapid introduction of new technologies, functionalities and product features can be difficult for users, governments, NGOs and society as a whole to follow. | Engagement between companies (who know the technology but less about its social impact) and stakeholders (who may know less about the technology but more about possible social consequences) becomes critical. |

## The end user is more significant – and companies and users can unite around a common cause

When the mainstream media first began reporting that Google, Yahoo! and Microsoft had agreed to filter search results or remove user generated content in China the issue was presented in typically simplistic terms: large and powerful companies were putting their own commercial self interests ahead of the needs, rights and interests of their users. Yahoo! was caught in the worst position of them all, accused of handing over personal information that led to the arrest and imprisonment for ten years of Shi Tao.[2] Cartoon images in the Financial Times perhaps summed this sentiment up the best, depicting the 'oo' in Google and Yahoo! as wrists in handcuffs.[3] The internet companies were no longer purveyors of freedom; they were now the major villains in freedom's demise.

The reality was, as it so often is, much more complex than this. The internet both allows and thrives on the free flow of information, and depends on a significant amount of user trust that companies making online communications possible will take a responsible approach to the privacy of personal information. Without these two features, the internet is dead. These three companies, steeped in the idealistic and optimistic world that is Silicon Valley, seemed genuinely taken aback by the dramatic shift in perceptions and reputations on a topic where they clearly felt that the impact of their services was a net positive. And it is this underlying assumption – that internet companies are ultimately on the side of the user in the cause of preserving freedom of expression and protecting privacy – that greatly informed the subsequent stance taken by the internet companies.

Indeed, the opening preamble to the GNI Principles contrasted the respective roles of governments and companies and framed the companies' responsibility first and foremost as a protector of the human rights of their users:

'The duty of governments to respect, protect, promote and fulfil human rights is the foundation of this human rights framework. That duty includes ensuring that national laws, regulations and policies are consistent with international human rights laws and standards on freedom of expression and privacy.

Information and Communications Technology (ICT) companies have the responsibility to respect and protect the freedom of expression and privacy rights of *their users.* [emphasis added]'

It is notable that the body of the GNI Principles and Implementation Guidelines is full of commitments made to the user in the face of threats that originate from governments:

'Participating companies will respect and protect the *freedom of expression of their users* by seeking to avoid or minimize the impact of government restrictions on freedom of expression…'

'Participating companies will respect and protect the *privacy rights of users* when confronted with government demands, laws or regulations that compromise privacy in a manner inconsistent with internationally recognized laws and standards. [emphasis added]'

Even more intriguing are the commitments that the GNI Principles and Implementation Guidelines make to specific actions that are designed to empower the user through transparency about the restrictions required by government:

'Give *clear, prominent and timely notice to users* when access to specific content has been removed or blocked by the participating company or when communications have been limited by the participating company due to government restrictions. [emphasis added]'

Indeed for Google, Yahoo! and Microsoft this transparency about censorship has been one of the powerful arguments they have been able to make for continuing to offer tailored services to markets with human rights risk – it is through this transparency that end users can first learn about the extent of censorship deployed by governments.

None of this is to say of course that the internet companies will seek to blindly protect users in all circumstances – there is a whole range of crime, from terrorism to child exploitation and hate speech – that requires cooperation, interaction and negotiation between companies and law enforcement agencies to protect broader social interests. But what we are witnessing is an intriguing alliance between the user and the company in defence of human rights.

This emphasis on the common cause between the end user and the company is a relatively recent development in debates around the responsibility of companies. In the past, we have developed a sophisticated understanding of how companies should uphold their responsibility with individuals and organizations with whom they have fairly direct relationships: the factory worker whose labor rights need protecting; the local communities near the extraction site whose property rights need respecting; the rural populations whose quality of life can be improved through the provision of services tailored to their particular needs.

However, by focusing on the end user, companies in the internet sector are directing their efforts at the rights, responsibilities and actions of someone who is both much further removed from the company and much closer to it. Much further away since in the internet world money rarely changes hands between the user and the company. Users are not, strictly speaking, customers – email, search, social networking sites, user-generated encyclopaedias, maps, satellite imagery, instant messenger, blogs and photo diaries are for the most part accessed and used for free. Indeed, it is this freedom to create, communicate and disseminate information that underpins the power of the internet to produce unprompted and user generated change.[4] However, the user is also somehow much closer to the company given all the personal information that the company holds.

All this means that the main human rights risks and opportunities from the internet arise not just from the direct actions of companies – important though they are, especially in the context of law enforcement – but also from the (often unpredictable) manner in which internet-based products and services are utilized, consumed and adopted by the user.

### Technology moves faster than the law – but the laws that do exist can conflict with internationally recognized human rights standards

The responsibility of companies towards the law has traditionally been framed as a fairly simple relationship: enforce the law at all times; go beyond the law when you can.

The example of labor conditions in factories illustrates this well. Companies seeking to improve factory conditions have long known that the relevant laws are largely predictable, straightforward and sound – but their implementation by suppliers and enforcement by local regulators is lax. So the challenge for companies becomes one of following laws known to be setting the right standard, and going beyond the law when you can (for example, by reducing working hours, paying higher wages or providing improved accommodation facilities for workers). Consider this extract from the Electronic Industry Code of Conduct (EICC), a standard widely applied in the ICT industry:

> 'Fundamental to adopting the Code is the understanding that a business, in all of its activities, must operate in *full compliance* with the laws, rules and regulations of the countries in which it operates. The Code encourages Participants to go *beyond legal compliance*, drawing upon internationally recognized standards, in order to advance social and environmental responsibility. [emphasis added]'[5]

This relationship between the company and the law – follow the law at all times; go beyond the law when you can – has come to dominate the sense of what society expects of business. So imagine the intriguing contrast that exists for Microsoft – a participant in both the EICC and the GNI – when it is now also expected to adopt an entirely different approach based on interpreting the law as narrowly as possible:

> 'Participating companies will respect and protect the freedom of expression of their users by *seeking to avoid or minimize* the impact of government restrictions on freedom of expression'

> 'When required to provide personal information to governmental authorities, participating companies will…*narrowly interpret and implement* government demands that compromise privacy. [emphasis added]'

In short, companies have historically tended to find themselves in situations where good law is accompanied by the absence of government enforcement; by contrast, here we find ourselves with a combination of bad law and an active over-enforcement by governments. And with this contrast has come a very different set of expectations for what a responsible course of action by a company should be.

One of the consistently remarked upon features of the ICT industry is the rapid pace of change and innovation – entirely new services and product features and functionalities are constantly being introduced. Twitter was only launched in March 2006 and, until fairly recently, interest in the service was restricted to the technology pages of a few broadsheet newspapers; by contrast, the role of Twitter in enabling communication and information dissemination about the elections in Iran was all-encompassing during July 2009. And the law can take a while to catch up; a number of human rights organizations have expressed concern that US export control law – written for all the right reasons – was unintentionally dampening the design and provision of internet services in the very countries where human rights activists want them the most.

In the absence of a settled legal framework – and in the face of governments increasingly turning to business to help advance their ends by restricting freedom of expression and privacy – companies carry an additional responsibility to explore, understand and investigate the potential social risks and opportunities related to their products and services and take action accordingly. In particular, companies should be identifying circumstances when freedom of expression and privacy can be jeopardized or advanced across a wide range of scenarios, including entering new markets, introducing new services or designing new technologies.[6]

Yahoo! has been particularly proactive in this regard. Recognizing that its products, technology and operating footprint increasingly intersected with human rights around the world, the company brought together a team from across the company, including Public Policy, Law Enforcement, Ethics & Compliance, International Legal, Public Affairs, Privacy, IT and the Operations teams to integrate human rights considerations into all business operations. An early result: after a Human Rights Impact Assessment, Yahoo! decided to manage and operate its Vietnamese language services out of Singapore so the services would be governed by laws with stronger user protections than in Vietnam today.[7]

A second implication relates to the role of companies in helping shape the law (when it is absent), change the law (when it is bad) and challenge its implementation (when it is over-enforced).

International Human Rights law is clear that there are legitimate circumstances when freedom of expression can be restricted. Article 19 of the International Covenant on Civil and Political Rights defines these exceptions as follows:

(a) For respect of the rights or reputations of others;
(b) For the protection of national security or of public order, or of public health or morals.

Common examples include actions necessary to tackle terrorism or to combat child exploitation. Similarly, it is recognized that companies can and should cooperate with law enforcement agencies and share personal information provided it is proportionate with the relevant purpose and consistent with the rule of law. However, there are many jurisdictions in which the law is simply not present on these topics – or at least not well established – and it is for this reason that companies may be well served to engage proactively with governments to reach a shared understanding of how restrictions to freedom of expression and collaboration with law enforcement agencies can take place in a manner consistent with international human rights law. In short, there is a capacity building role for companies in raising the governance standards and relevant laws and regulations in many jurisdictions around the world.

However, more challenging for companies are situations in which the law is bad or over-enforced. Indeed, the root of this question – what companies should do when international human rights standards and local laws and regulations are in conflict – was one of the toughest addressed during the negotiations to establish the GNI. Once it was agreed that the best route of action wasn't necessarily to leave the country (because of the potentially overall positive impact internet communications can have for human rights) the stark question remained: should the company obey the local law and potentially be associated with a human rights violation, or should the company disobey the local law and keep its hands clean from a human rights perspective?

The content of the final GNI Principles illustrate clearly some of the ways in which companies can attempt to deal with this dilemma. However, it is clear that ultimately the companies are in no position to practice civil disobedience and that a different route would be required:

> 'Challenge the government in domestic courts or seek the assistance of relevant government authorities, international human rights bodies or non-governmental organizations when faced with a government restriction that appears inconsistent with domestic law or procedures or inter-national human rights laws and standards on freedom of expression'

However, the GNI also recognizes that it is 'neither practical nor desirable for participating companies to challenge in all cases' – rather companies should choose when to challenge 'based on a range of criteria such as the potential beneficial impact on free-dom of expression, the likelihood of success, the severity of the case, cost, the representativeness of the case and whether the case is part of a larger trend'.

Implicit in this approach is the recognition that ICT companies will continue to be involved in restrictions to freedom of expression and privacy – that search results will continue to be filtered in some jurisdictions, that user generated content may continue to be removed and that personal information handed over when demanded, even if there is uncertainty about the nature of the case – but that the responsible thing for companies to do is to play a strategic game, in collaboration with like minded organizations, to challenge government interventions and advance the overall cause of freedom of expression and privacy.

## Technology is complex to understand, and its interaction with society unpredictable – so engagement with stakeholders becomes even more important

Over recent years it has appeared as if the large internet companies have been engaged in a crash course in human rights. Indeed they have, and continue to be reliant on external organizations to fully understand the human rights implications of their products and services. However, this is only half the story since civil society organizations have had their work cut out to fully understand how ICT can both jeopardize and advance human rights. And it is for this reason that engagement between companies (who know the technology) and stakeholders (who may know less about the technology but more about possible social consequences) has become critical to the common cause between the user and the company.

The ICT industry is characterized by constant change and the rapid introduction of new products and services. But underlying this constant change is a mindboggling complexity and technical sophistication sufficient to confuse many inside the industry, let alone those outside it. Yet to fully understand the responsibility of ICT companies to protect and advance freedom of expression and privacy requires a well developed understanding of the technology in question. It would be difficult, for example, to chart a practical path for companies without a basic understanding of questions along the following lines:

- How does search work, and how are results filtered?
- Under what circumstances is it technically feasible to take down content in one jurisdiction but not in the rest of the world?
- How is data transmitted across the telecommunications network? Where and how is this data stored? For how long?
- What is encrypted data, and what is the difference between http and https?
- What types of data constitute personally identifiable information?
- What information does a telecommunications service provider have about the phone calls a user has made?

These questions are just to skim the surface; the point being that the interaction between new technology and society is increasingly difficult to interpret and understand – and it is only through extended dialogue between companies and their stakeholders that the human rights risks and opportunities of ICT in diverse countries around the world can be fully comprehended.

Indeed, one of the huge benefits of the process to create the GNI was the sheer amount of learning that took place along the way. So important was this learning that the GNI's business meetings would often be preceded by a day-long learning session so that all participants could maximize what they could learn from each other and understand what real options existed for companies to be more responsible.

However, the decision by Google, Microsoft and Yahoo! – along with European telecoms companies Vodafone, France Telecom and TeliaSonera – to take such an open and constructive approach to engagement with outside organizations illustrates one of the dilemmas of responsible companies showing leadership: the risk that attention is diverted away from equally important companies who are either not in the public's attention or who have deliberately avoided public scrutiny.

**Our obsession with a few major brands can cause us to miss the bigger picture – and turn our attention away from where it is needed the most**

This chapter has so far focused on the role of Google, Yahoo! and Microsoft in establishing the GNI and taking steps to advance and protect freedom of expression and privacy. These three companies were in part pushed into this leadership role through the intense political and media scrutiny they faced – at the same time, the three companies deserve a huge amount of credit for proactively seeking collaborative solutions and for taking a bold stance in favor of human rights.

However, to let the story end here would be to miss the big picture. Indeed, a further exploration into the risks and opportunities faced by many of the companies not participating in the early stages of the GNI reveals that our collective obsession with a small number of major brands and a few simple questions – the type that easily become front-page news – can dangerously draw our attention away from the vast range of companies that require urgent attention.

We live and work in world in which the amount of information we create and communicate online increases exponentially each year. With this in mind it is worth taking a moment to reflect upon the human rights risks and opportunities that exist among the full range of ICT companies that have created and supported this information age – companies that, to varying degrees and with some notable exceptions, were largely ignored during the creation of the GNI in favor of a focus on three headline brands:

- Software companies who build and maintain vast IT infrastructures for the storage, analysis and processing of data.
- Internet security companies who provide solutions for the secure management of data and whose filtering technologies can have multiple applications.
- Telecommunications services providers who necessarily retain a vast amount of personal information about their customers and who are increasingly involved in the provision of content services over mobile networks.

- Telecoms equipment manufacturers whose network equipment contains the product functionality that enables interception, monitoring, surveillance and content filtering.
- PC manufacturers whose hardware products can potentially be sold pre-installed with filtering and surveillance software.
- Handset manufacturers whose products are increasingly designed with location-based services in mind and whose functionality can potentially enable surveillance and filtering.

Leading companies in all these sectors have proactive corporate responsibility programs in place and all are paying some attention to their human rights risks and opportunities. However, in the absence of focus and attention from the media, regulators and civil society organizations, it is perhaps not surprising that these companies were not active participants in the creation of the GNI.[8] And here's the point: the first human rights standard developed for the ICT industry on freedom of expression and privacy was written without these companies at the table and so is of uncertain value and relevance to them. To take one example, the role of companies in the development of internet infrastructure raises some intriguing ethical questions that were not able to receive the attention they perhaps deserved during the creation of the GNI:

- What ability does a telecoms equipment manufacturer have to design or control the functionality of products in order to minimize censorship or illegitimate access to personal information?
- What kinds of consulting services are provided alongside hardware that might advise customers on how to use products for censorship, or to facilitate illegitimate access to personal information?
- Is it possible for the company to 'get to know its customers' and not sell products to customers who may be engaged in human rights abuses – for example, 'public security'; customers in certain high risk locations?
- How can the company assess the risk that customers may use products to violate human rights?

- Are there ways to design future networks so as to minimize risks to freedom of expression and privacy at every stage in the ICT value chain?

During 2009 interest in the role of telecommunications equipment providers in Iran and the 'Green Dam Youth Escort' proposals in China – which would have implicated PC manufacturers in the provision of filtering (and perhaps monitoring) software – began to shift attention towards these companies. However, the lesson learned is that the creation of the GNI, a new, critically important and innovative development for the industry, was undertaken with a significant portion of the relevant participants absent.

## Conclusion

The rapid introduction of new ICT products and services into society brings with it all sorts of implications for the way we live and work. However, as has been discussed in this chapter, these products and services evolve at a great speed, are technically complicated, frequently outpace the law and can bring unpredictable consequences for human rights. Indeed, dynamics within the industry can change very rapidly as the unfolding story around Google's presence in China in early 2010 so clearly demonstrated. In these circumstances no one organization or sector – government, company, customer, user or civil society organization – has sufficient control over the social impact of business to act alone. These characteristics reinforce the need for an approach based on increased collaboration between stakeholders to achieve common goals.

# CHAPTER 7

# Innovation, regulation and complexity

## Business leads more social change than many people might think

The lifeblood of many businesses is their innovation pipeline, creating new products and services that offer benefits over the competition. Innovation can be both incremental – improving the efficiency of a process, or adding marginal benefits to a product – or breakthrough – creating a whole new product or service category. Breakthrough innovation is particularly critical for industries such as pharmaceuticals, creating new drugs, or in information technology, with products offering different combinations of services, such as internet enabled mobile phones that also play media. Incremental innovation is seen more frequently in fast moving consumer goods such as food and beverage and household products.

Often underestimated is the role that breakthrough innovation plays in social progress. Most of the technology that exists today was developed by businesses seeking to innovate. Sometimes the early breakthrough work was government sponsored, especially if there was a military application, but the significant social benefits are generally brought about by a technology being developed or popularized by a business. From mobile phones to car airbags, and from laptops to life-saving drugs, the benefits are all around us.

Such innovations are often developed in a collaborative way with universities and businesses working in partnership, exploiting the longer-term thinking and deep research capability of academics with the drive for direct saleable benefits for consumers that comes from business. The people driving innovation, both within business and within academia, are generally driven by their love of exploration, of creating something new, and getting there before others. These individuals have brought great benefits to society, but they are not universally trusted and their motivations, or at least those of the organizations they work for, are often suspected.

We will continue to require new innovations to meet the scale of the challenges that society faces on environmental issues such as climate change and water scarcity, and health crises such as HIV/AIDS and other global pandemics. From fuel cells and longer lasting batteries for electric cars, through to cheaper desalination equipment for fresh drinking water, billions of dollars are being invested around the world in clean technology innovations.

This chapter explores the role of both breakthrough and incremental innovation in achieving sustainability. It is through innovation that big business can make some of its greatest contributions to addressing our shared challenges – but to succeed this innovation will require new approaches from regulators and rapid uptake from the whole value chain.

## Eco-innovation has only just begun and requires the whole value chain

One of the most important contributions business can make is to create innovative products and services which deliver the same or a better quality of life for consumers but with a much lower environmental impact. Early work on eco-efficiency in the 1990s largely focused on waste reduction and was led by a range of concerned senior individuals at companies such as DuPont, the materials and chemicals group, and Interface Inc, the commercial textiles manufacturer. Whilst one of the key drivers was reducing operating costs, it was more than that. Self-empowered teams were formed at Interface made up of employees from all over the business, energized by the opportunity to cut waste and reduce environmental impact.

Interface, led by founder and chairman Ray Anderson, was one of the few businesses that challenged itself to go beyond eco-efficiency to eco-innovation, seeking to radically redesign its products to reduce the material inputs and wastes of the whole process. Interface created ultra lightweight floor coverings delivering the same performance and style, and 'random' design carpet tiles which could be laid in any direction, reducing on-site installation waste by 25% or more. However, Interface's even greater ideas – such as redesigning the way floor covering was sold through leasing rather than an outright sale, so that the raw materials were retained to make the next floor covering in a fully closed loop system – struggled to take off. This was largely because their customers were not ready to embrace these radical ideas.

This case demonstrates that for eco-innovation to work, the whole value chain needs to understand why sustainability is so important and be prepared to change – not necessarily to sacrifice the benefits of the product, but to be open to a different idea or new benefits. Recycling is now the norm in most homes in developed markets around the world, but it has taken 30 years for this to become the case in a widespread fashion. It's not because the technology wasn't there, because recycling has been possible for a long time. Rather it has taken a generation for families to be prepared to change their habits to the extent where local government enforcement of waste separation and recycling has become acceptable.

A further example of very simple home eco-improvements is energy efficient light bulbs. It took some years for consumers to shift to lower energy bulbs, even though they had been available for some time. It took the leadership of certain retailers to make them widely available and comparatively priced with old style light bulbs for them to succeed in the market place. Now we are seeing the second generation of this change, with the shift to LED lighting in the home occurring much faster now that consumers have gained experience changing the source of light in their homes. We will need consumers to be prepared for more and more change like this as companies begin to innovate more rapidly to reduce environmental impact.

Eco-innovation has significantly increased in the last ten years. From the widespread use of the LEED system (Leadership in

Energy and Environmental Design) in new building construction in the US, to the launch of laundry detergents which can wash clothes effectively at 30 degrees Celsius, we are finally seeing some significant change on a widespread scale.

But whilst leading companies have devoted resources to eco-innovation for some time, it is only now that the environment is seriously becoming one of the core themes of product innovation across the consumer products industries. All major fast moving consumer goods companies are using carbon and water footprinting tools to understand where the greatest impacts are in their value chain and considering how these can be reduced. Most major retailers are investing in communicating these issues to consumers, testing labelling schemes, in store education and incentives to see what level of traction these issues have with consumers. In the next ten years we will see a radical acceleration in eco-innovation to enable the world to meet the environmental challenge that we face.

## With developed markets reaching saturation, innovation 'favoring the billions' can generate both new revenue and significant social benefit

Some of the most important innovations of the last thirty years are those that have created significant social value by re-thinking the way business is done to benefit the poor. The development of micro-finance for poor communities whose only other access to credit was via expensive local money lenders is a good example. Muhammad Yunus, who founded the Grameen Bank in Bangladesh in 1983, won the Nobel Peace Prize in 2006 for his pioneering work in this area. Since the Grameen Bank was founded, micro-finance has bloomed around the world as a critical enabler of small scale, often rural entrepreneurs in developing countries.

The best social innovations not only provide direct local solutions for the poor but also create global connections which improve understanding, trust and commitment between communities. One of the most compelling examples is the development in 2005 of Kiva.org, which allows people anywhere around the world to lend money to a specific individual entrepreneur in the developing world through an existing local micro-finance institution. Kiva has taken the opportunity for greater personal connection provided by the web to a very different level, enabling an individual who wants to lend to do so in a way that would have seemed impossible before Kiva came along. In its first four years Kiva enabled over half a million funders to provide micro loans totalling $100 million to nearly a quarter of a million entrepreneurs in the developing world.

Big businesses are learning from the pioneering methods of entrepreneurs such as the Grameen Bank. The book 'The Fortune at the Bottom of the Pyramid' by C. K. Pralahad in 2004, documented a trend that has been growing in major multinational businesses to find profitable business models that meet the needs of consumers on very low incomes in developing countries. The business opportunity in these models is significant, but just as significant is the change in company thinking that has led to these products. Instead of taking products created for developed markets and adapting them for the developing world, companies which succeed in this area rethink their products based on deep insight into the needs of local consumers and a detailed understanding of the availability of local resources and infrastructure. This often results in some radically different products. Sometimes these products are facilitated by changes in technology, such as Vodafone's successful promotion of mobile communications technology in Kenya. People in rural areas can now use mobile phones for banking, paying for day to day goods and services and even paying school fees.

Products designed for these markets need to consider the irregular income stream of many poorer consumers, allowing for smaller sized packages for consumer goods such as food, beverages and cosmetics or 'pay as you go services' for communications. Unilever's single serve shampoo sachets in India allow consumers who can't afford to buy a whole bottle of shampoo up front still to be able to get the benefits of their products.

They also need to consider that operating conditions may be much harsher and therefore products such as laptops need to be more rugged, whilst many communications products such as mobile phones or computers may be shared amongst many users, rather than owned by an individual. Microsoft has created an approach where more than one user can utilize a computer at the same time through a split computer screen, and an additional mouse and keyboard.

One of the critical elements of these business models is keeping costs down, and local sourcing provides the double benefit of lower costs and creating employment elsewhere in the economy. SABMiller's Eagle lager, a sorghum-based beer developed in Uganda, is made from crops grown locally rather than from imported malting barley. It provides a high quality product at a much lower price than previously available and creates incomes for around 8,000 farmers, their dependents, and many more people in the distribution chain.

A further element of these new models is cross-sectoral partnerships. To make a new market work, companies promoting their products often need to invest in the local population to develop the skills and knowledge required to enable their value chains to operate effectively. This might be working with an NGO which knows the local community and can help educate local farmers about delivering their products on time, at the right quality and in the right quantities. Equally it might be working closely with other business sectors, such as finance, to ensure consumers can get access to a service. Nokia has worked with the Grameen Bank to develop the 'Village Phone' concept. An individual sets up a small business with a micro-finance loan, buying a mobile phone, and then rents out the airtime to local people who could otherwise not afford to use a mobile phone.

Operating successfully in these markets requires a different view of profit margins from the standard developed world view. Whilst the profitability per unit may be low on some of these innovations, the volume of opportunity is very large. Most importantly, these big businesses are viewing the world of innovation with a different lens, one which recognizes that people expect them not just to deliver innovative new products but also improve social wellbeing for people who earn very little.

## The rapid pace of change brings risks and can lead to social discomfort

Whilst innovation brings great benefits for society, it can also bring disadvantages or raise new ethical dilemmas. For example, the development of biotechnology touches on principles and beliefs that people may hold very deeply, perhaps not even being aware of it. Often this has a direct religious connection, but not always. The possibilities of using stem cells to grow new organs on demand may lead to a revolution in quality of life for some and, over time, extension of lifespans for those who can afford it, but understandably it also comes with many questions and challenges. These include highly inflammatory debates such as the source of stem cells: the use of embryonic cells for research has led to protests and discussion around the world. But beyond the issue of the source of the innovation, the abilities that we may soon develop in the biosciences lead to questions as fundamental as 'what defines my existence as a human being?' and whether it is right to specify the physical and medical attributes of a test-tube conceived child.

There are also significant risks that can arise from the pace of change. The new technologies being explored at the moment, such as the use of extremely small nano particles for a wide range of industrial and consumer applications, may have human or environmental health implications. The impact of a widespread release of specifically engineered particles into the world may well be unknown. Certainly those leading these innovations may well be more interested in the scientific breakthroughs themselves, or the profits these breakthroughs can generate, rather than a detailed mapping and testing of the risks that they might create.

It is for this reason that business cannot – and should not – make decisions about the pursuit and wide scale application of these innovations alone. For trust to be maintained in the process of innovation it is important that community and social interests are involved and represented during the process. Most often this can be through regulation by governments, but there are also other ways of involving the public in reviewing the benefits and risks of new innovations.

## Regulation is a difficult task

In a democratic market-based society there remains a critical role for government to play in regulating the way new technologies are developed and the impacts they may have on society and the planet. Most developed markets have a plethora of regulators who cover everything from food standards to human embryo research. There are sometimes movements of staff between industry and regulators – which contrary to popular belief regarding 'being in industry's pockets' actually gives regulators better insights into industry. Sometimes regulators are ahead of the game, setting out frameworks for research and parameters for testing which the innovators have to work within. But all too often they remain behind the game: the impact of complex and poorly understood financial products which led to the widespread instability causing the latest financial downturn is ample evidence of that.

One challenge regulators face is the fact that they were often designed to regulate an old technology when the pace of change leaves them grappling with a completely new paradigm. Take the case of telecommunications and media regulators and the rise of the internet. In the old world (1990s) of TV and telephones, there was a clear demarcation of content and communication. Only ten to fifteen years later a massive variety of content can be accessed online, in some places displacing traditional media such as newspapers, in other ways enhancing it such as TV re-players online. The recent debate around whether or not Google Voice (a web-based telecommunications service provided by Google) should be subject to the same rules and regulations as traditional telecommunications companies is a case in point.

Regulation can also fail in very basic ways. One of the most memorable cases in recent history in the UK was the bovine spongiform encephalopathy (BSE) crisis in the late 1990s, when much of the UK's cattle herd had to be killed in response to a breakout of that disease. It was ultimately found to be caused by contaminated feed including diseased animals being fed to cattle which are naturally herbivores. That particular case revealed a systemic problem which had been created by the search for the lowest cost in proteins for animal feed. For a period the government argued that the disease was confined to animals with no risk to human health. Eventually a link was made to the human form of the disease, variant Creutzfeldt-Jakob disease (vCJD), although so far the impact of this disease has been far lower that the predicted widespread deaths of the time.

The reputation and financial blow to UK agriculture was very large, with import bans being imposed on British beef for years by many of the UK's key trading partners. It had a deeper and longer lasting impact though in the form of creating a mistrust of the UK government's farming and food regulators, who were seen as defending the industry first and foremost and only agreeing to culls and food safety action when the problem had been known for some time. The decisions that the regulators faced were exceedingly difficult. The impact of acting too quickly, had the disease turned out to be less prevalent, might have been an unnecessary destruction of thousands of healthy cattle, destroying animals and livelihoods needlessly. Yet in the event it was far worse to have moved too slowly. Each new scare brings a new dimension which means that the previous models can't be used in the same way, so regulators face a tough role.

## Companies underestimate the importance of considering the public good

One of the areas that is most mis-understood and that has sometimes been critically undervalued by businesses is the role of a society-wide dialogue on a particular area of innovation and change. When innovation networks – including academics, businesses and others – charge ahead with their breakthroughs, there can be significant communication gaps with society and this can lead to a breakdown in successful innovation. This is more than just a public relations exercise, but rather a fundamental stage in sharing the benefits of a new idea with society and genuinely listening to public concerns.

The best example of this is the debate around genetically modified organisms (GMOs) in foods. When first introduced in the US in the 1990s there was some debate around both the human health and the environmental impacts of releasing modified plant DNA into the food chain and the wider environment. Field trials were carried out, as well as health trials, and despite some campaign group pressure in the US, the Food and Drug Administration (FDA) approved, over time, the widespread use of GMOs. Over ten years later, there have been no significant health issues reported in the US, despite extensive infiltration in the food system.

However the story in Europe and elsewhere in the world has been very different. When the GMO crops were first promoted by bio-tech companies to the public, it was not clear what benefits they offered consumers. It seemed to the public that they would see no change in the price or quality of their foods, whilst the agricultural companies and to a lesser extent some large scale farmers would make bigger profits. This left fertile ground for the campaign groups to sow the misgivings they had about the technology. However the campaign groups were smart: their concerns largely related to the environmental impacts of the release of GMOs, hence the key role in the campaigns by groups such as Greenpeace and Friends of the Earth. But their messaging to the public played on their health concerns, with images of 'Frankenfoods' and mad scientists. It is worth reflecting that the failure to introduce GMO crops into the UK and the surrounding public furore gave a major boost to the development of organic foods, through highlighting the 'artificial' nature of industrial farming.

This also positioned the campaign groups well with the instinctive public view, much more prevalent in Europe than the United States, that big business is out to exploit society for every penny it can get, and that anyone who opposes big business is an underdog who deserves support. As a result of campaigns resonating well with a receptive public sentiment, and a woeful failure by the promoters of GMOs to make a public value case, a very stringent anti-GMO regime was instituted in Europe which largely continues to this day.

Most interesting is the fact that the regulatory regime effectively followed public opinion. One of the enduring television images of the 1990s in Europe is Greenpeace and other NGO campaigners pulling up fields of genetically modified test crops. These crops had been licensed for growth following the development of detailed agricultural safety procedures, including buffer zones to prevent the spread of the genetically modified material to other plants. Yet the NGO activists had the public's support and relatively quickly politicians across Europe responded to this pressure by establishing a very tight regulatory regime. The cause of the NGOs was helped by the strong local farming lobbies on the continent who were also opposed to the increasing influence of multinational agriculture firms.

Would this case have been different had the regulators been trusted more? In the eyes of the public an industry perceived to be out to make a profit at all costs, and governments too weak to properly regulate them, is a toxic combination. Yet was this really the picture? Are GMOs all that bad for the environment? The lack of evidence from the US and elsewhere in the world of significant environmental damage as a result of GMOs suggests that the depth of the fear factor in Europe may be unjustified. However it seems clear that the GMO companies did not involve the European public in the development of their new products and did not effectively consider their needs or concerns – or if they did, then it wasn't effectively communicated to the public at large.

So with BSE in the UK and GMO crops in Europe we have two different examples of regulation not working. One where regulators arguably had allowed industry to go too far in cutting costs, leading to mass cattle slaughter; another where both industry and regulators were roundly beaten in a public campaign to stop GMOs which ultimately may turn out to have been too precautionary. Getting the science right is critical, as the BSE incident teaches us, but on its own it is nowhere near enough. Not only do regulators need to be trusted as independent, competent and prepared to stand up to big business, but those pushing the innovation – usually business – need to demonstrate that they are acting in the public interest as well as their own.

The GMO situation may well change in the future, even in Europe. A number of senior business people, including Peter

Brabeck, Chairman of the foods group Nestlé, have publicly come out in favor of GMOs as a solution to the world's growing food crisis.[1] This is a risky strategy given the history of GMOs in Europe, but it may be a more appropriate time to articulate what some of the benefits could be to the public at large. Population growth, greater meat consumption, climate change and water scarcity are all putting pressure on food supplies and GMOs do offer some benefits in terms of increased yields and crop resistance to harsher growing conditions, such as drought. If there is a global public good argument, rather than a private profit argument, the same technology may actually get a very different reception.

This would be a similar change in public opinion to the one that has recently occurred regarding nuclear power in countries such as the UK. In the 1990s it was unthinkable for a government to propose a new generation of nuclear power stations: a moratorium was the official policy of the incoming Labour government in 1997. Yet within ten years nuclear expansion was back on the table, advocated by both the Conservatives and Labour, with much reduced public opposition. The driver for this 'u-turn' in public acceptance has been climate change. It is clear that we cannot achieve the reductions we need in carbon dioxide emissions without significant changes in energy supply away from fossil fuels, and it is now increasingly argued that the scale and speed of that change means that nuclear needs to be part of the energy mix, along with renewable sources such as wind and solar. Even longstanding board members of Friends of the Earth UK have come around to that view, causing interesting splits in the green movement over the issue. If a clear public good argument can be made for a technology or an innovation, then it is far more likely to be accepted.

### Transparency and trust: a model for the future?

What can regulation look like in the future? The scale of the social and environmental challenges we face as a society requires great innovation, which means creativity, resources and commitment. But, as is clear from this chapter, innovation only really works when there is trust in those leading the process. How can transparency be improved in these types of situations, which can then lead to a greater trust in the process? How can the public feel that they are more involved? What is the role of the NGOs, the self-appointed independent interest groups who do not profit from the innovation and therefore are so highly trusted by the public?

There are some interesting approaches being piloted through the development of new technologies such as nano particles. Nanologue[2] was a collaboration between leading European environmental institutions such as The Wuppertal Institute in Germany and Forum for the Future in the UK, funded by the EU. It mapped the range of possible concerns regarding the technology, held detailed consultations with a range of stakeholders and then developed potential scenarios for how the technology might develop and how the world might respond.

In a similar vein The Innovation Society, a Swiss company, is the facilitator for an ongoing multi-stakeholder dialogue regarding the opportunities, risks and concerns surrounding the development of nano technologies.[3] The most significant insights coming out of this process concern the role of cooperation and coordination amongst the range of stakeholders involved and proactive public communication about the understanding of risks and benefits from the technologies as they emerge.

## Conclusion

Innovation lies at the heart of improvements in our quality of life, from medical developments to new ways of communicating, and will play an increasingly important role as new generations of products and services are required to take us to sustainability. Businesses drive most of this innovation, yet to do so without an understanding of public concern for the risks of new technologies is a mistake that big businesses cannot afford to make. Regulators play a key role in protecting society from innovations that go too far, but ultimately business would be well advised to increase its proactive engagement with the public, ensuring that its new products and services create more benefits for society than they do negative impacts, and continue to take on board ethical and moral concerns.

# Who is driving change?

## CHAPTER 8

# The government of big business

Ask who the largest telecommunications company is in the world and thoughts usually turn to large American companies such as AT&T and Verizon or European companies going global such as Vodafone or Telefonica. But in terms of the number of customers (522 million at the end 2009), size of the network (over 400,000 base stations on the same date) and market capitalization ($175 billion on 31st March 2009)[1] the answer by some considerable distance is a company present in only two markets, China and Pakistan: China Mobile. How China Mobile reached this point, and how it has done so, in part, through the provision of innovative services aimed at addressing real sustainability challenges, is an intriguing story about the interplay between government and business.

This chapter examines the relationship between government and big business in China and looks for insights on what it might tell us about the interplay between business and government in addressing sustainability challenges anywhere in the world. With businesses originating from emerging markets becoming increasingly global – three of the top five companies in the 2009 Financial Times Global 500 ranked by market capitalization were Chinese – it is a story of increasing significance to the future of global business.

## Strong direction by government can drive rapid changes that address sustainability challenges – and business benefits can follow

China Mobile serves two masters. On the one hand it is a Chinese State Owned Enterprise (SOE), 74.25% owned by the Chinese

Government. On the other hand it is quoted on the New York and Hong Kong Stock Exchanges with 25.75% of its stock owned by public shareholders. To meet the expectations of these two masters the company needs to meet two potentially conflicting ends: the return on investment required by its public shareholders and the broader public policy objectives of the Chinese Government. Yet so far the company appears to have successfully achieved both.

The Chinese Government has prioritized economic development in rural areas and the modernization of agricultural techniques. As a result China Mobile set about seeking ways to meet these public policy goals through the provision of new products and services. The company set up a Rural Information Network to be a primary source of agricultural, market and business information in rural communities, established new pricing structures that were affordable in rural communities and, as a partner in the Government's Village Connected Project, expanded its network to even the most remote areas of China.[2]

But rather than viewing these activities as a supplement to its core business, expansion in rural areas became a key factor in China Mobile's growth strategy – indeed, during this time around 50% of its new customers came from rural areas. This move was initially met with skepticism by traditional investors, fearful of the huge capital costs combined with far lower revenues per user. But China Mobile ploughed on – and with its success won over mainstream investors with rapidly expanding revenues.[3]

The point of interest here is that China Mobile's strategy was apparently not driven solely by the profit motive: that approach may have resulted in a narrower focus on high-value content-based services in urban areas. Rather, it was also inspired by the social and economic public policy goals of government and by thinking innovatively about how to meet the real sustainability needs of its potential customers. As a result China Mobile innovated in ways that it might not otherwise have done and challenged underlying assumptions in the telecommunications industry about sources of profit and revenue growth. Today this view is commonplace in the global industry, including within powerhouses such as Vodafone and Telefonica.

This isn't to argue that the Chinese form of corporate governance should be replicated elsewhere. Indeed, the problems arising from the 'dual masters approach' to ownership are numerous and raise real questions about the rights of minority shareholders, who are ultimately subject to the will of the majority owned by the state. It also raises questions regarding whether the corporate governance standards established in accordance with the requirements of the New York Stock Exchange are real or illusionary. However, the China Mobile case does point to the sustainability and financial benefits that can accrue when a government provides clear and unambiguous direction in its public policy goals for business. Indeed, the approach taken by China Mobile is reminiscent of the conclusion put forward by Jim Collins and Jerry Poras in their highly influential classic 'Built to Last' or Arie de Geus's 'The Living Company' – that the most successful companies place a lower priority on shareholder return or profits, but are instead driven by a strong sense of identity and progress.[4]

It's not just Chinese SOEs that stand to benefit from the growing emphasis placed by the Chinese Government on the role of business in the country's sustainable development. An intriguing example is also provided by GM, a company whose recent history has been dominated by a rapidly shrinking business in the US that ultimately resulted in a dramatic intervention by the US Government, massive restructuring and bankruptcy. The reasons for GM's collapse in the US are complex and numerous, but among the accusations frequently made are that the company was far too slow to respond to the trend towards smaller and more fuel efficient vehicles and that, rather than embracing the climate change challenge, the company dragged its heels in a way that eventually damaged its business.

Yet this stands in stark contrast to GM in China, where the Government has set clear direction in favor of an automotive industry based on more efficient vehicles and alternative fuels. Indeed, even after the intervention of the Obama administration in 2009, the fuel efficiency standards in China were of a higher standard than those in the US.[5] The result? In China, reassured by the certainty and clear direction set by local policy, GM chose to invest heavily in alternative fuels and more energy efficient cars through a $250 million research hub.[6]

While the reasons are many and complex, it is worth noting that GM in China has 13% of the market (competing with VW for the top spot) and apparently does not face the same profitability challenges that held it back in the US.[7]

These two examples, China Mobile and GM, illustrate the benefits that can arise from clear and unambiguous direction from government in favor of sustainability, and how profitable business can arise from the ambitious pursuit by business of public policy objectives. However, these two cases also spring from a country where civil society is weak and government is strong – it provides a stark contrast with India for example, where family owned businesses, a strong philanthropic tradition and a thriving civil society has provided the means of promoting change. And of course public policy interventions from governments may not always push companies in the right direction, as Google, Yahoo!, Microsoft and other internet companies have increasingly discovered at their cost in many countries around the world.

It is perhaps unsurprising, therefore, that in China it is government, not civil society, which has become the source of change for corporations. However, this needn't always be so. Indeed, one of the key things governments can do is mandate from business the transparency that is required to enable greater participation from civil society in helping to drive progress towards sustainability.

## Transparency can support rapid changes in behavior and performance

Governments in countries with weak civil societies are often reluctant to put in place the reforms necessary to encourage civic activism. Yet this might be exactly what governments need to do if they are to promote sustainable development, especially when it comes to the contribution made by big business. Making this change will require two significant reforms:

- Making information about corporate sustainability performance more transparent to decision-makers and to the public at large;

- Establishing a local and national culture in which sustainability performance information is used to make decisions and influence the actions of corporations.

Surprisingly, one of the mechanisms to achieve this radical change could be the humble and much maligned sustainability report – though perhaps only when combined with the liberating and democratizing power of the internet.

Over the past decade in the US and Europe there have been two developments in corporate sustainability reporting that display an interesting contrast. On the one hand, corporate reporting of sustainability performance has moved from the exception to the expected and is increasingly in the mainstream. KPMG's regular survey of corporate reporting shows that nearly 80% of the world's 250 largest companies worldwide now issue reports, up from about 50% in 2005.[8] Perhaps the turning point in the US was the decision by GE – frequently referred to as 'America's business school' – to adopt a leadership stance on reporting, making it nearly impossible for other companies not to follow suit.

On the other hand, a chorus of voices have criticized sustainability reporting as at best a waste of time, money and resources with little impact on sustainability performance, and at worst a deliberate and meaningless greenwashing effort intended to mislead the public into thinking that business is making more progress than it really is.

However, the breadth, depth and sophistication of the information being published by companies over the past decade has progressed significantly and major improvements have been made in the quality and comparability of reports. Reports are much more likely than ever before to focus on the sustainability issues that matter the most, to be used in decision-making by investors and other stakeholders, and eloquently describe the companies' future strategy, objectives and targets for sustainability.

However, the time is right for governments and the relevant regulators around the world to enable increased transparency from business on sustainability performance and to set standards that ensure greater comparability across all businesses. This could mean, for example, a framework in which all large companies issue sustainability reports, not just the 80% of the Fortune 250 that have voluntarily decided to disclose. Earlier in the 20th century regulations were increasingly put in place to ensure that the market operated on the basis of reliable and transparent information with which people could make confident investment decisions. Governments took this route after various unscrupulous and, by today's standards, extraordinarily corrupt practices undermined people's confidence in the market. Given how critical the sustainability transition is today the question businesses and governments all over the world have to ask themselves is 'Why are sustainability disclosures any different from financial disclosures?'

This approach becomes all the more important as companies from emerging economies are increasingly prevalent in the lists of the world's largest companies. Consider once more the case of China. Just a few years ago there was very little reporting of sustainability performance by companies – much like the early 1990s in the west – leaving most of us to guess, and assume the worst, about the extent to which social and environmental issues were being proactively managed inside Chinese companies. But the view of the Chinese Government has changed dramatically, and the results may well prove to be significant.

The rate of growth in sustainability reporting in China has been rapid, with the number of reports increasing from just four in 2004 to over 130 in 2008.[9] And this growth wouldn't have happened without significant encouragement from the Chinese Government, manifested in some important public policy signals.

However, what appears to be truly significant is the way in which Chinese companies are beginning to use reporting on their sustainability performance, not just as improved communications, but as a capacity building exercise for improving sustainability performance management and strategy too. The achievement of China Mobile – not only becoming the first company from mainland China to make a serious attempt to disclose its $CO_2$ emissions, but the first also to be listed on the Dow Jones Sustainability Index[10] – could be the sign of things to come. By subjecting corporate sustainability performance to the discipline of public scrutiny, the Chinese Government is helping to drive

**State-owned Assets Supervision and Administration Commission (SASAC) of the State Council 'Guidelines on Fulfilling Social Responsibility by Central Enterprises'**

The SASAC is the entity that manages and supervises Chinese SOEs on behalf of the Chinese Government. In late 2007 the SASAC issued a highly-influential guideline stating that corporate social responsibility should be the main way for SOEs to attain sustainable development. The Guideline called on SOEs to:

- Establish divisions in charge of corporate social responsibility
- Integrate corporate social responsibility into their strategies, culture and activities
- Monitor corporate social responsibility performance
- Consult with stakeholders
- Publish corporate social responsibility reports
- Learn from the best of foreign corporate social responsibility, while tailoring their approach to the Chinese situation

In addition a number of other influential guidelines for corporate transparency have been introduced, including from the Shenzhen and Shanghai stock exchanges and the Shanghai Banking Regulatory Bureau.

significant performance improvement and the implementation of strategies that could become critical to China's sustainable development. The challenge, just as in the west a decade or so ago, will be to make high quality and comparable reports the mainstream and not the exception, and to ensure that the full range of companies leading China's rapid development are integrating sustainability into the core of their operations.

It would be wrong though to let this story rest having considered only the reporting of sustainability performance information into the public domain: the real test will lie in how this information is used by decision-makers and enables the development of a strong civil society able to participate more actively in the pursuit of sustainable development. Here too, government action to establish and enforce transparency will be pre-requisite for change. We can turn again to China for two examples of how Government action shows signs of beginning to support the ability of civil society to promote change:

- The Chinese 'Measures on Open Environmental Information', adopted by the State Environmental Protection Administration of China in February 2007, requires that local government agencies make public a list of local environmental policies and a list of businesses that violate these rules. Businesses falling foul of these rules must disclose environmental performance information – opening up the possibility that companies won't just be held accountable by regulators, but by civil society too.[11]
- The 'China Water Pollution Map' displays information relating to water quality, emission levels and the source of pollutants in China, as well as a 'pollution ranking' and 'environmental information transparency index'. An accompanying 'China Air Pollution Map' takes a similar approach to air quality.[12]

The question now is the extent to which these measures will encourage the performance improvements that they are intended to incentivize, the credibility of the information, and the extent to which Chinese civil society will be able to use the information to enforce and campaign for improved environmental standards from business. The answer is that it is far too early to tell, and that China still has a long way to go in terms of the management of company sustainability performance.

However, despite this uncertainty, something very important is happening in China that has huge implications for corporate responsibility. The development of new urban centres and rural economies in China requires the efficient use of energy and material resources and this is a huge challenge for the country with obvious and significant implications for global sustainability. The Chinese Government has rightly recognized that SOEs have a significant role to play in this development and has chosen government-led approaches to corporate responsibility as one tool to channel that development in a sustainable direction. Moreover, this approach has wider implications: in China, it influences the approach taken by large private enterprise that are not owned by the state and, intriguingly, western companies with a significant market presence in China; outside of China, it raises all sorts of interesting questions about whether the corporate responsibility approach encouraged for Chinese companies at home will be replicated overseas.

## Big business and governments need to collaborate to build effective public governance – a move away from over-simplistic notions of 'too much government interference in business' or 'too much business influence over government'

In this chapter and in this book we've been arguing for more collaboration between governments and business to solve sustainability challenges. This point of view – that companies and governments should form a closer bond – often brings with it one of two responses: that we risk too much interference of government in business, or that we risk too much influence of business over government.

Of course, both of these risks are ones that we need to be careful to avoid. We need frameworks from government that set clear direction and provide the incentives for business to deliver social value and public goods. And we need laws and regulations that prevent corruption and the undue influence of business over government.

However, to suggest that either of these two points of view should prevent government and business working together to achieve public goals is over simplistic and dangerous. In fact, there is a great deal of common cause between the two, especially in emerging economies or in countries where civil society is less strong.

A leading example of this common cause is provided by GE's activities in emerging markets, a key source of revenue growth for the company. As a company, GE is scrupulous in its identification of priorities, believing that its approach to corporate responsibility needs to be focused on the issues that matter the most. And right there, near the top of its list, is capacity building and the rule of law in emerging markets. According to Karan Bhatia, Vice President and Senior Counsel, GE International Law and Policy:

> 'There are many business-related reasons for multinationals to promote rule of law in emerging markets. Rule of law fosters a level playing field on which to compete. It promotes stable, durable economic growth in prime export markets. The predictability it brings helps business managers anticipate commercial needs and constraints. Rule of law also helps to create an environment where multinational companies morally and ethically feel comfortable doing business.'[13]

It is notable that GE sees its role and purpose in emerging markets as not just being about the generation of profit but also about the development of stable, sustainable and just forms of governance and the rule of law. Examples of putting this into practice include close relationships with law schools in China and Vietnam, financial grants to support rule of law initiatives and partnerships with organizations promoting conflict and change management methodologies.[14]

GE isn't alone in realizing that business has a critical role to play in raising standards of governance around the world. During 2008 the World Economic Forum's 'Global Corporate Citizenship Initiative' took a similar view when it published 'Partnering to Strengthen Public Governance: The Leadership Challenge for CEOs and Boards' with the aim of developing a framework for business engagement in promoting more effective public governance:

> 'everyone – the citizens of weak governance zones, international and local businesses, home and host governments – has much to gain from strengthening public governance: enhanced human welfare, higher sustainable growth and the creation of new markets...[we] acknowledge that the business sector is a valuable partner in public sector reform, one

that can do much to create and sustain the impetus for reform.'[15]

Indeed, this challenge, of business partnering with civil society and government to promote more effective public governance, is illustrated well by the topic of freedom of expression and privacy on the Internet covered in the previous chapter. Here one of the principle concerns of the participating companies is the extent to which they are being subject to demands from governments that do not comport with international standards of due process or the rule of law. The internet companies don't necessarily want less governance; they want better governance – and one of the primary ways to secure that is through proactive efforts to promote the rule of law and due process.

This encouraging trend – of companies seeking more stable and sustainable governance – results directly from the realization that, over the longer term, the existence of shared risks means shared responsibilities, and that profits will require sustainable development.

## Global companies need to become invested and integrated in local markets and their social and environmental challenges – sustainability requires commitment for the long haul

A traditional and skeptical narrative for the activity of 'big business' operating in emerging markets runs something like this: the large company initiates operations overseas to take advantage of cheap labor and poor environmental standards and to reap greater profits as a result. The investment in the country is transitory and the company soon leaves to take advantage of the next 'cheap labor' location and in doing so leaves behind conditions much worse than it found them.

It's an attractive point of view to take and, frankly, one that has sometimes had a lot of truth to it – concern about this exploitation by companies of people and the environment explains the very origins of the corporate responsibility movement.

However, as we have seen in the discussion on building effective governance, business has the opportunity to write a different story, and it is beginning to do so. The trailblazers in this regard are not the retail companies with manufacturing supply chains shifting from location to location as labor cost fluctuates, nor the mining, oil and gas companies, extracting from the country with the natural resources and transporting to the country without.

Rather, the trailblazers are the companies that have become invested in many markets around the world and who see themselves as global companies with global operations and global markets – and who are invested in these places for the long term. These companies have an interest in sustainable economic development all over the world, and view themselves as direct beneficiaries of local growth.

Perhaps the most high profile example – but by no means the only one – is IBM and the introduction in 2006 of the notion of a 'Globally Integrated Enterprise', a new type of business organization, made possible by IT, that integrates its production and value delivery worldwide: 'state borders define less and less the boundaries of corporate thinking or practice'.[16] This bold stance was rapidly followed by the company's 'Smart Planet' positioning, the notion that the company would find revenue growth through the application of IT and analytics to solve some of the world's greatest social, economic and environmental challenges. IBM's Corporate Service Corps is similarly innovative, a highly popular scheme – it is heavily over-subscribed – that sends high potential employees to emerging markets to immerse themselves in local challenges and develop solutions that meet local needs. It's a business strategy based on the notion that out of these experiences will come new ideas and revenue opportunities.

GE's strategy is similar, its 'company to country' approach aimed at identifying local needs and the development of products that are designed and produced locally. And Japan's Hitachi is building a turn-around strategy for its business based on revenue growth outside Japan resulting from the provision of 'social infrastructure' – think everything from trains

to elevators and energy equipment to water treatment plants
– in emerging markets.

But for this approach to succeed it requires a fundamentally
different approach to global business. Gone are the days when
managers from the home country could hop from one country
to another, enjoying the comfortable life as an ex-pat but
never really becoming an active part in the local community;
here instead are the days of integration, where global companies are encouraging two-way movement between the head-
quarter country and the local markets and where company
senior management and boards are globally representative.

It is in the execution of this global approach that business has
the greatest room for improvement. Many fine words have been
spoken about developing a global outlook, but to return to the
theme of this chapter, the relationship between government and
big business, it is involvement in local public policy processes
– to inform them, to learn from them and to respond to their
trends – that big business has the furthest to travel. It is only by
listening to the voices prevalent in local markets that companies
are going to fully understand how to develop successful product
and service strategies. And it is only by engaging constructively
– promoting high standards of governance, ethics and integrity,
and by faithfully championing high social and environmental
protections – that western business can reconstruct trust in their
intentions, both at home and abroad.

It must be remembered that this alternative narrative of 'big
business' outside of their home countries – becoming invested
in local and sustainable economic development – shouldn't just
apply to the big brands from the west; it just as significantly
applies to the large private and SOEs from rapidly growing
emerging markets that are becoming some of the world's largest
companies and global brands of the future. Corporate responsibility must be a global pursuit, or else it fails. However, this
implies two things: first, that western business and governments
will only have the moral authority to press this new narrative
when their companies do the same; and second, that it suggests
an approach of engaging in, rather than avoiding, the countries
of high risk and poor governance.

Of course this latter point – engage in, rather than avoid, countries with poor governance records – runs directly counter to some of the assumptions that sparked the original growth of NGO interest in holding companies accountable, which was just as likely to campaign against operating in certain high-risk countries. Nowhere is this dilemma more graphic today than in the Democratic Republic of Congo (DRC), where, spurred by the ongoing civil war, electronics companies are increasingly being asked to identify the origins of the metals used in their products, especially tin, tantalum, tungsten and gold. The instinctively attractive position to take is one of avoidance: screen metals originating from the DRC out your supply chain and source from elsewhere. Putting aside for one moment how extremely difficult (though perhaps not impossible) this might be – the smelting and refining of minerals often combines minerals from multiple sources, and once this happens is can be extremely difficult to trace the origin of the minerals – the question that really needs to be asked is whether this is the best approach for peace and sustainable economic development in the DRC.

Perhaps we're better off asking what interventions need to be made by governments to bring peace to the DRC and, importantly for corporate responsibility, what role companies at all stages of the minerals value chain might play in the creation and development of a sustainable and responsible trade in minerals in the DRC. This could mean, for example, establishing efforts to bring development-orientated metals to market by identifying communities where the benefits of mining are shared locally, or building the human rights capability of the smelters, refiners and processors that have more direct relationships in the DRC. Engaging with such intractable problems would no doubt be messy business, but the result for human rights, social justice and environmental sustainability would be far more enduring.

## Conclusion

Governments are intended to be the ultimate protector of the public interest. For this reason governments around the world have both the responsibility and the ability to establish the framework conditions in which business can make a stronger contribution to sustainable development. However, to achieve this will require the smarter use of the three main policy levers – tax, public expenditure and regulation – to incentivize behavior change from business. But governments can't do this alone; the transition to global sustainability will require the proactive, constructive and innovative engagement of big business to help solve some of the world's most intractable challenges. Business will also be well advised to prepare for the fact that, while governments are increasingly interconnected and coordinated in their policy approaches, the balance of policy levers will likely vary significantly from market to market as governments experiment with different approaches.

## CHAPTER 9

# Everyday champions

There can be times when business is discussed as if it is run by a group of men in suits sitting around a shiny boardroom table at the top of a tall building making highly logical profit maximizing decisions that are then flawlessly put into effect. All that would need to be done to achieve corporate responsibility under these circumstances would be to convince these powerful men to make different decisions – invest in renewable energy, for example – that could then be just as easily and effortlessly put into effect.

It is true, they are usually men.

But business is more complex, creative and unpredictable than is suggested by this stereotyped imagery. Getting things done and driving change in business – whether it is improved customer service, higher quality products or more efficient procurement – is a complicated undertaking that requires champions and leaders well beyond those in the boardroom. Change is not always clean and methodical; it can just as easily be messy and complicated. And as we describe in the introduction, businesses around the world are ultimately made up of millions of people just like you and me, people who want to have fulfilling jobs in which they are able to pursue goals, impacts and outcomes beyond the simple pay cheque.

The transition to corporate responsibility will not depend on boardroom decision-making and high-level strategy alone, important though these aspects are. Rather, the creation of corporate responsibility will involve a more complicated interplay between leadership from the CEO and boardroom on the one hand and the hearts and minds of the millions of talented employees around the world who create change through their everyday work on the other. And to be sustainable both of these dimensions of leadership will require systemic changes inside the company – its vision, management framework and performance incentives – and in the broader economic, financial and regulatory context within which the company operates.

## There is plenty of room in business for 'everyday champions' to drive change towards corporate responsibility

There was once a time when if you wanted to pursue social justice and environmental sustainability then politics or the NGO world were the only places for you. These would be the sectors through which social change could be driven; business, by contrast, was a place to make money rather than pursue change.

Less than a decade ago, one of the authors remembers being in a business meeting for 'young leaders' in which, as an ice-breaker, a senior executive asked all those who had organized a student demonstration in the past to raise their hand. The author was the only one and soon turned red with embarrassment as 40 suited young people all looked towards him slightly amused at this author's obvious error of judgment. But much to everyone's surprise the senior executive went on to say how disappointed he was with the poor response; this senior executive wanted to see more business leaders who were so dissatisfied with the status quo that they want to disrupt the current way of doing business.

The senior executive was making a serious point. Successful businesses thrive on disruption, change and innovation, on discovering new and improved ways of delivering products and services better than the competition. He was looking for leaders willing to challenge the status quo and enhance the way his business performed. And here is a surprising conclusion: seeking change in the pursuit of sustainability can just as easily work with the grain of business, rather than against it. Far from being a barren place to purse sustainability, a business culture that encourages change, innovation and speed can be the perfect place for the impatient everyday champion to thrive.

London Heathrow Airport's energy manager, James Brittain, provides a case in point. His job is to ensure that the airport is as energy efficient as possible, a big task given that Heathrow handles 70 million passengers a year and with a flight taking off or landing every 30 seconds at peak times. James's job isn't to do it all himself but to mobilize the many people who know the airport and its terminal buildings inside out and to give them the tools they need to save energy. He's done that by building strong relationships with people across the airport, at every level, by running a visible energy saving campaign and by bringing a good dose of infectious enthusiasm to his work. The approach has delivered results – significantly cutting energy use, carbon emissions and also costs – and has received positive feedback from airport staff, who have been concerned about environmental issues but not always sure what they can do at work to help.

However, where once these 'everyday champions' would be working somewhat undercover in big business – disguising their passion or quietly getting on with their tasks lest someone tell them to stop – over recent years business leaders have begun to recognize the value brought to their organizations by these change makers and increasingly made them a deliberate component of business strategy. For while 'everyday champions' are pursuing their passion to create social benefit and environmental protection through business success, the benefits of their actions are accrued not by the individuals concerned or by wider society alone; the benefits are realized by their employers too.

The reason for this is simple: by being provided with the space to pursue their passion in business, these everyday champions are able to identify opportunities for innovation (or risks to avoid) that individuals focused primarily on the profit maximizing motive alone would miss – there can be a powerful link between a sense of purpose, social good and innovation. Far from undermining business, employees with a broader outlook and purpose are a critical asset, and this is increasingly true in a world where economic frameworks and financial incentives are being transformed to reward the companies that are addressing the world's social and environmental challenges.

## The leading businesses of tomorrow are turning 'everyday champions' into a deliberate strategy, led by CEOs

It is perfectly possible for 'everyday champions' to pursue change within their organizations without high profile support from the Board or CEO – new policies on supply chain labor conditions and incremental environmental improvements are frequently made without the need for explicit direction by a CEO or Board. However, the ability of this 'bottom up' change alone to cause the transformational redirection of business that is needed to achieve sustainability is severely limited.

Rather, there is an important 'top down' leadership role to be played by CEOs in promoting responsible business throughout their organization. This is true for the integration of sustainability with business strategy – discussed elsewhere in this book – but it is equally true for the unique role of the CEO in setting the right tone throughout the business and providing 'everyday champions' with the mandate to pursue change. The successful CEOs of the future will be the ones that deliberately provide the space and permission for 'everyday champions' to succeed and who recognize that some of the best ideas may originate from those who keep a much closer eye on what is going on outside the company rather than inside it.

Sir Terry Leahy, Chief Executive of Tesco, is a prime example of the CEO providing top level leadership and setting the right tone in the company for sustainability to take hold. Speaking at a Sustainable Consumption Institute conference in October 2009, Sir Terry committed Tesco to becoming a zero-carbon business by 2050 without purchasing offsets, in addition to its existing commitment to a 50% reduction in emissions from 2006 levels by 2020. Sir Terry also emphasized the important role played by consumer behavior in tackling climate change, concluding that for Tesco 'a revolution in green consumption is a fantastic opportunity: once and for all to break the link between consumption and emissions, and in doing so to satisfy a new consumer need, and grow our business…that is the goal of a sustainable business'.[1]

This pro-sustainability tone-setting approach from CEOs has become increasingly prevalent in recent years and there has been a noticeable advance in the comfort, sophistication and directness of CEO interventions on the topic of sustainability. A key attraction of BSR's annual conference – a gathering of over 1,000 corporate responsibility professionals – are the key note speeches provided by leading CEOs, which are always taken as a reasonable bellwether on the extent to which the CEO community is really driving sustainability. And at these conferences it has become increasingly noticeable that CEOs are relying less and less on pre-prepared speeches and more and more on their own personal interpretation of sustainability and what it means for business. Where once they were uncomfortable, CEO's are increasingly talking about sustainability with a fluency and confidence that they would any other part of business.

Quite how far this CEO leadership agenda had progressed became clear at BSR's 2009 annual conference when Alcatel-Lucent's CEO, Ben Verwaayen spoke very favorably about the need for mandatory public sustainability reporting by large companies. Immediately after his speech, in a smaller break out session held to discuss the topic of 'mandatory versus voluntary reporting', speaker after speaker got up to express their concern about how complicated mandatory reporting would be and explain why they were personally against it. Where once the in-house sustainability team would need to convince the CEO, here we had a CEO who was one step ahead.

Those who go into business to work on environmental or social impact often end up in the sustainability and corporate responsibility functions that, while small in size, are increasingly prominent in the world's largest companies. However, while these functions are important in creating overall coordination and strategy, the most significant champions for sustainability and corporate responsibility will increasingly be found deeper in the core business – the scientists, the buyers, the marketers, the lawyers, the sales people and the operations managers.

Gerry van den Houten is Technical, Supply Chain and Enterprise Development Director for SABMiller in Africa. His day to day role includes guidance of the purchasing of $100 million or so of agricultural raw materials, packaging and other products and services required to make the brewing company's operations work. Yet much of his time is spent on establishing new local sourcing partnerships across Africa, working to establish new products utilizing smallholder grown crops like cassava and sorghum. He works with the corporate sustainable development team to build partnerships with global and local NGOs and governments to ensure that local smallholder sourcing brings the benefits that both the business and the local communities need.

## The business case for corporate responsibility needs to stack up and responsible businesses still need to make money

There is plenty of room in business for 'everyday champions' to drive change and innovate to improve profitability and social and environmental impact. However, it would be wrong to assume that just because 'everyday champions' have found this space to experiment that a business case is not required or that wider systemic changes to the global market place do not need to be made. The success of individuals pursuing sustainability will not come of its own accord or without a supportive company infrastructure and rationale for change; and it certainly won't come without the wider changes to our global economic system (such as that right government policies and economic incentives) that will allow companies to benefit from the innovations of their 'everyday champions'.

GE's CEO Jeff Immelt was remarkably candid on this point at BSR's 2008 annual conference. Admitting that he once had a 'healthy dislike for most environmental NGOs' he went on to down play his previous personal commitment to environmental issues, having 'never camped' and 'not gone fishing'. GE's recent environmental commitments were certainly not due to 'one big green dream one night'. Rather, Immelt explained, GE's environmental strategy was born from work undertaken by three teams, one studying the science (which they concluded was pretty irrefutable), one talking to customers (who had serious environmental challenges needing solutions) and one looking at government policy (where there was clearly a trend towards more policy action). Spotting a significant business opportunity in the making, Jeff Immelt turned himself into a major champion of environmental sustainability and made a number of significant strategy announcements – doubling green research and development to $1.5 billion by 2010, for example. Jeff Immelt openly recognizes that he was not an environmentalist at heart, but he had been won over by the business case. As GE became fond of saying, 'green is green'.

This case illustrates that for the 'everyday champions' to succeed in business two conditions need to be met:

• *First, a logical business case for action that is tailored to the specific needs of the company and the market place in which that company competes.*

No matter how smart the innovation, the lack of a business case will certainly doom the 'everyday champion' to failure. However, one of the most significant features of the past decade of corporate responsibility has been the extent to which the business cases deployed by 'everyday champions' have become both more sophisticated and more deeply integrated into mainstream business strategy.

Vodafone took the ultimate step – described in its 2008 report 'One Strategy' – of making it clear that the company's business strategy and corporate responsibility strategy were 'inseparable' and that 'growth both in emerging markets and through "total communications" are closely linked to responding to society's challenges'. But Vodafone was only able to make this step after years of work by its 'everyday champions' making smart business cases for individual aspects of its corporate responsibility program. They showed that: revenue growth can result from socially-orientated product and service offerings and pricing structures geared towards customers on low incomes; efficiency gains can result from addressing climate change; and customer trust can be gained by providing a safe internet experience that respects privacy. With supportive CEO's providing the space, Vodafone's 'everyday champions' have been able to turn a company with minimal activity in corporate responsibility at the start of the decade into a company with one of the most sophisticated and integrated corporate responsibility strategies around.

- *Secondly, reforms to the overall market framework that reward companies making innovations for sustainability*

Just as companies need to encourage the work of 'everyday champions' as business strategy, so governments too need to put in place the policies, regulations and financial incentives that allow the 'everyday champions' at these companies to succeed. Be it 'cap and trade' systems that increase the price of carbon, investments in new technologies such as electric vehicles and 'smart grids', or integrating labor and environmental standards into trade agreements, governments have huge potential to increase the space available for 'everyday champions' to make an increasingly meaningful contribution to business success. Going back to the GE example, no matter how hard its 'everyday champions' may have tried, there would have been limited success without governments sending a clear signal to business that a transition to a low carbon economy was on the horizon and that companies with products enabling that transition would most likely be the winners.

## 'Everyday champions' can drive change, but processes, structures and incentives need to be put in place so that change outlasts the individual

The case has been made then that there is room in business for 'everyday champions' to drive change, especially when armed with business case arguments that enable them to justify their proposals and favorable reforms to the broader economic framework. However, relying on such individuals alone is not sustainable and it would be foolish to let change come to an end when the individual leaves the company. Rather, it is important that these 'everyday champions' are supported by the right organizational infrastructure – strategies, incentives and processes – that both support the 'everyday champion' while they are there and outlast them after they have left. Change for sustainability and a transition to corporate responsibility needs to be viewed in business terms, and that requires an alignment of company strategy, goals, incentives and culture to support the success of 'everyday champions'.

One of the beauties of business is that no two companies are the same and each experiments with its own approach to everything, be that new products, a different way of delivering customer service or the introduction of new technologies. Indeed, the contribution that can be made by an 'everyday champion' will of course vary significantly between companies: an oil and gas company requires a very different type of change from a telecommunications firm or retail company. For these reasons there are no right or wrong ways to support these 'everyday champions' that are driving change. However, there are a few key features that frequently re-appear in the businesses making the greatest attempt to engage their employees in the pursuit of sustainability:

| Vision | Companies leading the transition to corporate responsibility are bold in describing their vision of sustainability as a core part of the company's purpose and reason to exist, providing a framework in which change-orientated employees can innovate and contribute to the company's future business success. |
| --- | --- |
| | IBM's recent Smart Planet approach espouses the notion that the company has the technology, skills, employee talent and experience to help solve the world's problems in areas such as healthcare, water, transportation, urban development and climate change. Similarly, Hitachi's Environmental Vision 2025 is based on the $CO_2$ emissions that can be reduced through the company's products (everything from clean forms of energy to public transportation) and forms a critical part of the companies 'Social Innovation' business strategy. |

| | Both companies are sending clear signals to their employees, the wider market place and investors that the success of their businesses in the future will hinge on their ability to address big social challenges – and in doing so they are providing fertile ground upon which 'everyday champions' can succeed. |
|---|---|
| Key Performance Indicators for Sustainability | Vision alone is not enough; companies also need to support 'everyday champions' by demonstrating that company performance is understood and measured through more than simply financial indicators alone. Starbucks, BT, Vodafone and Cisco are all examples of companies establishing non-financial 'key performance indicators' that attempt to express how well the company is performing across a range of success factors such as customer service, employee relationships, supply chain ethics and environmental impact. This approach only works if it is accompanied by a clear expression of how these non-financial performance areas make a significant contribution to the ultimate financial success of the company, but the message established by these 'key performance indicators' is clear: there are multiple ways in which employees can contribute to the performance success of the business. |
| Pay, Reward and Incentives | It remains uncommon for companies to create a clear link between sustainability performance and the pay and bonus structure for its employees. Intel provides a rare exception here, when in 2008 it linked a portion of its annual bonus for employees – from the front line right up to the CEO – to the achievement of criteria in the energy efficiency of its products, reputation for environmental leadership and completion of renewable energy projects and purchases.[2] |

| | It is much more common for an individual's pay and reward to be linked to goals closer to their immediate and personal sphere of influence on issues relevant to responsible business. However, if 'everyday champions' really are to be supported and encouraged across the whole business – rather than just in corporate responsibility or sustainability functions – then it will be important for leading companies to take a more comprehensive and bold attempt at linking pay and reward to corporate responsibility performance. |
|---|---|
| Employee Engagement and Communications | Finally, and working on the premise that most (though not all) employees come to work for more than a pay cheque, it is important for companies to engage with the broad base of their employees on the sustainability issues and challenges most relevant to the company. While some employees – the biggest champions – will always be on the look out for a chance to participate in sustainability initiatives, and some employees – the biggest skeptics – never will, this still leaves a huge swathe of employees in the middle that are ripe for increased engagement and participation in a companies sustainability efforts. |
| | For many companies the opportunity exists to utilize employee engagement and communications efforts to increase the enthusiasm by which employees can contribute to the companies sustainability goals and, through that, feel more loyal to the company. |

## Corporate responsibility will be advanced if more people switched between sectors during their careers

It is sometimes remarked that there is nothing more depressing than hearing a government civil servant trying to talk about business, a world with which the public sector employee will often only have a fleeting familiarity. The same is almost certainly true in reverse: there are plenty of people in business who are shockingly unfamiliar with the methods and workings of government. Indeed, it is striking to draw a contrast between three different features of the world we live in today:

- First, that thanks to rapid innovations in communications technology, the world is interconnected like never before.
- Second, a running theme through this book, that increased collaboration between all sectors in society – business, government, NGOs, academia, investors – is required to address our most pressing sustainability challenges.
- Third, that despite these changes and with some noteworthy exceptions, most of us continue to have one-sector careers in which we become intimately familiar with one sector but distant from the other parts of society with whom we need to collaborate to achieve sustainability. This is despite the fact that demographic change points to careers in the twenty-first century getting longer, not shorter.

This is both a missed opportunity for the existing 'everyday champion' – who will be more likely to drive the change that's needed for sustainability when armed with an holistic view of how the world works – and a missed opportunity to create new 'everyday champions' who are more likely to be inspired by a diverse set of experiences and employment challenges. But these missed opportunities can be overcome with deliberate action by both business and government.

From the business sector there is a need to provide employees with opportunities to broaden their horizons and experience diverse challenges during their employment with the company. IBM's Corporate Service Corps is a leading example of what these opportunities may look like in practice. Targeted at its highest performing individuals and future leaders, the aim of the Corporate Service Corps is to provide employees with the opportunity to work outside of their home country and traditional office environment by experiencing global teams, diverse cultures, and society's greatest sustainability challenges.

By the end of 2009 IBM had sent over 52 teams to locations including the Philippines, Vietnam, China, Malaysia, Brazil, Tanzania, Ghana, South Africa, Nigeria, Egypt, Romania and Turkey, and by the end of 2010 hopes to have expanded the number of employees participating in the program to around 1,500. Projects have included establishing business incubators with leading universities in Ghana and helping a social welfare program in Nigeria determine the best information system for monitoring and recording child and maternal health. The rationale of this program for IBM is not just more highly motivated employees; it's also a business strategy based on the assumption that employees experiencing the program are more likely to lead the innovations that both solve sustainability challenges and help IBM's make the most of new market opportunities.[3]

This approach is suited to the IBM business strategy because it supports the company's desire to grow revenues outside the US and to generate business from the use of IT to help solve global problems. But while the exact program may not be directly transferable to every big business, the underlying assumption – that by giving employees the opportunity to experience situations from which unexpected innovations and business opportunities can arise – is directly transferable. However, there are also opportunities to encourage a greater churn of employees between sectors – including academia, business, government and NGOs – which creates an even greater range of experience and is something business has the potential to experiment with in years to come. Rather than being the route taken by failing or under-performing employees, greater use of extended secondments or transfers to other sectors should be encouraged, especially for high potential employees and future business leaders. The leaders of the future will be those who can be the businessperson, government policy-maker, campaigner, educator and consumer all at the same time.

There is a role for governments here too, most significantly in the design of education systems and the underlying learning philosophies that support them. This book has made the case that increased collaboration between all sectors in society – business, government, NGOs, academia, investors – is required to address our most pressing sustainability challenges. But achieving this collaboration requires the supply into the global marketplace of a workforce equipped with the outlook necessary to put this into practice through a holistic understanding of the role each sector and every profession in society can play in the transition to sustainability. We need trained scientists who understand government, campaigners who have an instinctive feel for business, and academics who have spent time in industry.

A strong case can be made that the leading business of tomorrow – ones that will both shape and win in the sustainable economy – should seek leaders who have a broad range of experiences and an established record of achievement across a variety of sectors of society. While these board members exist today as non-executives, it is our contention that we need more of them, especially in the executive rather than non-executive ranks.

## Conclusion

This chapter has made the case that the journey to corporate responsibility and sustainability requires the development of and contribution from 'everyday champions' who are provided with the leadership, space and the permission to drive change and innovation in their companies. These 'everyday champions' exist today in ever growing numbers, but their role will only increase in significance and we need many more of them.

These 'everyday champions' tend to be positive, creative and solutions-orientated in their outlook. They are alert to the world around them and its implications for their business. These are people whose response to a problem is not resignation, doom or gloom, but instead a sense that challenges are there to be addressed and problems to be solved. But these 'everyday champions' are also not afraid to engage with the people, institutions and approaches that they disagree with or that make them feel uncomfortable. They have the perseverance to do this successfully and see it as their mission to challenge the way things are done now. Adversarial conflict is not the only outcome of course; the 'everyday champion' frequently succeeds, over time, to turn those who are initially critical into the most vocal champions of all for sustainability. The visionary companies of the future will be the ones that embrace these 'everyday champions', not run away from them.

# The view from here – a vision for successful companies in a sustainable world

## Setting the scene

In our final section we draw together the key conclusions from the preceding chapters as a foundation to explore the broad themes that are already shaping the world of big business today and that we believe will do so much more in the coming decades.

The world today is facing social, environmental and economic challenges on a scale previously unknown. How global society tackles climate change while lifting more than a billion people out of extreme poverty will be the defining challenge of our generation.

While many have seen big business as part of the problem, there's an increasingly widespread recognition within companies and beyond that they need to be, and can be, be part of the solution. The logic is powerful: these challenges won't go away, big businesses share in the risks that they pose, and can benefit from the opportunities presented by the sustainability agenda. As a result there have been significant shifts within leading companies which are integrating sustainability concerns into their mainstream strategy.

That fundamental change is being driven by a variety of people across different levels of business. The CEO plays a fundamental role in setting the overall leadership tone for a company, but leading companies are also increasingly creating the space for 'everyday champions' in their organization to drive change and develop solutions. Companies are also working with NGOs and governments in a new 'collaboration zone' to develop shared solutions to common problems.

Sustainability is an increasingly important part of a company's relationship with its customers. A growing portion of consumers want to know that they are buying from a company that they can trust to 'do the right thing', and companies are responding by differentiating their products and services based on their environmental or social performance. But as they innovate to find new technological solutions to sustainability challenges, companies will need to ensure that they engage with consumers. Innovation has driven many improvements in our quality of life, and will be critical in the future, but big business will need to understand public concerns and ensure that their innovations create more benefits than negatives.

The optimistic picture that we have painted doesn't mean that the business community has changed overnight. Not all companies are changing and there are limits to voluntary action. It is clear that many challenges will only ultimately be solved by public policy. Positively, leading companies are increasingly embracing this reality and are helping to develop and support government intervention to address sustainability challenges.

## Looking backwards to look forwards – the last 35 years

It is often said that if you look back ten years ago on a particular cause or campaign, not much may have changed, but if you look back a generation, roughly 35 years, things have transformed dramatically. Good cases of this include the recognition of civil rights in the US, the role of women in the workplace in the UK, and gay rights almost anywhere in the developed world. Perhaps on a global scale the most noticeable and important change has been the move towards a capitalist-based economic system, first in the old Soviet Union, and now, through a different method, in China.

Technology, cultural norms and resource exploitation have all dramatically changed over the past 35 years, changing the operating context for almost all big multinationals. In the mid 1970s air travel was only just starting to become the form of mass travel that we know today, personal communication was limited to fixed line telephones, correspondence was done using a pen, paper and the postal system, and personal banking and investments were all undertaken face to face via a trusted broker whom you got to know personally.

Reviewing society's fears of that period can be instructive. The big fear in the western world was nuclear war with the Soviet Bloc, a concern that 35 years later has changed to a fear of micro terror cells or smaller states with weapons of mass destruction. There had just been an oil crisis and personal economic welfare was close to top of mind for people, perhaps not dissimilar to recent economic events. Poverty in the developing world was not high profile in the west ahead of the Ethiopian famine of the mid 1980s which would bring it to world attention. The mindset change was still ongoing from the colonial model – Zimbabwe was still Southern Rhodesia – and a generation was in power who grew up with a colonial approach to Africa and Asia. The European Union was just a fledging economic community. There were the first signs of the environmental crises to come: Rachel Carson's book Silent Spring had been published in the US regarding waterway pollution in the Love Canal and its effects on biodiversity. Greenpeace and Friends of the Earth had both been recently founded on different sides of the globe in Canada and England respectively.

Watching old television science programs from that period is insightful. Their expectations for personal communications and information technology have probably been significantly exceeded, with changes brought by mobile phones, the internet and online social networking largely unforeseen. Much focus was on the exploration of space and widespread air-based personal transportation within countries and cities, but progress in this area has been no way as substantial as they imagined. Biotechnology, with the opportunities for the growth of human limbs from stem cells, and the extent of our insight into our DNA and its manipulation, was also not widely foreseen.

## Looking forwards: Four themes for the future

How do we look forwards whilst being mindful of the pitfalls of either dreaming of too much or expecting too little? Below we explore some broad themes, rather than specifics, that we believe are beginning to shape the world of multinational companies already and which will do so much more in the coming 35 years.

Different businesses plan over different timeframes depending on their capital investment and innovation timelines. But all businesses will need to think much longer term and with greater flexibility to deal with the different but inter-related challenges the world now faces. Those businesses that flourish in the coming decades will do so in part because they are able to cope with the social and environmental challenges they face. Indeed, some of the most successful entrepreneurs of this century may well be those who develop solutions to our environmental resource constraints and human needs.

However, the changes taking place in the world do not only have implications for businesses. Governments, investors, international organizations and NGOs all need to respond to a change in their operating environments. Most of all, there is a need for all of these institutions to work better together to address the world's sustainability challenges.

### 1. Environment: a very different world

Back in the early 1970s the environment movement was still in its infancy, with green issues just beginning to enter mainstream public consciousness. Through the 70s, 80s and early 90s mainstream concern with environmental issues fluctuated, with peaks of interest generally revolving around specific issues, often in specific locations: acid rain in northern Europe for example, tropical deforestation, or the hole in the ozone layer in the southern hemisphere. And the companies that got to grips with the environment agenda tended to be those in the spotlight for particular issues.

As we've outlined in this book, the last ten years have marked a shift in the profile of environmental issues in many parts of the world and the corporate response has evolved significantly over that period. So what do the next three decades hold environmentally, and what implications does that have for companies?

*Climate change, climate change, climate change*

Looking back to when he first began his tenure as the UK Government's Chief Scientific Adviser in 2000, Sir David King described climate change as something that the government felt could be solved within one part of one minister's department.[1] That's no longer the case, he says – there's now a recognition that this is an issue that needs to be addressed by all areas of government. It's clear that over the last decade climate change has established itself as *the* overarching environmental challenge, and that's set to continue going forward. UN Secretary General Ban Ki Moon has described it as 'the defining challenge of our age'.[2]

Looking ahead, it's clear that climate change will be one of the issues shaping the landscape in which business operates. The current scientific consensus identifies the need for carbon cuts globally of 50% by 2050, with developed countries needing to reduce further still – by 80%. That virtual decarbonization of the economy will have far-reaching effects. And while targets for emissions cuts that set their end-point in 2050 can feel pretty distant to most people, experts are increasingly focusing on the need for global emissions to peak as early as 2020 – now only a decade away.

Carbon will come with a cost attached to it, and that cost will rise as policies make the right to emit carbon an increasingly scarce resource. Companies will need to understand their 'value at risk' from the carbon agenda. Those businesses that don't understand the impact of operating in a carbon constrained world will struggle to survive. On the flip side, there's a significant opportunity out there for those companies that can innovate the lower-carbon products and services that we will need to confront the climate challenge.

Consumers will also become increasingly 'carbon-aware' and will look to companies to help them to understand the carbon impact of what they are buying – one only has to look at how 'health literate' consumers have become over the past 35 years to get a sense of how 'carbon literate' they may become in the next 35 years. But as we saw in Chapter 5, communicating in grams, kilograms and tonnes of carbon is complex, and leading businesses will need to help educate consumers. The companies currently trialing 'carbon footprint' labels on products are likely to be in the vanguard of a trend that all companies will eventually be expected to embrace.

Carbon also increasingly looks set to become the lens through which many other environmental issues are viewed. Avoiding tropical deforestation, for example, has a range of benefits, from species preservation to flood alleviation. But it's the ability of forests to sequester carbon, and the opportunity to harness that for a financial return, that has the potential to really transform efforts to save the rainforests. At a consumer level, carbon may well become the common currency used to describe a host of other environmental issues – the benefits of recycling, for example, or of reduced water use.

One of the big questions for companies is whether the policy response that drives carbon into business decision-making will be a coordinated global one, or a more piecemeal regional approach. The aviation industry provides an illustration of the challenge. Europe has been in the vanguard of moves to address aviation's climate impacts by including flights in its carbon trading system. Within Europe some national governments have also introduced environmental levies on airlines. In the continued absence of a global policy to tackle carbon from flights, a patchwork of similar policies could develop around the world and that creates risks for airlines that operate globally: it creates more uncertainty, will cost more to comply with and is likely to be less effective environmentally. That means that it will be in the long-term interests of global airlines to help develop a credible international solution. Leading airlines have recognized this need and set up the 'Aviation Global Deal' group – working with not-for-profit The Climate Group to develop a proposal to include flights in a global cap and trade scheme. This challenge isn't unique to airlines; there will be a fundamental role for all companies to develop and support the right government policies to address climate change.

This also points to a key role for government in creating the policy certainty to enable companies to scale up their response to climate change. In the aftermath of the Copenhagen negotiations the verdict of the 950 companies from over 60 countries that signed the Copenhagen Communique was pretty clear on this point: 'a legally binding deal is needed as a matter of urgency to provide business with the confidence it needs to invest in specific low-carbon technologies and infrastructure'.

### It's not just about cutting carbon, but about adapting to inevitable changes

Alongside measures to reduce emissions, there's also the challenge of adapting to the climate change impacts that we are already locked into globally. The Copenhagen Accord sets an international goal of limiting temperature rise to no more than two degrees Celsius. That may sound a relatively modest rise, but would lead to some wide-ranging impacts, including:

- a 20–30% decrease in water availability in some regions such as Southern Africa and the Mediterranean
- 5–10% declines in crop yields in tropical regions
- 40–60 million more people exposed to malaria in Africa
- up to ten million more people affected by coastal flooding each year[3]

When temperature rises beyond two degrees the impacts are correspondingly more dramatic. Companies will need to understand the potential physical impacts of climate change at a number of levels: their own operations and infrastructure; their supply chain; and their customers and markets.

### Carbon won't be the only scarce resource

With the world's population forecast to rise to up to nine billion people by the middle of this century, carbon won't be the only resource in scarce supply.

The same kind of pricing policies that we've outlined for carbon dioxide will apply to other forms of pollution that overload the limited carrying capacity of the environment. That includes solid waste, for example, already subject to stringent taxes in parts of the world to divert it from landfill sites to more productive uses like recycling or energy generation. It also includes dirty water produced as a by-product of industrial or agricultural activities, where legislation will make pollution more expensive.

It's not just pollution, but also the natural resources that we rely on to support us that will become scarcer, particularly as development continues in some of today's rapidly emerging economies. Land will be under pressure, with more people to feed and soil degradation already taking place in some parts of the world. Per capita availability of freshwater is decreasing globally, a trend that's set to continue as population grows and incomes improve. Meanwhile demand for minerals and metals for consumer products will continue to boom.

Scarce supply is usually reflected in rising prices and the environment will be no exception. Natural resources like energy, water and minerals that have historically been cheap will become more expensive – significantly more in some cases. Companies in the most environmentally intensive industries that fail to anticipate and adapt to the environmental limits most relevant for their industry are likely to struggle. But by the same token, resource scarcity will drive major technological innovation by academic researchers, entrepreneurs and big businesses, all seeking to do more with less. As we've outlined earlier in the book, there are already many examples of companies innovating in response to environmental challenges. To be successful in the first half of the 21$^{st}$ century, all companies will need to follow that path – driving significant resource efficiencies in their products and services.

### Pricing or rationing?

One of the most critical questions will be how environmental limits are managed. Currently, as discussed in Chapter 1, most products and services are not priced to reflect the scarcity of the resources they depend upon, or the cost of cleaning up the pollution they create. One option for governments is to regulate further to ensure that all consumer products include these costs. To do so governments can use cap and trade schemes, like the European Union Emissions Trading Scheme. Once tight environmental caps are imposed through cap and trade schemes, it is likely to lead to increases in prices for goods. This will stir companies to find ways of innovating to provide the same product benefits for a much lower environmental impact, as discussed in Chapter 7. However internalizing environmental costs may also lead to consumers consuming less.

It is quite possible though that the political debates about equity and fairness that such cost internalizing strategies would bring might also lead to alternative outcomes. A different option to internalizing everything into a product's price is to allocate scarce environmental resources, essentially a rationing system. This might lead to caps on resource use for companies, individual consumers, or both. At the company level absolute limits on use of scarce resources such as water might be set, with no option to get more of the resource, even if you are prepared to pay more. Suddenly being eco-efficient would become an even more important priority to enable business growth. At the individual level each person in a country might be given a personal budget for the amount of water they consume, the carbon they emit and the domestic waste they produce. There might also be a combination of both systems, with some form of allocations supplemented by trading schemes which then affect price. In less democratic economies, companies may simply be told what their eco-efficiency target is and be expected to achieve it, or face penalties such as fines or plant closures.

It is likely that different governments will experiment with different approaches over the coming years. This will lead to major challenges for global businesses which prefer a consistent global approach with standardized systems. Rather, businesses will have to ensure that their senior managers around the world are up to speed on resource constraints and how they might play out in their local markets.

## 2. Changing consumers and their greater demands

The first great boom of consumer awareness on environmental issues was in the 1980s, when societal debates as diverse as saving the whales, eliminating animal testing on cosmetics and the wasteful grain mountains, wine lakes and butter vats of European agricultural subsidy all hit the press regularly. For a brief period being green became cool, in particular as an antithesis to the prevailing 1980s material excess *zeitgeist* in the US and western Europe. Environmental entrepreneurs founded companies to deliver consumer products with much lower impacts, such as the Ecover cleaning products company, founded in 1980 in Belgium. Others such as Anita Roddick sought not just to change the impact of a business value chain, such as her Body Shop cosmetics which were not tested on animals, but also to use business as a campaigning platform. She used the power of the Body Shop brand and its shop windows to engage consumers in causes such as human rights and even took on Shell regarding the impact of its operations in Nigeria.

However, whilst some campaigners and entrepreneurs in the 1980s expected radical change in a short space of time, they were sorely disappointed. Change throughout the 1980s and 90s was slow, despite seminal events in the international political arena on the environment with the Rio Earth Summit in 1992 and the signing of the Kyoto Protocol in 1997. Although public interest in various environmental issues has peaked at certain points in the last three decades on specific issues, overall growth in awareness has been slow and this has translated to only incremental changes in consumer behavior.

In part this was due to a lack of available products of the right quality to meet consumers' needs whilst also being more ethically responsible or environmentally friendly. Companies such as Ecover and The Body Shop grew from ethical niches to be successful businesses by the 1990s, but overall the range of consumer products offered as ethical or environmentally friendly remained limited until the late 1990s. Since then the dominant companies in certain FMCG segments first bought up many of these pioneers, and secondly began to incorporate these concerns into their industry strategies. L'Oreal bought the Body Shop. Unilever bought Ben and Jerrys, the premium ice cream label, whilst Cadbury bought Green and Blacks, the UK Fairtrade chocolate pioneer. Certain start-ups, such as Cafedirect, the charity and cooperative owned UK Fairtrade coffee and tea market leader, remain independent, but many of the pioneers have been absorbed by established businesses. The rationale for those purchases was clear: ethical products, in particular organic and Fairtrade offerings, have been some of the most rapidly growing retail segments in recent years. In 2008 Fairtrade sales in the UK increased 40% to £700 million, whilst the UK organic food market is worth over £2 billion – the global organic market is over $23 billion.

A number of companies have also championed specific issues with consumers. IKEA, the Swedish furniture business, led the way on promoting low energy light bulbs with reasonable performance at a comparable cost to the dominant incandescent style. Tesco, the UK retailer, has been one of the pioneers of carbon labelling, putting carbon footprint indicators on a range of own brand goods including orange juice, laundry detergent and potatoes.

Most recently a number of the large FMCG businesses have integrated environmental and ethical concerns into their mainstream brand developments. Ariel, a laundry product from P&G, has been formulated to provide cleaning at much lower temperatures, saving energy bills and carbon emissions. Cadburys has made Dairy Milk, its iconic chocolate brand, entirely Fairtrade, whilst Starbucks UK and Ireland has announced that all of its coffee will be Fairtrade too. Retailers are also playing a key role. In the UK all the main food retailers have organic or Fairtrade own brand lines for commodities such as coffee, tea, chocolate and bananas and they are taking it further into beer, wine and other categories.

So there is now a wide enough range of high quality products which enable consumers to take easy steps to buy the right product to match their beliefs in this area. The question is what change we will see in the coming decades?

*High consumer awareness, but low consumer understanding*

As consumers begin to care more about the environmental footprint of the products they buy, they will demand changes. Public knowledge of the impacts of climate change is now relatively high in Europe and the US. Whilst research suggests that some consumers remain in denial that their lifestyle is causing it, this cannot continue much longer. When consumers do start to demand much more from the companies and brands they trust, those companies had better be ready.

In Chapter 3 we outlined the various labelling schemes that have arisen to advise consumers on the sustainability and fairness of the products they buy. There is no doubt that consumer interest in these issues is increasing and that demand for further information is growing. In response Walmart, the world's largest retailer, has developed a product sustainability index, with an end goal of communicating clearly and quickly to consumers the sustainability of all the products on its shelves. It is difficult to communicate effectively just through labels though, particularly given the limited space. Sustainability issues are complex and may involve trade-offs, for example between the land required to grow food and the land required to grow biofuels for low carbon transport. Consumers don't just need labels but a broader understanding of the critical issues and how they interact.

For this reason a greater coordinated effort to engage with consumers will be needed. This is where NGOs have a great deal to offer both companies and consumers, in terms of the trust that the public hold in key NGO brands such as WWF, the Sierra Club, Greenpeace, Friends of the Earth, Care International, Oxfam, World Vision and others. Although these organizations often prefer to remain publicly independent of business, in the future companies, NGOs and governments will need to work together to communicate a clear and consistent message to consumers.

This is where reviewing the opportunities for an individual company's competitive advantage, versus ensuring a common and consistent approach amongst all companies in a sector, becomes important. In recent years this conundrum has been dealt with by leading companies differentiating themselves through being the first to adopt a demanding sector wide standard such as the FSC label for sustainably sourced timber or the Fairtrade label for global consumer commodities. But if the scale of the challenge, particularly on environmental issues, requires all goods of a particular type to conform to a certain standard, then where is the next opportunity for differentiation?

The future for competitive advantage lies in two places. First, in terms of environmental impact, competitive advantage will be found in the control of scarce resources through well-managed value chains. Businesses which move first to secure the resources they need – whilst ensuring that they are operating in a transparent, trusted, environmentally sound and socially responsible way – will win. These businesses will be able to best control the costs of scarce resources, ensure that their supply chains have lower environmental impacts and therefore offer consumers the most sustainable choice.

Second, there will remain an opportunity for differentiation through how companies enable consumers to engage directly with the sustainability issues themselves. This can include guidance for consumers on how they can improve their own environmental footprint, such as tools to use in the home to monitor their own impact. It can also include enabling consumers to interact with the distant suppliers of their products, ensuring first hand that the products they buy are meeting the standards for environmental impact and ethics that they would expect. The internet allows incredible interactivity between consumers and their ultimate suppliers and so far companies have only begun to scratch the surface of what that could mean.

The ability to provide independent reviews of products and services, from TripAdvisor.com on hotels to amazon.com for books and other products, has begun to create new communities around purchasing behavior. This will accelerate and consumers of certain products may group together in ways that manufacturers do not expect, perhaps undermining some of the power of brand control, with important implications for corporate reputations.

### The disruptive consumer-employee

In 2001 Charles Handy published his book The Elephant and the Flea, which envisions a world of corporate outsourcing to thousands of individuals who act as mini-consultancies, rather than having large fixed workforces. Slowly mobile working and broadband connections at home are enabling a world where this might be more possible. However, freeing employees to be empowered in this way also means they are more likely to be disruptive. Employees who are less bound to the business, providing services to two or three major businesses as a consultant, are more likely to be prepared to share their views on the business publicly. It is no longer simply a one way employer–employee relationship, but rather a set of thousands of interactive relationships with employees who are also likely to be customers, commentators and critics.

Already, employees blogging, twittering and uploading Youtube videos cause management headaches around the world, as the carefully crafted global face of the corporation of old gives way to a greater visibility and insight into the thousands of employees that make up companies and what each of their views is. Access to information means that transparency will be a key feature of our future whether business leaders like it or not, and employees are increasingly likely to use the web to share their real feelings. Despite attempts to control this, it is likely that in the end businesses will have to get used to operating in a more open and accountable way.

*Measuring happiness?*

An important dimension of sustainability is the question of how we value the lifestyle we have. For a number of years now the New Economics Foundation, a UK NGO, has been researching different ways of measuring human progress in a way that captures our wellbeing as well as our relatively narrowly defined economic performance as measured by GDP. They argue that although UK wealth has doubled since 1973, our happiness in life has not changed over that period. This begs the question of whether our extra effort to produce more, earn more, consume more and do more in life actually leads to an improved quality of life. It is a theme that the French President Sarkozy emphasized during the recent economic crisis, commissioning Noble prize winning economists Joseph Stiglitz and Amartya Sen to set up a Commission on the Measurement of Economic Performance and Social Progress. These measures consider the positive impacts of economic growth whilst netting off the negatives of pollution, reducing the 'capital' we share in the form of natural resources, and considering social issues that reduce our quality of life such as congestion and road accidents.

Whilst this debate has remained largely amongst the intelligentsia on both sides of the Atlantic, it is possible that it will enter consumer consciousness in a more fundamental way in coming years. Governments have an important opportunity here to facilitate this analysis of quality of life to ensure that their citizens have clear insight into the changes in their own lives.

## 3. A world of greater equality?

The Millennium Development Goals (MDGs) are the key objectives for human development that the international community has set to be achieved by 2015. Some of the recent trends have certainly been positive. One of the main development measures is the number of people living in 'extreme poverty' – defined by the World Bank as getting by on an income of less than $1.25 a day and therefore not able to meet basic needs. Those living in extreme poverty accounted for almost half of the developing world's population in 1990, but that had fallen to slightly more than a quarter in 2005.[4] The same period also saw an encouraging trend in terms of eradicating hunger, access to safe drinking water and universal primary education.

But progress on some of these goals has been affected by the global downturn which started in 2008 – with the numbers of people living in extreme poverty and the prevalence of hunger both increasing that year.[5] And on other issues progress has been less strong, including child nutrition, maternal mortality and sanitation. The United Nation's latest assessment warns that despite many successes, overall progress has been too slow for most of the targets to be met by the 2015 target date.

Leading economist Jeffrey Sachs has highlighted the risks of failing to tackle extreme poverty, saying that abandoning any part of the world to it would seriously jeopardize the health, security and economic progress of the rest of the planet, leaving us facing a world of 'instability, failed states and uncontrolled pandemic disease'.[6] But he also remains optimistic, stating that 'Ours is the generation that can end extreme poverty'.[7]

We saw in Chapters 2 and 7 that leading businesses are focusing on what they can do to help tackle the challenges posed by global poverty, and also what business opportunities this may present for them. That trend will continue in future. With strong global businesses depending on a strong global society, big companies also stand to suffer from the world of instability that Sachs warns of. So there's a shared interest for companies that have a global reach in contributing to global development. There's also the opportunity presented by focusing product development strategies on low-income consumers in the developing world. As we saw earlier in the book, for some companies that is already happening and this trend is also likely to continue.

The growth of global business players from China, India, Brazil and some of the world's other big emerging economies is likely to further drive those trends. Companies from those countries will be closer to consumer markets at the 'bottom of the pyramid' and well positioned to develop the business models needed for success there. Companies will also need to position themselves for success as development starts to drive changing consumption patterns amongst the emerging middle income consumers in the developing world. As wealth grows, we are likely to see increased awareness of and interest in environmental and social issues by consumers around the world.

The most significant challenge for global development remains sub-Saharan Africa. Throughout the last two decades we have seen increasing instability in a number of central and eastern African countries which have implications for global security. From pirates off the coast of Somalia to terrorist cells in Sudan, a lack of governance allows instability which further undermines economic wellbeing and therefore allows criminality to thrive. Corruption, a challenge by no means unique to Africa, continues to throttle growth in markets rich in natural resources and slows the pace of institutional improvement.

However, Africa is also a place increasingly rich in entrepreneurship, which remains valued for the variety of natural resources it holds and which is beginning to play an increasingly important political role, as its profile at the talks at the Copenhagen climate summit in December 2009 showed. South Africa is a nation of increasing global presence and influence, with the football World Cup in 2010 focusing global attention on its achievements and progress.

Major global businesses are widely present in Africa and operate very successfully. Indeed some businesses such as SABMiller have grown from African origins to be sector leaders on a global level. Yet the ability of businesses to promote more rapid growth is restricted by the institutional challenges of ineffective government, poor infrastructure and continued corruption. To see growth, businesses will have to become more involved in partnerships to improve governance, infrastructure and public and business ethics. Business Action for Africa, a group of major businesses which co-operate to call for better public policy in Africa and to deliver development benefits on the ground, is a good example. We need to see a greater commitment to such collaboration for development across the continent from more businesses.

One of the central questions for Africa in the coming decades is whether the effects of climate change can be effectively managed to protect development, or whether its impacts will undermine the fragile growth that does exist. Climate change will further exacerbate the droughts that the continent frequently falls victim too, whilst also leading to greater floods as rainfall events become more intense. The floods in Mozambique in 2000 are unfortunately an example of what we may see more of across the continent throughout the coming century. The most important next step to deal with this climate challenge is to understand what climate change will mean for different sectors in different parts of Africa, to help businesses, governments, farmers and health professionals understand what their future operating environment might look like, and to develop flexible ways of managing these climate challenges as they unfold.

## 4. Changes in the global balance of power

The financial crisis in 2008–2009 and its ongoing implications for public finances in the west have brought a realization that the speed of change in the global balance of power might be more rapid than previously thought. Growth has returned much more rapidly in China and India – where the growing internal markets continue to demand energy, natural resources and consumer products to meet the needs of wealthier consumers – than it has in the sluggish west.

However, although it is much commented upon and characterized, this is not a simplistic shift, with China and India on the ascendancy whilst the US, Europe and Japan slowly demise. Rather, a more complex, multipolar world is emerging, with Brazil, Russia and others also playing key roles, whilst the US, Europe and Japan retain much power. China and India have massive consumer markets; Russia has vast energy reserves; Brazil has forests and agricultural land which supply much of the world's soya, beef and, increasingly, biofuels.

The negotiations regarding a global climate change agreement, discussed elsewhere in this book, have shown that power dynamics in this multipolar world can be surprising. The leadership shown on occasion by both Brazil and China, in discussing their own carbon emissions reduction targets, shows that 'moral' leadership is not a one way discourse from west to east, or from north to south, as US governments in particular have sometimes seen it.

The dynamics of the economic strength of the BRIC nations will continue to change geo-politics in coming years, but it won't be simple. Each of the BRIC countries is big enough and powerful enough to chart its own course and change partners on global issues as it suits them, leading to an intriguing set of global political dances on different issues, from security to human rights.

The role that China is playing as a sponsor of Africa's development is a good case in point. Whilst there is a clear motive for China to access the vast mineral resources of Africa, in addition to the value of agricultural land to feed a growing population, there are further dimensions to the relationship. African nations also play an important role in supporting China through the United Nations system with votes at the General Assembly and in critical bodies such as the Human Rights Council. There is no doubt that Africa is reaping benefits from China's involvement

– improved infrastructure, delivered quickly, and accompanying public services such as healthcare clinics, are supporting development in a way that western aid hasn't quite delivered, at least not that quickly.

Domestically, the governance models within the BRIC nations differ greatly. Whilst economic freedom in China increases, there remains a strong grip by the state on public speech. The political system that shapes the living environment of the largest group of consumers in the world is bound to have a significant impact on how global companies think about the products and services they will develop in coming years.

As attractive as it is to many in the west to think that material wealth will inevitably bring democracy and an increased respect of individual human rights to consumers from China to the Middle East, we cannot assume this will occur. Whilst consumers may be becoming more outspoken, the system is surely likely to evolve in a different way from the Anglo Saxon capitalist model. There are some instances where it is clear that consumers in China are becoming more active. When the scandal of contaminated milk occurred in 2008, with six babies dying and up to 300,000 people made ill,[8] public reaction was vocal and the government had to move fast to contain it and the reputational damage it was doing to China's dairy industry.

In the last 30 years NGOs have played an important role in bringing to the attention of western consumers the environmental and social impact of major companies. In China, the NGO sector is far more controlled and outspoken campaigns are unlikely to be tolerated in the same way. Also interesting is to ask what implications would exist for western consumers if the balance of corporate power shifts over time to China and other emerging markets? If internet-based technologies and services developed for the Chinese market provide greater opportunities for governments to monitor individuals, will those same products and services be trusted by western consumers?

In the same way that a different style of capitalism has developed in the US and UK from other major nations such as France and Germany, so a different form again is likely to continue to evolve in China and other large emerging markets. It is quite possible that with a different cultural model of capitalism growing in power, the individual rights model might fade slightly. For example, in the coming decades the scale of the resource challenges may actually move the world towards models of shared risk and shared accountability rather than individual property rights, so instead of market-based trading schemes we could see greater state-led allocation of resources.

*The shift of corporate power centres means more than just a change of HQ*

If there is a visible shift in power from the west to the east, it is probably the corporate world in which this change will be most directly felt. It is quite possible that many of the headquarters of the global companies we know well today will relocate to China because of the sheer scale of the consumer base and economic opportunity. In particular, if being successful in this market requires having a good relationship with the government that influences that market, having your senior management close to that government makes sense. HSBC's CEO's recent move to Hong Kong will challenge other companies to consider whether their senior management might need to be closer to their biggest opportunity, as well as demonstrating their commitment to the Chinese market. Yet the changing location of western multinationals' headquarters is probably of much lesser importance than the role that growing emerging market originated multinationals will have on the rest of the world.

In the last decade Chinese and Indian businesses in particular have expanded out of their home markets through buying major companies, including some iconic brands, in the US and Europe. Lenovo buying IBM's laptop business in 2004, Tata buying the historic British car marques Jaguar and Landrover in 2008, as well as the Tetley Tea company a few years earlier, are all good examples. But this trend doesn't stop at a few examples: in the utility sector, Wessex Water, a regional UK water utility, is owned by YTL, a Malaysian conglomerate; and a number of famous UK football teams are now owned by Russian oligarchs, Middle Eastern oil families and Asian businessmen. Stakes taken by emerging market state-controlled companies in industries that the west considers of strategic importance have raised new questions for political leaders. The arguments for freedom of ownership seem to disappear surprisingly quickly when the purchaser of a stake in a major company is seen as being an extension of foreign government policy. One of the major dimensions is that whilst many of India's largest companies are family owned, the largest Chinese, other Asian and also Middle Eastern businesses are often state owned enterprises (SOEs) or state-controlled entities.

In 2008 the purchase of a large stake in Rio Tinto, the mining group, by the Chinese aluminium company Chinalco led to discussions of China's intentions regarding control of key commodities. When Dubai World, a state-owned company in the United Arab Emirates, took over P&O, a UK-based company in 2006, one of P&Os activities that came with the deal was the management contracts for six major US ports. Although approved through the relevant US government security clearance procedures, a media storm developed. In the end, after a media debate on the merits of free trade versus the security concerns of a Middle Eastern government effectively controlling some major US transport infrastructure, Dubai World agreed to sell the American part of the business to an American company.

This question about state influence via large state-owned or controlled companies in global business will only grow as these businesses become more powerful in the world. Armed with the scale provided by large domestic markets and strong cash flow to support acquisitions, Chinese SOEs are likely to play a more powerful role in global business in the near future. In 2009 the head of the government body overseeing China's SOEs stated that in the first half of 2009 150 SOEs had sought advice about buying overseas companies.[9] The question is at what pace this will happen, and how governments and the public in the west will react. So far the response, especially in the US, has been more protectionist than the country's official trade policies would suggest.

## Closing thoughts

This book has detailed why and how big business is becoming energized to help create a more sustainable future. Our closing thoughts reflect back on the five emerging realities set out at the beginning of this book and their implications not only for business but also for NGOs, governments and others.

First, shared risks mean shared responsibilities. Big business needs to continue to understand the real risks to its continued viability presented by trends such as climate change and water scarcity. Only by sharing the responsibility of addressing these challenges will business remain successful in the long term.

Second, these shared risks are best addressed through collaboration. Big business needs to feel much more comfortable working with others in their industries and up and down their value chains, as well as with governments and civil society, to address these shared challenges. Here we particularly emphasize the importance of entire industries moving together – not allowing the lesser known brands to get away without scrutiny or responsibility – and of recognizing that systemic change of the scale required dictates more than voluntary action alone.

Third, being trusted has never been more important, and this will require ever greater amounts of transparency and accountability. Public disclosure of sustainability performance needs to be as regular, comparable and regulated as disclosure of financial performance. Companies can benefit from becoming increasingly frank and open about the real obstacles they face in operating in a more responsible way, so that other parties such as governments are also required to play their part.

Fourth, smart and effective regulations and fiscal incentives can encourage business activities that support sustainable development. As long as policy is established based on sound research and widespread dialogue, then appropriate new regulation should be encouraged by leading businesses – and they should play a key role in shaping it. Sustainability requires systemic changes applied consistently and governments have an important role in ensuring this occurs.

Fifth, the successful companies of tomorrow are already treating sustainability as an opportunity for innovation, not simply as a risk to be mitigated. Helping consumers understand some of the complexities of sustainability is important, as 'dumbing down' the message will reduce transparency and discourage consumers from taking responsibility for their own consumption decisions.

As we have described in many parts of this book, the NGO community has been particularly important in convincing big business of the scale and significance of the sustainability challenge and has been extraordinarily effective at shifting the public discourse on corporate responsibility. However, we believe the time has arrived for a new approach from the NGO community. Whilst the role they have developed in recent decades of 'exposers' of corporate malpractice will no doubt continue, we believe that the NGO community would serve the cause of sustainability better by acting with less overall suspicion of the business community and more frequently welcome businesses as partners in the change that we all want to see. Increasing numbers of influential people in big business are ready to play that role. Most of all we believe that NGOs can much more effectively immerse themselves in the realities of business life: understanding their products, services, markets, consumer demands and operating pressures. In doing so we believe that NGOs will be much more able to engage with business and offer their expertise to support an increased pace of change.

We leave government with one clear message: business action in this area has accelerated, but (with some notable exceptions) government is struggling to respond fast enough. The Copenhagen climate summit provided a clear picture of that, where governments failed to respond to the many global businesses calling for clear government action. Governments need to match the pace of business change.

In recent years the sustainability game has changed. Companies are now just as likely to be working in partnerships with NGOs as they are to be boycotted by them and consumers are more likely to learn about their environmental footprint from their retailer than from a government campaign. There is much further to go before all big businesses call truly call themselves visionary in their impact on the world around us, but leading companies are offering an increasingly compelling vision of how big business can help society collectively address our shared social, environmental and economic challenges.

# NOTES

## Introduction

1　http://www.unctad.org/Templates/webflyer.asp?docid=2426&intItemID= 2079&lang=1
2　http://www.foreignpolicy.com/articles/2009/04/15/the_next_big_thing_h20
3　BSR Conference 2009

## Chapter 1

1　http://www.un.org/millenniumgoals/
2　http://www.imf.org/external/pubs/ft/weo/2009/02/weodata/index.aspx
3　http://www.unilever.com/sustainability/reports/news/inseadreport-launchedatworldeconomicforum.aspx
4　http://www.sabmiller.com/files/reports/2009_insead_report.pdf
5　http://www.pewclimate.org/facts-and-figures/international/by-sector
6　http://www.carbontrust.com/publications/CTC740_business_rev%20v5.pdf
7　http://www.fairtrade.org.uk/what_is_fairtrade/facts_and_figures.aspx

## Chapter 2

1　Edelman, 2009, *Edelman Trust Barometer*, http://www.edelman.com/trust/ 2009/
2　Boston Consulting Group, 2009, *Capturing the Green Advantage for Consumers*, http://www.bcg.com/documents/file15407.pdf
3　Ibid
4　M&S, 2009, *How we do business*, http://corporate.marksandspencer.com/ howwedobusiness/hwdb_reports
5　http://plana.marksandspencer.com/
6　M&S, 2009, *How we do business*, http://corporate.marksandspencer.com/ howwedobusiness/hwdb_reports
7　Greenpeace, 2005, *A recipe for disaster*, http://www.greenpeace.org.uk/ files/pdfs/migrated/MultimediaFiles/Live/FullReport/7281.pdf
8　Walmart, 2009, Walmart Sustainability Report, http://walmartstores.com/ sustainability/
9　www.bp.com, http://www.bp.com/productlanding.do?categoryId=120& contentId=7047744
10　BP, 2009, *Sustainability Report 2008*, http://www.bp.com/sectiongeneric-article.do?categoryId=9027837&contentId=7050758

11  See reference in Chapter 2
12  Oxfam, 2009, *A business case for fighting poverty*, Briefings for Business No. 2, http://www.oxfam.org.uk/resources/policy/private_sector/downloads/business_case_poverty.pdf
13  GSK, 2009, *Corporate Responsibility Report 2008*, http://www.gsk.com/responsibility/message-from-ceo.htm
14  Oxfam press release, *GSK breaks industry ranks to improve access to medicine*, February 16th 2009, www.oxfam.org.uk/applications/pbas/pressoffice/?p:3735
15  International Telecommunications Union in Vodafone, 2009, *Vodafone Group CR Report 2008–9*, http://www.vodafone.com/start/responsibility.html
16  Quote in *Vodafone Group CR Report 2008–9*, p. 11, http://www.vodafone.com/start/responsibility.html
17  Vodafone, 2009, *Vodafone Group CR Report 2008–9*, http://www.vodafone.com/start/responsibility.html
18  Speaking at INSEAD's 17th Executive Sustainability Roundtable, in collaboration with the INSEAD Social Innovation Centre, November 2007, http://knowledge.insead.edu/Bottompyramid.cfm
19  Ibid
20  P&G, 2009, *2009 Sustainability Report*, http://www.pg.com/en_US/downloads/sustainability/reports/PG_2009_Sustainability_Report.pdf

# Chapter 3

1  Opening remarks to the UN Climate Change Summit Plenary, 22nd September 2009, http://www.un.org/apps/news/infocus/sgspeeches/statments_full.asp?statID=582
2  Copenhagen Communique, 2009, http://www.copenhagencommunique.com/
3  Forest Stewardship Council website, www.fsc.org
4  Ibid
5  UN Food & Agriculture Organisation, 2005, *The State of World Fisheries and Aquaculture*, http://www.fao.org/newsroom/en/news/2005/100095/ index. html
6  www.msc.org
7  Ibid
8  Walmart, 2009, Walmart Sustainability Report, http://walmartstores.com/sustainability/
9  www.msc.org
10  www.ghgprotocol.org
11  Source: Watch website http://www.sourcewatch.org/index.php?title=Global_Climate_Coalition
12  Speech to Stanford University, 19 May 1997, BP website speech library http://www.bp.com/productlanding.do?categoryId=120&contentId=7047744

13 Letter to Tony Blair in advance of Gleneagles G8 Summit, July 2005, Corporate Leaders Group on Climate Change, http://www.cpi.cam.ac.uk/our_work/climate_leaders_groups/clgcc/uk_clg.aspx

14 Ibid

15 Press release marking launch of Copenhagen Communique, September 2009, http://www.copenhagencommunique.com/news

16 Ibid

17 www.ethicaltrade.org

18 See for example BSR's 'Beyond Monitoring' program at http://www.bsr.org/consulting/working-groups/beyond-monitoring.cfm

19 See ref in Chapter 2

## Chapter 4

1 See http://www.sprint.com/responsibility/environment/productresponsibility.html, accessed on 2nd October 2009

2 GE's report can be found at www.ge.com/citizenship

3 See http://www.api.org/resources/members/index.cfm and http://www.uscap.org/ accessed on 2nd October 2009

4 More about the EICC can be found at www.eicc.info

5 Carbon Disclosure Project 2009, *Global 500 Report*, www.cdproject.net

6 Kingfisher, 2009, *Kingfisher 2008/09 CR Report*, www.kingfisher.com/cr

## Chapter 5

1 Boston Consulting Group, 2009, *Capturing the Green Advantage for Consumers*, http://www.bcg.com/documents/file15407.pdf

2 The Fairtrade Foundation, http://www.fairtrade.org.uk/what_is_fairtrade/facts_and_figures.aspx

3 The Fairtrade Foundation, http://www.fairtrade.org.uk/what_is_fairtrade/faqs.aspx

4 Sustainable Consumption Roundtable, 2006, *I will if you will – towards sustainable consumption*, p. 19, http://www.sd-commission.org.uk/publications.php?id=367

5 The Grocer, March 2009, *Organic sales slump is worse than predicted*, http://www.thegrocer.co.uk/articles.aspx?page=articles&ID=198223

6 Sustainable Consumption Roundtable, 2006, *I will if you will – towards sustainable consumption*, p. 19, http://www.sd-commission.org.uk/publications.php?id=367

7 Sustainable Consumption Roundtable, 2006, *I will if you will – towards sustainable consumption*, p. 19, http://www.sd-commission.org.uk/publications.php?id=367SDC

8  Ibid, p. 17
9  Ibid
10 The Carbon Trust, 2008, *Climate change – a business revolution? How tackling climate change could create or destroy company value*, p. 5, http://www.carbontrust.com/publications/CTC740_business_rev%20v5.pdf
11 Stern, N., 2006, *The Economics of Climate Change*
12 Carbon Trust, 2009, *Product carbon footprinting: the new business opportunity. Experience from leading companies*, http://www.carbon-label.com/casestudies/Opportunity.pdf
13 Ibid
14 Ibid
15 Ibid, p. 22

## Chapter 6

1  For an authoritative survey of the extent of internet filtering, censorship and surveillance around the world see the OpenNet Initiative at www.opennet.net
2  For an excellent description of the Shi Tao case and other incidents around the same time see 'Shi Tao, Yahoo! and the lessons for corporate social responsibility' by Rebecca MacKinnon at http://rconversation.blogs.com/rconversation/2008/01/yahoo-the-shi-t.html
3  Financial Times, February 15th 2006
4  For an excellent description of the growth of the internet and the characteristics that enable user generated innovation and change, Jonathon Zittrain's 'The Future of the Internet and How to Stop It', Yale University Press, 2008
5  The full EICC code is available at www.eicc.info
6  For an insightful analysis of the increasing burden being placed on companies by governments and the implications for business ethics see John Palfrey 'Reluctant Gatekeepers: Corporate Ethics on a Filtered Internet', Global Information Technology Report, World Economic Forum, 2006–2007
7  See 'A wired – and safe – Vietnam' at http://ycorpblog.com/2009/03/12/a-wired-and-safe-vietnam/
8  One exception was 'China's All-Seeing Eye' by Naomi Klein, Rolling Stone Magazine, May 2008

## Chapter 7

1  Financial Times, 23 June 2008, *Nestlé asks EU to soften line on GM*
2  www.nanologue.net
3  www.nanoregulation.ch

## Chapter 8

1 FT Global 500 2009 and chinamobileltd.com
2 China Mobile has become a leading publisher of corporate responsibility reports in China, and this rural strategy is well described in its CSR reports at www.chinamobileltd.com
3 Chandler, C., *China's mobile maestro*, Fortune Magazine, 31st July 2007
4 Collins, J.C. and Porras, J.L., 1994, *Built to Last: Successful Habits of Visionary Companies*, and de Geus, A., 1999, *The Living Company*
5 Bradsher, K., *China Is Said to Plan Strict Gas Mileage Rules*, New York Times, May 27th 2009
6 *GM Launches Strategy to Support China with Energy, Environmental Challenges*, General Motors Press Release, October 30th 2007
7 *General Motors' car sales surge in China*, Guardian Newspaper, October 9th 2009
8 KPMG, 2009, *International Survey of Corporate Responsibility Reporting 2008*
9 SynTao, 2008, *A Journey to Discover Values*, 2008
10 http://www.sustainability-index.com/
11 The full text of the measures can be found here: http://www.epa.gov/ogc/china/open_environmental.pdf
12 The China Water Pollution Map can be found here: http://en.ipe.org.cn/. The China Air Pollution Map can be found at http://air.ipe.org.cn
13 GE, *Corporate Citizenship Report 2008*, p. 22
14 Ibid, pp. 30–31
15 World Economic Forum and Business for Social Responsibility, January 2008, *Partnering to Strengthen Public Governance: The Leadership Challenge for CEOs and Boards*
16 Palmisano, S., *The Globally Integrated Enterprise*, Foreign Affairs, May/June 2006

## Chapter 9

1 Just Food, 22nd October 2009
2 Intel CSR report 2009
3 IBM CSR report 2009

## Conclusion

1 Speaking on BBC Radio 4, *Today Programme*, 22nd December 2009
2 Quoted in New York Times, November 17 2007, http://www.nytimes.com/2007/11/17/world/europe/17iht-climate.1.8372066.html

3  Stern, N., 2006, *The Economics of Climate Change*, p. 157
4  United Nations, *Millennium Development Goals Report 2009*, http://www.un.org/millenniumgoals/
5  Ibid
6  Sachs, J., 2008, *Common Wealth – Economics for a Crowded Planet* (book website – http://www.sachs.earth.columbia.edu/commonwealth/index.php)
7  Ibid
8  http://news.bbc.co.uk/1/hi/7843972.stm
9  http://www.marketwatch.com/story/caution-urged-for-chinese-state-owned-enterprises-in-foreign-ma-2009-09-05

# GLOSSARY

| | |
|---|---|
| BICEP | Business for Innovative Climate and Energy Policy |
| BLIHR | Business Leaders Initiative on Human Rights |
| BRIC | Brazil, Russia, India, China |
| BSE | Bovine Spongiform Encephalopathy |
| BSR | Business for Social Responsibility |
| CEO | Chief Executive Officer |
| DFID | Department for International Development |
| DRC | Democratic Republic of Congo |
| EICC | Electronic Industry Citizenship Coalition |
| EITI | Extractive Industries Transparency Initiative |
| ETI | Ethical Trading Initiative |
| EU | European Union |
| FDA | Food and Drug Administration |
| FDI | Foreign Direct Investment |
| FLA | Fair Labor Association |
| FMCG | Fast moving consumer goods industry |
| FSC | Forest Stewardship Council |
| GCC | Global Climate Coalition |
| GHG | Greenhouse gases |
| GMOs | Genetically Modified Organisms |
| GNI | Global Network Initiative |
| ICT | Information and Communications Technology |
| ILO | International Labour Organization |
| IPPC | Intergovernmental Panel on Climate Change |
| LEED | Leadership in Energy and Environmental Design |
| MCS | Marine Conservation Society |
| MDG | Millennium Development Goals |
| MSC | Marine Stewardship Council |
| NGO | Non-Governmental Organization |
| OFR | Operating and Financial Review |
| RSPB | Royal Society for the Protection of Birds |
| RSPCA | Royal Society for the Prevention of Cruelty to Animals |
| SASAC | State-owned Assets Supervision and Administration Commission |

| SOE | State Owned Enterprises |
| UDHR | Universal Declaration of Human Rights |
| vCJD | variant Creutzfeldt-Jakob disease |
| WSSD | World Summit on Sustainable Development |
| WWF | Worldwide Fund for Nature |

# INDEX

cost of capital, and other inventory costs) for delivery at short notice, rather than "selling" the inventory (and the obligations for the inventory costs) to the customers. The customers can reduce the time inventory is carried. Unless the supplier modifies internal processes to provide quicker production response, or introduces inducements (such as better quantity discounts) to move inventory to customers, the supplier can find inventories expanding.

6. There is some evidence of "regret" about participation in IT-supported business networks, but usually at a time when this has become "the way business is now done." Escape from the system may not be a viable commercial option.

late to organizations that did not understand
ng in IT-based business networks. There are
ig from airline reservation systems through a
advanced systems in which considerable inte-
rred across organization boundaries and new
d the competitive strength of the participants.
enhance the performance of participants but
to the participants. "Win-win" situations are

nsequences (and benefits) to chance, it is sug-
les and benefits of business networks can be
zation to recognize the benefits and their sus-
maintain advantage or to compensate for the
is probably not whether an organization par-
t how and when it participates.
cases is that where competitive advantage was
uently accompanied by imaginative enhance-
ned in the IT systems supporting the business
vork to handle additional business processes.
ion of the technical potential of IT has been
ple electronic connection (or EDI system) into
customers are introduced to new products and
g up new product introductions, new pricing,
ie "winners" were organizations that (1) had
d rapidly exploit additional ideas and extend
ed an imaginative management that perceived
ie network and more deeply "penetrate" their
:s, it seems that one of the organizations has
ther organization.

simple solution to the problem of finding the spark of genius on demand but rather some approaches that will create an environment that will help to stimulate this spark.

## Some Basic Principles

In considering business network opportunities, the value chain or Value Process Model (as discussed in Appendix D) provides a convenient tool for the exploration and assessment of opportunities. This approach requires that the models be developed for both the organization itself and the other parties in the business network. The more that is known about the other parties in the value systems, the greater the potential for determining linkage and integration opportunities, implications, and implementation issues. It may be necessary to start with very simple models and little cost information; but even a primitive understanding of the broad processes is useful and can be refined as the exercise proceeds and discussions with the other parties occur.

A number of factors need to be considered:

1. Business relationships range from loose/open relationships (between a large number of organizations) to tight/closed relationships (between a limited number of organizations).
2. Technology considerations are based on connections and applications and depend on whether these are standardized (and potentially widely available) or unique and proprietary (and available to a small or controlled population).
3. Strategic options derive from the interplay of business relationships and technology considerations.
4. Integration scope is the depth of penetration of the system into the internal processes of the participants in the business network.
5. Participant roles are related to the IT systems used or shared.

As an aid to the conceptualization of IT-supported business networks, it is observed that many exhibit the characteristics of a hub-and-spoke structure. An example of a hub might be a chain of do-it-yourself retailers, and the spokes might be the various suppliers of tools, paint, wood, fittings, and so on. In general, both hubs and spokes can be buyers or sellers. While hubs are generally surrounded by spokes, in some circumstances the business network may involve the interconnection of hubs in peer-to-peer relationships.

## Business Relationships

An important point is the extent to which the parties in a business network are biased, whether by the systems/business processes or by commercial agreements. Hubs may wish to operate "electronic markets" among competing suppliers, the spokes (a loose relationship), or they may wish to build close relationships with the spokes to ensure that suppliers are operating to standards of quality (with supporting internal quality processes) that avoid large-scale quality functions being performed by the hubs when goods are received. In an electronic business network, hubs may invite competitive bids from spokes (a loose relationship) or may share marketing information and volume expectations and requirements with chosen suppliers, and use the network to negotiate a supply program (a tight relationship).

## Technology Considerations

At one extreme we find highly standardized applications systems, based on both standard interfaces and standard applications, and at the other extreme are proprietary links and applications systems. In practice, mixes of standard or proprietary elements can exist, such as standardized interfaces and message formats but customized trans-action processing systems.

Proprietary interfaces or applications do not necessarily imply tight coupling—this is a separate issue. Rather, the proprietary interfaces and applications may act as a form of technology constraint, temporarily at least, on those participating in the business network.

### Strategic Options

When the business relationship is loosely coupled and a high degree of technical stan-dardization exists, there is little more to the network than an electronic infrastruc-ture. An unbiased electronic market has probably been created. Participation is easy. The primary decision factors influencing transactions are price and availability. Examples of such systems exist in currency and commodity markets.

For hubs, such systems provide access to multiple suppliers or customers. For both hubs and spokes, they can give access to a market. For competing hubs sharing the same business network, limited scope for differentiation is provided by the net-work, and differentiation must be created within the hub. For competing spokes, the basis of competition is essentially price and availability.

When a loosely coupled business relationship is combined with proprietary interfaces and applications, the potential exists for short-term competitive advantage. Such networks tend to be dominated by the standards setter. Hubs may have limited access to alternative suppliers or other customer networks, and spokes may find their market opportunities restricted. Whoever creates the proprietary standards has the best chance of maintaining competitive advantage, but this will probably be limited and short-lived unless the business network changes to a tightly coupled situation, with potential for integration and major network redesign.

When a tightly coupled business relationship is combined with strong standards, this provides opportunities for, and depends on pursuit of, collaborative advantage. Participation needs to be "by agreement," and there may be functional linkage. The advantages depend on collaboration such as achieving cost reductions through the sharing of financial risks, or the shortening of product development cycles.

When a tightly coupled business relationship is combined with unique and pro-prietary standards or applications, then the potential exists for radical business net-work redesign. Note that the interconnections may be "standardized," but the appli-cations may be proprietary and unique. The potential exists for movement of functions from one organization to another, with advantages from specialization or economies of scale. Such arrangements can be manifested as an enhanced innovation potential, greater in total than the innovational potential of the individual partici-pants. Figure 6-6 illustrates the interrelationships of these options.

### Integration Scope

This reflects the business network role and derives from the nature of the information carried by the IT system supporting the business network. Four roles are proposed:

*1. Transactions.* Here the applications are limited to the exchange of "action items," such as line item orders, line item delivery information, invoice infor-

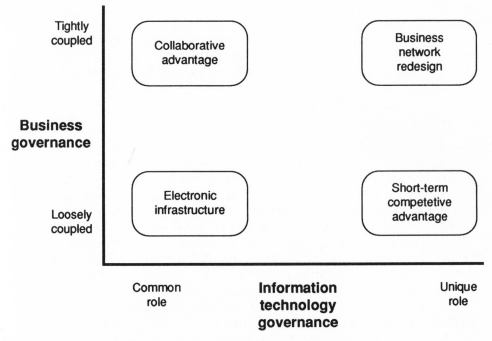

**Figure 6-6.** Strategic options. (From N. Venkatraman)

mation, payments, and so on. The system is essentially providing an electronic analogue of a paper system.

*2. Inventory/availability.* The IT system is used to "offer" products and services and options (such as volume or delivery-related prices) which a "buyer" selects and orders. The system may automatically differentiate between the products offered to various buyers or customers.

*3. Process linkage.* The IT system provides direct linkage between the processes of the two organizations, and a high degree of functional integration between the two organizations is effected through the system. High-level information may be exchanged. Process completeness depends on the linkage. A typical example is where one organization exchanges design information with another which translates the information into tooling and production information. The design process in one organization is linked to the tooling processes and production processes of another.

*4. Negotiation, dialogue, and knowledge sharing.* This role covers interconnection of "soft processes," such as might apply to the development of a product specification, or sharing access to "hard codified processes" (such as expert systems). In the latter case, an advanced form of process linkage is assumed. An example might be an exchange of design information leading to production (process linkage), but the relationship can be extended to include access to expert systems to "exercise and diagnose" problems in the products provided through this relationship.

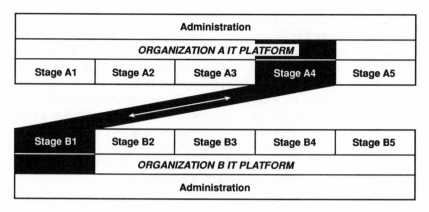

**Figure 6-7.** Simple IT platform connection.

## The IT Roles of Participants in the Business Network

The simplest form is a localized linkage between functions in two organizations; typically purchasing in one organization connects with the sales order processing activity in another organization. Each organization will have an independent (integrated) IT platform. The connection is "localized," in the sense that it relates to only a single process element in each participating organization. Figure 6-7 shows this.

However, one participant in the business network can assume (or seek to establish) a role as a "focal organization" and extend the internal IT platform into other organizations in the network. At this stage the boundaries of the various participants in the network have become blurred. This is shown in Figure 6-8.

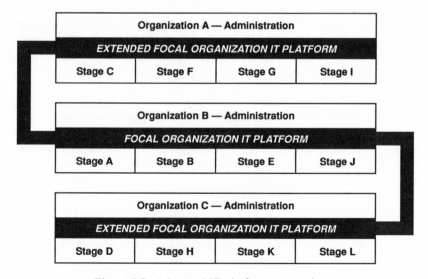

**Figure 6-8.** Advanced IT platform connection.

When a very broad-based collaboration exists, such as a "virtual networked corporation," this approach is appropriate. A participant whose natural role (power) in the business network may be weak, and even disadvantageous, might use such an approach to position the organization more effectively and, by providing additional services, establish "binding" with key participants in the network. (A supplier in a monopsonic relationship with customers may choose to extend the IT platform to the customers as a means of both adding value and achieving binding.) In such situations, the focal organization may gain information access advantages by carrying and/or processing the transactions of competitors. The focal organization is in a far better position to understand the commercial structure and trends of the business network, which may provide vital competitive advantage.

## Roles and Benefits

The four roles (or forms) of business networks provide different levels of potential benefits. The scale and sustainability of the benefits can be related to the area of benefit. Five broad classes of benefit are proposed, as follows:

1. Operating efficiency benefits arise when the network reduces the operational costs of the business processes, typically reducing administration costs, either directly or through "quality effects."
2. Financial structure benefits arise when the network leads to shifting the location of capital, typically when the network causes the relocation of inventory in the value system.
3. Market positioning benefits arise when services provided by the network enhance the attractiveness for a participant because of such factors as ease of doing business.
4. Participation conditions benefits arise through the development of formal or informal "binding" between suppliers and customers, either through contracts, as a condition of participation in the network, process linkages that are difficult to "unpick," advantages that derive from the general principle of belonging to the network, or information disclosure that enhances competitive advantage.
5. Strategic capability benefits arise where participation in the network enhances the combined capabilities of the participants, the "two plus two equals five or more" situation.

Two frameworks are shown which illustrate the typical benefits that may arise for different network roles (Figure 6-9) and the sustainability of those benefits or the factors necessary to ensure sustainability (Figure 6-10). Both frameworks are self-explanatory and are an expansion of Figures 5-14 and 5-15. Some notes on the frameworks follow.

### Transactions

Operating efficiency is reflected by reduced costs, either because the electronic system is more economical than the paper system or because the system shifts the responsibility for data entry to another organization and offloads costs. This may lead to a reduction in errors, with consequent advantages to both parties. Because simple

| Roles | Examples of benefits | | | | |
|---|---|---|---|---|---|
| | Operating efficiency | Financial structure | Market positioning | Participation conditions | Strategic capability |
| **Transactions** | Reduced costs; reduced errors | Reduces "float" | "Easy to do business"; first-mover effects | Standards weaken linkage | Low |
| **Inventory/ availability** | Reduced errors; orders confirmed before placement | "Just-in-time" offloads inventory upstream | Presentation effects; least resistance; new products | Contracts and variable terms | Channel expansion |
| **Process linkage** | Simplification of procedures | Potential for shared benefits | Process timing and simple customization | Process integration | Product derivatives and specials |
| **Expertise** | Direct | Exposure of opportunities | Fast channel for needs | Rapid response to new requirements | Collaboration |

**Figure 6-9.** Benefits in business networks.

| Roles | Benefits | | | | |
|---|---|---|---|---|---|
| | Operating efficiency | Financial structure | Market positioning | Participation conditions | Strategic capability |
| **Transactions** | Temporary | Limited | Temporary first-mover benefits | Unrestricted — temporary benefits | Low |
| **Inventory/ availability** | Ongoing if channel developed | Shifts downstream | Limited unless channel developed | Contract restrictions | Limited |
| **Process linkage** | Time and service effects | Shared but tends to shift downstream | Differentiation but need "maintenance" | Specialized contract restrictions | Innovation timing |
| **Expertise** | Long-term potential | Investment "triggers" | Unique relationships | Strong potential for exclusivity | High |

**Figure 6-10.** Sustainability of benefits in business networks.

transaction systems are relatively easy to imitate, the differential benefits, in terms of operational efficiency, will tend to be temporary.

The financial structure may be affected either by the reduction of "float," throughout the business network, or by shifting of inventory responsibilities upstream, toward the producers and material sources.

Market positioning benefits will derive from the "easy to do business" arguments and first-mover effects. Again, because simple transaction systems are easy to imitate, such benefits are temporary, particularly the first-mover effects.

There is a strong tendency for hubs to adopt standards for interfaces and transaction formats. These tend to weaken linkages, and, where participation is unrestricted, benefits may be temporary except for large hubs operating an electronic market. Participation condition effects are at best temporary. Because of the limited content of the transactions and the limited nature of the relationships between the organizations implied by simple transaction exchange systems, the strategic capability is low, and the potential for innovation within the network is very limited, almost nonexistent.

### Inventory/Availability

Paperwork savings may contribute to operating efficiency, but the cost of errors is seldom recognized as a major cost that such systems can reduce. Availability can be confirmed before the placement of orders. By the use of appropriate "pointers" (use of cursor or mouse) or "option menus," the information content of the eventual transactions can be derived from the availability display, and hence "data quality" is improved.

Although slightly more difficult to emulate, such systems tend to generate temporary operating efficiency benefits. However, if the systems are developed to the point that the network provides a "marketing channel," operating efficiency benefits can continue. Essentially, the business network has become a substitute for part of a marketing/sales operation.

The financial structure effects are similar to those of transactions systems, and inventory tends to drift upstream. Benefits tend to drift or shift downstream. New pricing options, encouraging "program purchasing," and other similar tactics can ameliorate this tendency.

Market positioning can be enhanced by presentation effects, such as "first-line" or "first-screen" effects, which can bias customer selections. Likewise, order quantities can be influenced by highly visible (and possibly selective) differentials in prices or supply terms. Particularly where marketing channel capability is developed through the system, new products can be introduced extremely simply and at very low cost. The marketing positioning benefits can be considerable, initially, although they will tend to weaken unless channel capability is developed.

Participation conditions can be a powerful binding factor. In exchange for giving access to inventory information, a supplier can establish participation conditions that may also be related to value or volume.

Strategic capability is subject to limited enhancement, related to the development of a channel. Upstream suppliers may achieve greater volume through the channel capability that is developed downstream.

*Process Linkage*

The prime contribution to operating efficiency derives from simplification of procedures and reduced intervention. Further benefits can derive from time and service factors.

Financial structure benefits can be considerable for both parties, with inventory costs of both being reduced by integrated processes. These benefits tend to be shared, but there is a tendency for them to drift downstream.

Market positioning effects can derive from process timing and efficient product customization. This can be a powerful differentiator, but it needs maintenance in order to preserve the advantage. The breadth and depth of the relationship need to be extended.

Participation conditions can be more stringent because of the requirement for process integration. For the duration of projects, the binding force can be extremely strong.

When a process linkage relates to innovation, the strategic capability deriving from this linkage can be considerable, contributing to timing of the introduction of innovations and to quality effects.

*Negotiation, Dialogue, and Knowledge Sharing*

Operating efficiency benefits can derive directly from time-scale and quality effects. These can be long-term effects.

Financial structure effects can derive from investment optimization, and triggering requirements can be exposed.

Such systems provide a very fast channel for the exchange of requirements information and the negotiation of product specifications. In terms of market positioning, such business networks can develop unique relationships.

Because relationships are so "intimate," participation conditions can be exclusive. Rapid response to requirements or problems is an essential basis for participation.

Strategic capability developed in such circumstances is extremely high, and a collaborative relationship is developed.

## Process for Business Networks Redesign

Our experience suggests that there are three stages in developing strategic opportunities derived from business networks:

1. Development of the process models.
2. Exploration of opportunities for integration across organization boundaries.
3. Recognizing needs for internal business process redesign.

The processes for Value Process Model preparation and information assembly, described in Appendix D, all apply. The approach is the same, although the process elements that should receive most attention are those at the organization's boundaries. However, the potential for shifting "internal" process elements to "external" boundaries should also be reviewed.

The main difference relates to the need to develop an "external vision," partly by developing Value Process Models for customers, suppliers, collaborators, and so on, and partly by looking at the organization through the eyes of outsiders.

## Dynamics

Developing or changing business networks can have competitive effects. Such systems may lead to shifts in "traditional" buyer/supplier power relationships. As networks are developed, particularly with standards, interrelatedness is introduced into trading relationships. These changes can provoke major competitive reactions.

It should also be remembered that various forms of business networks can introduce competitive disadvantage at some stages for certain participants. This may occur in the form of enhanced buyer/supplier power or in the shift in the capital structure. There may be little option but to absorb this disadvantage, but it is well to be aware that it may arise; otherwise, the participant may be subject to unanticipated "benefit drift."

Where benefit drift can be anticipated, the need to review internal processes becomes even more important. As a result of the improved responsiveness that an electronic order processing system may provide, a supplier may find that enhanced inventories must be carried to meet customer requirements. This may then require revisions in internal processes either to provide better responsiveness or alternatively to change commercial trading practices to ameliorate the additional inventory carrying costs. Realizing what may happen may not be a reason for not participating in a business network, but it can influence the nature of participation and other strategies to reduce the disadvantageous effects or compensate for them. Anticipation provides the opportunity to prepare corrective action.

Preserving competitive advantage appears to imply two types of continuous development: (1) the progressive enhancement of the scope of the network, and (2) the repositioning of the linkage in terms of the strategic options.

Thus, participants who are initially concerned only with transactions may be able to gain advantage by developing an inventory/availability approach and then in due course moving on to the building of process linkage between suppliers and customers. In parallel, negotiation and dialogue systems may be introduced for the fast resolution of problems and the determination of requirements.

Alternatively, as standards become established and a drift toward an unbiased electronic market occurs, by the provision of additional functionality, a unique role may be reestablished. Also possible is the manipulation of the relationship, so that a more tightly coupled relationship can be developed, leading to collaborative advantage from which development into a more radical network redesign becomes possible.

Business network redesign is largely within an organization's control. As such, it is a logical area in which to invest effort. The 1990s research and/or practical experience have shown it can have large impacts. However, it is often the case that major benefits can also come from a redefinition of scope—a subject addressed next.

## BUSINESS SCOPE REDEFINITION

This level of business transformation seems to involve two separate but interconnected concepts:

1. Using IT to enlarge the business domain, extending the "reach" of the organization into new markets, but without changing the essential nature of the business.
2. Using IT to change the nature of the business, reducing dependency on existing markets, entering new and different markets, which may imply a very different business from that which applied without the exploitation of IT.

Otis Elevator has enlarged its business domain with IT—although the servicing potential has been expanded, the business is still essentially concerned with the supply and servicing of elevators. Individual tax preparation (U.S. practice), when IT is applied, creates opportunities for a range of financial services that are a long way from the original "simple" market for tax return preparation services.

There is no simple solution that will proceduralize the generation of the spark of genius. However, what may have been done to prepare for the examination of opportunities for business process and business network redesign will help to create an environment in which latent ideas can emerge. Understanding what actually goes on in internal processes, whether administrative or operational, and how interorganizational relationships work (and what they imply to both parties) provides excellent starting points for the consideration of opportunities for expansion and change. The measurement methods that have already been discussed briefly are equally applicable.

Experience with business scope redefinition is still sparse. However, we have found that the concepts of the capacity and reach of an organization can be useful ways of operationalizing this stage.

### Capacity

The concept is well understood in the context of plant capacity or similar ideas. It can be applied to an organization as a whole, with particular relevance to the potential for exploiting the capacity to expand the business without implying the corresponding expansion of resources/costs. A service organization that already exists and is calling regularly on customers potentially has the capacity to service other products already installed in the serviced base, or to service other products not necessarily installed with existing customers but requiring skills already available.

The earlier review of internal processes can readily expose the capacity of the organization and the extent to which this capacity is fully exploited. The exercise needs to cover the existence of skills possessed by the organization and the uniqueness of those skills (such as existence, deployment, and distribution). The relevance of those skills to other organizations can be addressed while addressing the redesign of the business network. This is a typical element of a comprehensive SWOT (strengths, weaknesses, opportunities, threats) analysis.

While this approach has wide relevance and does not apply uniquely to IT, it should be noted that the organization's ability to apply and exploit IT represents both a skill and a business capacity. The question that can be addressed is whether IT can be used to enhance the skills and capacity of the organization or be an instrument for releasing those skills and free capacity to be applied to enlarging the business domain pursued by the organization.

Besides the cases described in Chapter 5, there are a number of other simple examples. A financial services organization has expanded the range of its products to the point that the sales representatives are unable to decide which product to offer. A simple expert system, implemented on a lap-top personal computer, now assists the representatives in becoming financial advisers, gives the representatives an enhanced professional image, analyzes the prospective customer's affairs, and helps the representative to choose the products to be offered. The system also produces a personalized presentation of proposals, and, if the prospective customer wishes to purchase the offered service, then the information has been collected for most of the order processing and subsequent documentation. This simple expert system has allowed the organization to implement a major expansion of the product line, and this has increased business volumes, without a major expansion of training costs and documentation distribution. The "standard" program capsule is changed as new products are introduced or old products discontinued.

There are many cases of business networks at the inventory/availability level, where the role of the system has been developed to provide a "marketing channel." Order entry clerks are prompted to offer additional products or services, the system becomes the means of displaying the "catalogue," and new products or new commercial terms are introduced through the system.

In all these examples, there was potential capacity for IT to enhance the performance of human resources and thus expand their capacity, or IT itself had the capacity, once implemented, to enlarge the business opportunities available to the organization.


## Reach

Consideration of business network redesign can expose both a good understanding of the current reach of the organization and, through consideration of Value Process Models, suggest opportunities for extending reach, either upstream in the value system to suppliers or downstream to customers or through channels to customers. The question to be addressed here is whether or not IT provides the mechanisms for extending the reach of the organization in either direction.

The implications of extended reach cover deeper penetration within the existing value system, extend to cover more participants in the business network, or shift into new value systems.

Constructive broadening of the supplier base can create an electronic market and change supplier power relationships, but it can also expand a product range, with both upstream and downstream implications and effects (as in the financial services example mentioned above). As downstream IT linkages are created, the IT system not only can be the instrument for introducing new products or serving more customers but can provide the mechanism through which customers can communicate their need and the focal organization identifies new opportunities.

## The Information Component

The fact that information collected during the course of business becomes a product that the organization can, in turn, sell to others is well known. Although not necessarily a direct revenue source, information can be used to "enrich" the products offered (such as analysis of consumption information or the provision of remote computer-aided problem diagnosis). These are examples of IT enhancing the competitive value of products, at the very least, and also contributing directly measurable revenue.

However, as business network redesign reaches the negotiation, dialogue and knowledge network role, the IT systems can become the delivery vehicle for codified knowledge. This can be a business opportunity in its own right, and not just a means of adding comparative competitive value. A supplier of agricultural chemicals offers farmers a service based on analysis of soil and crop plans, from which are derived fertilizer recommendations (and possibly pesticide or herbicide recommendations as well). What was originally considered to be a marketing aid was recognized to be a valuable service and has become an important new source of revenue.

## Implications

Recognition and expansion of capacity and reach through IT and the addition of the information component apply to business process and business network redesign and to both aspects of redefinition of business scope. In considering the last of these, it seems that separate consideration of enlargement or shifting of business scope is an unproductive refinement. In fact, these issues are best addressed as a natural part of the consideration of either business process redesign or business network redesign.

Where opportunities for business scope redefinition are found, these will probably require a review of business processes to provide the required capacity, or a review of the business networks of which the organization is a part in order to extend the reach.

## STRATEGIC ALIGNMENT

In working with the concepts in Part II of this book, it has become very apparent that one of the most important is that of alignment between an organization's business strategy and its IT strategy. In working with the research ideas throughout this report, our practical experience has suggested the beginnings of a Strategic Alignment Process. This has been captured in a tentative SAP which is the result of the initial attempts by some of the sponsors to operationalize this alignment task. This is built on the concepts developed by Henderson and Venkatraman (1989a and 1989b) during the 1990s program and is spelled out in Appendix E.

## CONCLUSION

The process of taking research results and working to translate them into ideas that change the way the organization operates is a challenging one. However, it is also rewarding, and even though the process steps that have been laid out in Appendices C, D, and E are only a first step, they do provide a flavor of the powerful results that can be captured by an organization. The nature and pace of business change as a result of turbulence in the marketplace are forcing us to rethink our strategic posture. The work by Saloner and Venkatraman is central to this task.

## REFERENCES

Henderson, John C., and N. Venkatraman. 1989a. "Strategic Alignment: A Framework for Strategic Information Technology Management." MIT Sloan School of Management, Management in the 1990s, working paper 89-076.

————. 1989b. "Strategic Alignment: A Process for Integrating Information Technology and Business Strategy." MIT Sloan School of Management, Management in the 1990s, working paper 89-077.

Porter, M. 1985. *Competitive Advantage.* New York: Free Press.

# PART III

# THE ORGANIZATION AND MANAGEMENT RESPONSE

CHAPTER 7

# The Networked Organization and the Management of Interdependence

## JOHN F. ROCKART AND JAMES E. SHORT

This chapter focuses on the three forces highlighted in Figure 7-1. Information technology has the inherent characteristic of being able to shrink the effects of time and space and provide humans with information support. Thus, electronic tools such as workstations can leverage a human's mind, shorten the time needed to accomplish tasks, and through networks speed up information flow. The time between an event and its consequences, such as placing an order or changing a design, is shorter than ever before. This shortening of work and information flow changes the dynamics of the organization. These new dynamics have major implications for how the organization operates and is managed. The rapid spread of the just-in-time (JIT) system, which has the effect of removing organizational buffers, is a partial example of this.

Organizations have always had to manage coordinating the functions, markets, products, divisions, and geographies that make up the large corporation, but now this is increasingly done without the luxury of buffers of assets or time lags. A central task facing management in the turbulence of the 1990s is learning how to apply the new IT capabilities to manage more effectively the interdependence inherent in all large, dispersed organizations.

This chapter lays out the attributes of the networked firm and documents the move to networked organizations. Organizations are integrating both across the value chain and across particular functions. The former is exemplified by linking customer service to manufacturing, and the latter by the numerous examples of shared service organizations, such as in the financial and personnel areas. There is also a move toward more emphasis on market forces and less emphasis on organizational hierarchy. The Ryder Company taking over the transportation departments of several major companies or Federal Express's handling of IBM's repair inventory out of

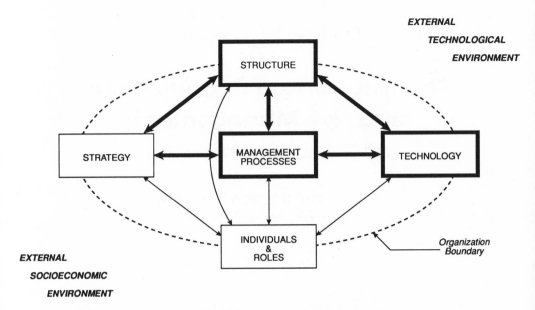

**Figure 7-1.** MIT90s framework—Chapter 7 emphasis.

Memphis are two examples. This chapter goes on to lay out a managerial perspective that emerged from the research which improves an organization's ability to manage the new levels of interdependence that the competitive environment is demanding.

The turbulent competitive environment, discussed in Part II of this book, when combined with the enabling forces of IT, results in the need to move toward a more flexible organization. As more and more members of the organization do an increasing portion of their work on or through workstations, and as these workstations become easily linked to pervasive networks, we move toward the possibility of a truly flexible organization. One dimension of such an organization is that any member can easily link to any other person, or information, horizontally or vertically. This enables the organization to make use of ad hoc teams to accomplish tasks as they arise. One's contribution to a team is based on relevant knowledge, not formal position or title. Such ad hoc teams and "virtual" organizations, when combined with the speed-up flow of information, present real challenges for the measurement and control systems as well as for management.

These new levels of interdependence increase the complexity of roles and the levels of skill required. They also require new kinds of planning and control systems and measurement systems. The classical cost accounting, budgeting, and planning systems that exist in most firms are not able to handle the requirements of the organization of the 1990s. The research reported in this chapter suggests seven dimensions of change that must be dealt with before an organization can move to a more networked approach.

An IT-enabled networked organizational approach is a major design challenge for management. Until the right skills, attitudes, and systems are

in place, an organization cannot exploit the potential opportunities in the
environment that are enabled by IT.

Parallel to most firms' efforts to increase performance, set competitive strategy,
or alter strategic market positioning is the need for organizational innovation and
change. More specifically, organizational innovation may take the form of new
modes of production processes—in short, how work is defined and accomplished
within the firm. Conversely, innovation may take more of a traditional, structural
form, whereby key pieces of the formal organization—that is, structure, roles, and
hierarchy—are changed to produce different modes of work allocation or reporting
relationships. Of course, we think of organizational change as encompassing many
more dimensions than that of simply work production or work allocation and structure, but these are clearly major dimensions, if not the most important ones.

This chapter is about one form of organizational innovation, the networked
firm, and the role of IT in making the many networks operating within the firm more
effective. A major premise is that IT-enabled networks permit us to more effectively
manage organizational interdependence, or the firm's ability to achieve concurrence
of effort along multiple dimensions of the organization.

The emergence of networks as an innovative, organizational design seems
largely based on two related concepts. First, from a *design standpoint,* networked
firms are usually conceived of as communication-rich environments, with information flows blurring traditional intracompany boundaries. Networks are also seen to
foster and utilize important role changes in individual managers. Networks increase
role complexity and require greater skill on the part of both workers and management.[1] In short, the organization is seen as information-rich, and by connecting
information, people, and skill (talent) together more effectively within the firm, the
firm in aggregate is more effective. Although important, these benefits (which are, for
the moment, implied; we will take each one up later in the chapter) are not new.
Galbraith, Lawrence and Lorsch, Bahrami and Evans, Child, and others have
detailed the importance of enabling and enriching internal communications and
information processing capability within the firm to increase performance. What is
new about networks, however, is the tight meshing of the design of networks with
the information technology required to enable them. In short, IT is seen as a design
factor in organizational change and innovation, and not just as an enabler of
more effective, organizational functioning once a given design has been put into
place.[2]

Second, from a *performance standpoint,* networked organizations are seen to
allow firms to retain small company responsiveness while becoming larger and more
complex. All other things being equal, management practice tells us that size determines complexity. The more complex the organization, the more it has to be organized along the principle of size.[3] We have tended to build large and complex organizations to produce multiple, integrated products and services. Then, using the same
organizational form, we have tried to streamline and simplify the firm's key processes
to enable flexibility and responsiveness to local market needs. In short, we have typically decentralized large firms to ensure responsiveness. Conversely, very rarely have
we successfully built large, complex, and flexible organizational forms. The attractiveness of the networked firm as such is that by adding IT as a design factor, we may
be able to design firms that can simultaneously increase size, complexity, and
responsiveness.[4]

## DEFINITION AND ATTRIBUTES
## OF THE NETWORKED FIRM

Network concepts have been used primarily to study either inter- or intraorganizational activities.[5] In a world increasingly populated by strategic alliances, partnerships, and other forms of horizontal communications both within and between firms, however, this inter- and intraorganizational distinction is itself increasingly artificial. In investment banking firms, for example, Eccles and Crane argue that because so many people in the bank are directly tied to the bank's environment (through clients, etc.), changes in the environment are rapidly translated into changes in organizational structure.[6]

We have chosen, therefore, to think of networks more as interrelationships within or between firms to accomplish work than as "formal" organizational designs per se. In short, we think of networks as one part of the firm's overall system of interrelationships to accomplish work. Note that this definition does not assert that networks are the *only* way in which work is done within or between firms, nor does it state how many networks operate to accomplish any specific work task. Networks may be the most effective way to design and accomplish many kinds of work, but this does not say that all work, or even most work, is done in networks.

For work that can be usefuly networked, then, what are the key attributes of the more networked approach? We see seven:

1. *Shared goals.* Networks typically organize around shared goals or objectives. (Note, however, that this does not mean people uniformly agree on how to achieve these goals.)
2. *Shared expertise.* Networks allow for the sharing of expertise and knowledge across the firm.
3. *Shared work.* Networks allow for the sharing of work across groups not normally part of the local structure.
4. *Shared decision making.* Networks allow for shared decision making, mainly through enhanced access to critical information across the firm. As a result, more expertise is brought to bear on specific decisions. Note, however, that although better-quality decisions may result, they may not be faster decisions.
5. *Shared timing and issue prioritization.* Networks allow for, and depend on, shared prioritization and time horizons for critical issues and action steps.
6. *Shared responsibility, accountability, and trust.* Networks depend on the sharing of responsibility, accountability, and trust in the organization. Trust is a critical and difficult issue. We have depended largely on face-to-face interaction to develop and solidify trust among people in most of our firms. A more IT-enabled, networked approach will eventually replace, or significantly reduce, many forms of face-to-face interaction with a technology interface (electronic mail, videoconferencing, design station to design station electronic connection, etc.). This raises serious questions about how trust will be established and developed in this kind of environment, or, conversely, the use of networks cannot be truly effective until a certain level of trust is established in the organization.[7]
7. *Shared recognition and reward.* Implicit in the effective functioning of networks is shared recognition and shared rewards for cooperative work.

A final point is that although networks depend on and enhance the sharing of work, expertise, responsibility, decision making, and so forth within the firm, a major effect of networks in many cases is to enhance internal conflict. Eccles and Crane state that "network structures of investment banks are flexible, flat, complex, and rife with conflict."[8] Their point about conflict echoes Lawrence and Lorsch's observation that "recurring conflict is inevitable" in differentiated organizations.[9] To paraphrase the point, the high degree of differentiation resulting from high degrees of specialization and the resulting effort to integrate across all dimensions of this specialization mean that conflict is inevitable in the networked firm. Eccles and Crane go on to identify several organizational capabilities for resolving this conflict (basically, flexibility and good communications), a number of which we address later in this chapter.

## WHY NETWORKED FIRMS NOW?

Though we are getting slightly ahead of our story here, we need to introduce one additional concept and a simplified framework of key points before we stop to outline our chapter. This concept will help us to address the question, Why the move to networked firms now?

We can summarize the concept as follows. In a firm's efforts to change strategic market positioning, set strategy, or increase performance, the need to manage effectively the interdependence of subunits and people within the firm is increasingly recognized. By effective management of interdependence, we mean the firm's ability to achieve concurrence of effort along multiple dimensions of the organization.[10] Our research in sixteen firms suggests that the need to manage interdependence is growing significantly. Moreover, it is a major managerial thrust today as executives cope with the demands of both managing complexity and increasing responsiveness across the organization. (See also Part II of this book.)

The firm's ability to continuously improve the effectiveness of managing interdependence is the critical element in product, service, or strategy innovations in the marketplace (the proactive dimension to strategy) and in effectively responding to new competitive threats (the reactive dimension). Networks, designed and enabled by information technology, are key to effectively managing this interdependence.

Figure 7-2 illustrates our points in simplified form. (A more detailed summary is provided in Figure 7-3.) The essence of the framework is outlined in five boxes, from left to right. As firms position themselves in the competitive environment, there is a need to manage the size and complexity of the organization while ensuring responsiveness and flexibility. Firms typically select areas of performance emphasis to manage this balance at the customer interface, in areas such as quality service, risk management, and cost or product quality. In order to improve performance in these emphasis areas, firms must more effectively manage interdependence across the organization. Although there are several ways to do this (examples are Galbraith's liaison roles or Drucker's team concepts, both discussed later), the key to effectively managing this interdependence is IT-enabled networks. Critical IT capabilities include advanced communications and data accessibility and the steadily improving cost-

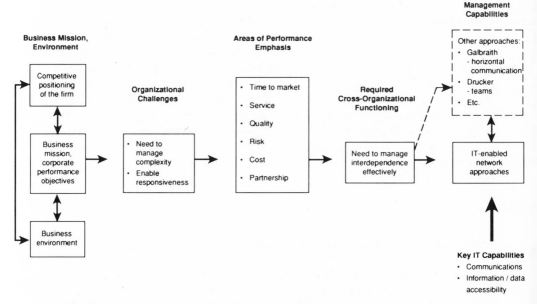

**Figure 7-2.** The move to networked organizations.

performance of the technologies themselves, leaving the machines, software, and communications more broadly available than ever before.

## CHAPTER OVERVIEW

Our research program over the past two years has studied the impacts of IT on organization structure, roles, and behavior in a sample of sixteen major firms. Our approach has been case-oriented and longitudinal. In earlier published work, we argued that the current IT impacts literature was incomplete and sought to refocus the issue by arguing that IT provided a new approach to one of management's oldest organizational problems: effectively managing interdependence.[11] This chapter suggests another dimension that has grown out of a rethinking of that research. Although we did not explicitly address networks during the research program, it is clear that the management of interdependence is heavily based on the set of IT-enabled networks supporting the required inter- and intraorganizational functioning. Our interest in networks, therefore, became a natural outgrowth of our research into managing interdependence.

Figure 7-3 illustrates our approach. In column I, we discuss the two key forces driving today's dynamic, technology-enabled, global business environment: new and powerful competitors and new and powerful information technologies. Next, we identify several areas of the business where firms are attempting to increase performance. We then link these areas of performance emphasis with the increasing need to manage interdependence effectively and identify the importance of IT-enabled networks in managing this interdependence.

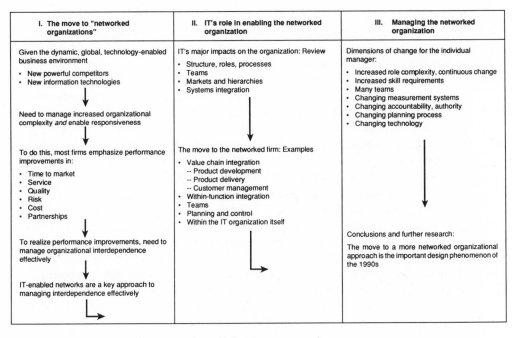

| I. The move to "networked organizations" | II. IT's role in enabling the networked organization | III. Managing the networked organization |
|---|---|---|
| Given the dynamic, global, technology-enabled business environment<br><br>• New powerful competitors<br>• New information technologies<br><br>↓<br><br>Need to manage increased organizational complexity *and* enable responsiveness<br><br>↓<br><br>To do this, most firms emphasize performance improvements in:<br><br>• Time to market<br>• Service<br>• Quality<br>• Risk<br>• Cost<br>• Partnerships<br><br>↓<br><br>To realize performance improvements, need to manage organizational interdependence effectively<br><br>↓<br><br>IT-enabled networks are a key approach to managing interdependence effectively<br><br>↳ | IT's major impacts on the organization: Review<br><br>• Structure, roles, processes<br>• Teams<br>• Markets and hierarchies<br>• Systems integration<br><br>↓<br><br>The move to the networked firm: Examples<br><br>• Value chain integration<br>  -- Product development<br>  -- Product delivery<br>  -- Customer management<br>• Within-function integration<br>• Teams<br>• Planning and control<br>• Within the IT organization itself<br><br>↳ | Dimensions of change for the individual manager:<br><br>• Increased role complexity, continuous change<br>• Increased skill requirements<br>• Many teams<br>• Changing measurement systems<br>• Changing accountability, authority<br>• Changing planning process<br>• Changing technology<br><br>↓<br><br>Conclusions and further research:<br><br>The move to a more networked organizational approach is the important design phenomenon of the 1990s |

**Figure 7-3.** Chapter overview.

Column II provides examples of how IT enables a more networked approach to the firm in our sixteen field research organizations. We identify five organizational contexts where IT-enabled networks have strikingly improved a company's ability to effectively manage its functional, product, or geographic subunits: value chain integration, within-function integration, IT-enabled team support, within the planning and control system, and within the IT organization itself.

Column III addresses the managerial implications of moving to the networked, organizational approach. We discuss the key dimensions of change from the perspective of the individual manager and conclude with several thoughts on needs and implications for further research.

## THE MOVE TO NETWORKED ORGANIZATIONS

### Drivers: A Dynamic, Global, Technology-Enabled, Increasingly Competitive Business Environment

The need to effectively coordinate the activities of individual organizational subunits is vastly greater in 1989 that it was even a few years ago. Competitive pressures are now forcing all major firms to become global in scope, to decrease time to market, and to redouble their efforts to manage risk, service, quality, and cost on a truly international scale. The dynamic, global, increasingly competitive business environment is driven by critical forces:

*New and powerful strategies and competitors who have changed the rules of global competition.* Hamel and Prahalad argue that a small group of highly innovative firms, many of them in the Far East, have defined a whole new approach to competitive strategy and altered the rules of global competition.[12] The major impact of this has been to remove the many traditional buffers enjoyed by firms in inventory, people, space, time, quality, and lack of consumer knowledge. Removing these buffers has two direct effects. First, it reemphasizes the need to share information and to work cooperatively across the organization. Second, it prompts managers to focus on horizontal work groups, such as teams, to facilitate the required cooperation and information sharing. Both emphasize the need for increased integration of effort within the firm.

*Information technology.* The rapid diffusion of key information technologies into the business environment has created new business markets and dramatically affected the cost structures of traditional ones. Familiar examples include airline reservation systems, cash management accounts, automated teller machines, and automated order entry systems. Technology provides firms with the technical capability to more tightly couple the firms's key internal business processes and to coordinate externally with major suppliers, customers, and other firms (alliances and so on) in new and different ways. See Chapter 4 of this book for more detailed discussion of these effects.

The combined effects of new competitors and new information technologies has produced a new, dynamic, global, technology-enabled, increasingly competitive business environment (see Figure 7-4). The growing demands of this environment have dramatically affected the firm's competitive positioning and the need to increase performance against growth, profitability, quality, marketplace, and customer goals.

## The Need to Increase Organizational Performance

As firms set new strategy objectives, experiment with new organizational forms, or work to improve internal performance in response to the increasingly global business environment, competitive pressures challenge firms not only to increase performance in conventional terms (marketshare, ROI, customer satisfaction, quality measures, etc.) but to reexamine how they measure performance in the first place. The network firm will require new, and perhaps unconventional, measures of firm performance. For example, individual performance measures that track span of authority and control for compensation and promotion purposes (dollar volume of business managed, number of employees) have little to do with the more diffuse, cooperative, and shared work and authority environment necessary for effective networks. As one executive with considerable team experience told us. "I know very well who works effectively in teams. What I don't know is how to separate out individual contributions from that of the team, or whether I should really be trying to do this in the first place."

To achieve the company's revenue growth, profitability, market share, or other aggregate financial objectives, most firms in our sample were working aggressively to improve internal operations and increase effectiveness in all "customer facing" activities. Additional significant emphasis is being placed on the following areas:

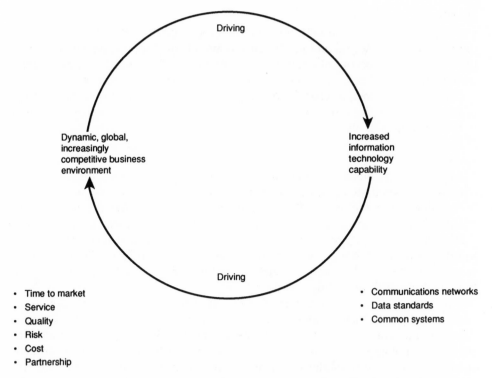

- Time to market
- Service
- Quality
- Risk
- Cost
- Partnership

- Communications networks
- Data standards
- Common systems

**Figure 7-4.** What is pushing the move to networked organizations?

### Time to Market

Today's marketplace demands more rapid new-product introductions and more effective management of existing product lines. "Time to market" refers to the firm's ability to design, produce, and bring to market new products quickly, or to better manage existing product lines. Black & Decker, for example, now brings new products to market in half the time it took before 1985. Xerox has made similar product design and manufacturing improvements in its copier division. And Ford shortened its usual product development cycle more than a year in the introduction of its Taurus/Sable vehicle line. In each case, compressing time to market required increased integration of effort among departments such as design, engineering, manufacturing, purchasing, distribution, and service.[13]

### Service

Effective service to the customer requires an effective service orientation throughout the business.[14] Service, of course, is based not only on the effectiveness of a single person or team in charge of a customer account but also on organizationwide knowledge of the customer's status, current problems, and anticipated problems. The need to improve service is therefore a driver for management's increased attention to integration across many tiers of the organization.

### Quality

*Quality* has come to mean both product and process quality. *Product quality* refers to the accuracy of the end product design and manufacturing processes (for example, the number of defects or failures in a specific part or final assembly). *Process quality,* defined in terms of customer outcomes, refers to the degree of conformance to customer needs. In short, assessing process quality is assessing how well the ultimate product or service delivered to the customer meets the customer's needs, measured in the customer's terms.[15]

### Risk

Market volatility, business complexity, and competitive pressures can easily overcome a firm's ability to accurately track and manage its business risk. Merrill Lynch, for example, lost more than $250 million in less than a week when the firm failed to adequately oversee an employee trading a complex form of mortgage-backed securities.[16] And Banker's Trust New York reported in 1988 that it had overstated its fourth quarter 1987 foreign exchange revenues by more than $80 million—in effect stating that the bank had not accurately valued its currency trading position over a full quarter's worth of trading activity.[17]

In addition to growing business risks, the rapid development of key technologies and their effects on markets and companies carries with it growing technology risks. There are three dimensions to technology risk: (1) the risk of not keeping pace with current technologies; (2) the risk, conversely, of investing in new, unproven, or inadequately understood technologies where the payoff may never come; and (3) the risk of not understanding how the rules of competition change in electronic markets.[18]

### Cost

Cost management and cost reduction are concerns for all organizations. In response to the drivers noted earlier, manufacturing firms, for example, have moved increasing amounts of manufacturing offshore in search of lower labor costs. Other firms have worked to rationalize product lines to capture global scale economies. Still others have mimicked Japanese practices, including instituting quality circles and just-in-time production techniques.

Another trend has been to consolidate shared activities across subunits within the company into one (or a very few) centralized operations to reduce costs and improve service quality. For example, several functions in auditing, cost accounting, some research activities, and some transaction processing of routine business tasks have all been candidates for consolidation into shared services organizations in firms such as Citicorp, General Electric, American Express, Dupont, Baxter Healthcare, Sun Company, and IBM. Of course, consolidating people and work to leverage expertise and to achieve economies of scale across the firm is nothing new. What is new in these cases is the role of IT in redefining what functions are consolidated and how these functions are then performed in the new services organization.

### Partnership

A final area of performance emphasis is in the firm's external links with supplier, customers, and other firms. Firm-to-firm linkages through electronic data interchange (EDI), value-added networks, partnership programs, and strategic alliances have grown markedly in recent years. In the automotive industry, for example, "arm's-length" supplier relationships common just a few years ago now operate more as "strategic partnerships," where one company may contract out part of its own value-added chain to the other. Ryder Truck, for example, now handles key pieces of Ford Motor Company's inbound and outbound logistics for vehicle assembly and distribution.

A second example is McKesson Corporation, well known to IS professionals for its successful leveraging of IT to improve customer service and cut order entry costs. As pointed out by Johnston and Lawrence, however, McKesson also transformed itself into the hub of a large value-adding partnership, successfully defending itself against its primary competition, the large vertically integrated drugstore chains.[19]

The point of the Ryder-Ford and McKesson examples, however, is that each firm's individual financial performance is increasingly tied to that of its major trading partners. For these companies, therefore, there is increasing need to develop effective internal and external procedures to define, track, and manage joint performance across these partnerships and/or strategic alliances. For additional discussion of partnerships see Chapter 5 of this book.

## The Need to Effectively Manage Interdependence

As firms work to improve performance in these areas of emphasis, the need to improve work coordination and cooperation and to share information, decision making, and responsibility across many tiers of the organization is increasingly recognized. We have earlier identified this need for increased concurrence of effort along multiple dimensions of the organization as effectively managing interdependence. We asserted that the firm's ability to continuously improve the management of interdependence is the critical element in responding to new and pressing competitive forces. Unlike in previous eras, managerial strategies based on optimizing operations within functional departments, product lines, or geographical organizations simply will not be adequate in the future.

Managers, of course, oversee innumerable large and small interdependencies every day. What happens in one function or product line affects others. Specialists in one area of the company must communicate effectively with specialists in other areas of the firm. It has long been understood that the activities in each of these dimensions, and in each of the subunits within these dimensions (for example, branch offices or manufacturing locations), are far from independent, as shown in the following examples.

Production engineers rely on product designers to design parts that can be easily and quickly fabricated. Conversely, designers depend on product engineers to implement design concepts faithfully.

Sales representatives for a nationwide or worldwide company are also interdependent. The same large customer may be served by many sales offices throughout the world. Common discounts, contract terms, and service procedures must be maintained. Feedback can be important.

Companies themselves rely on other companies to supply parts and services. When Toshiba faced the possibility of major economic sanctions for its sale of defense-related technologies to the Soviet Union, several U.S. computer manufacturers, including DEC and IBM, filed briefs in support of Toshiba's case. These U.S. firms feared that sanctions against Toshiba would harm them as well, given the high degree of interdependence in the industry.

In short, interdependence is a fact of organizational life. What is different today, however, is the increasing need to manage interdependence, driven by the competitive environment, and IT's role in enabling a more networked organizational approach to help meet this need.

## Managing Interdependence in the Networked Firm

How do companies today manage interdependence? Several approaches have been proposed, each with the goal of producing the concurrence of effort necessary to allow the organization to compete effectively in the marketplace. Mintzberg, for example, argues that firms coordinate work through five basic mechanisms: mutual adjustment, direct supervision, standardization of work process, standardization of work output, and standardization of worker skills.[20] Lawrence and Lorsch found that successful companies differentiated themselves into suborganizations to allow accumulation of expertise and simpler management processes driven by shared goals and objectives. Conversely, these same successful firms adopted integrating mechanisms to coordinate work activity across suborganizations. Lawrence and Lorsch postulated five mechanisms to manage the needed integration: integrative departments, whose primary activity was to coordinate effort among functional departments; permanent and/or temporary cross-functional teams; reliance on direct management contact at all levels of the firm; integration through the formal hierarchy; and integration via a "paper-based system" of information exchange.[21]

Galbraith later expaned the intellectual understanding of managing integration through people-oriented mechanisms.[22] He noted that direct contact, liaison roles, task forces, and teams were used primarily for lateral relations, permitting companies to make more decisions and process more information without overloading hierarchical communication channels. He also introduced the concept of computer-based information systems as a vertical integrator within the firm.

The IT-enabled network has now been added to this list of approaches. Several leading-edge firms are working to redesign basic business processes through a more IT-enabled networked organizational approach with the goal of dramatically improving performance in the six emphasis areas noted earlier (market, service, quality, risk, cost, and partnership). We address specific, company examples below, following our discussion of performance in networks.

## Performance in Networks

Effective networks operating within the firm are assumed to contribute readily to improved aggregate firm performance.[23] Implicit in this view are two key assumptions. First, the improved sharing of information, work, decision making, and responsibility improves aggregate work performance (in short the more information

**Network characteristics**                                    **Operational performance objectives**

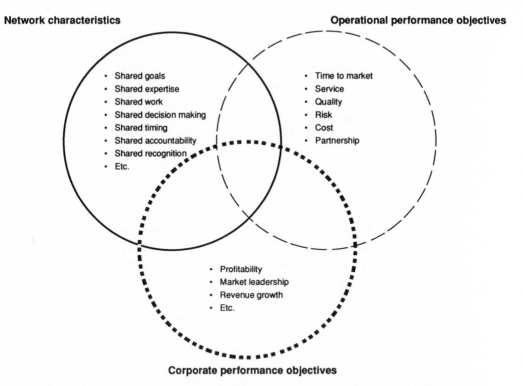

**Figure 7-5.** Linking network characteristics with areas of performance emphasis within the firm.

and cooperation in accomplishing work, the better). Second, we have a well-trained and motivated work force with adequate management philosophies and procedures to enable, manage, and maximize the benefit.

Our research, however, underscores the need for a way to link specific characteristics of networks with specific performance objectives of the firm. In other words, we seek to answer the question, In what way will the networked firm help to improve, for example, time to market, quality service, or cost?

Figure 7-5 is our initial attempt to draw together several generic performance objectives with the characteristics of how networks function. The reader will recognize this as a preliminary attempt to identify several key dimensions of networks and of firm performance with the intention of associating the two. The exercise we have in mind is to ask, How does the improved sharing of work, enabled by improved information technologies such as EDI, CIM, or office automation, contribute to our aggregate ability to service customers or to produce and bring to market new products quickly?

To address this question in a specific business situation, take, for example, IT support for currency trading in commercial banking. In the past several years, foreign exchange trading has become one of the largest profit generators in many of the nation's biggest banks, including Citicorp, Chemical Bank, Banker's Trust, and Manufacturers Hanover. As trading has become more profitable, and riskier, significant emphasis has been placed on improving trading-floor performance in three critical areas: time to market (quickly developing and bringing to market new financial instruments), risk management (accurately assessing global risks across multiple financial instruments in multiple trading markets), and cost management (driving costs out of low-value-added activities, such as clearance and settlement, and moving investment into high-value-added activities, such as product development or risk management). Significant IT investments are now being made by most banks in the following areas:

> Enhanced trader workstations. Better, faster-trading "front end" (better user interface, better decision support tools).

> Enhanced back office. Faster clearance and settlement of completed trades.

> Integration of front end and back office. Ensuring front-end and back-office systems integration and ultimately "seamless" electronic trading.

> Integration across trading markets and across financial instruments. For example, position and risk management across foreign exchange and municipal bond markets and across spot, futures, and swap transactions.

Whether these IT investments have enabled a more networked approach to trading is far less clear, however. Traders are highly individual and highly entrepreneurial as a professional group. This is very much the culture, which is reinforced by measurement and compensation systems that reward individual entrepreneurship. In some of this IT investment we can see potential significant enhancements to individual work productivity (in, for example, improved workstations). We can also see, however, the potential for greater monitoring of individual trader behavior. Back-office systems will not only clear trades but integrate with the trading "front end" to provide real-time global position-reporting capability. Which is it, better traders or better control of traders? The technology is there to enable either possibility. We can only speculate at this moment, but clearly there will come the time when continued investment in individual productivity tools will yield diminishing marginal returns. At that point we expect to see increased attention to a more team-based, cooperative, integrated approach to trading. Similarly, if the aggregate bank risk of this still highly individual, entrepreneurial activity continues to grow, fueled in part by IT investment, integration of trading from a management control and risk perspective will move onto the trading floors very quickly.

## Implications of Our View of Networks

There are a number of key assumptions and implications embedded within our view of networks:

> *Networks can be thought of as capabilities for organizational functioning.* Networks allow for dynamic multidisciplinary coalitions to form. Authority is derived not through a vertical chain of command but through characteristics of how networks function—in short, through the sharing of work,

expertise, decision making, and responsibility, as detailed earlier. This capability can lead to responsive and adaptive organizational functioning, but it also may not (see next point).

*Networks do not mean automatically that the organization is flat, flexible, or responsive.* There is no "organization law" that states whether the networked firm is flat or responsive. Some networked firms, as pointed out by Eccles and Crane, are rife with conflict. They may not have the time to be responsive to the customer. Similarly, there is no organizational law that states networks have to operate in flat organizations. In theory, they can operate just as effectively within traditional, hierarchical organizations as within any other.[24] Our point is simply that flatness, responsiveness, and flexibility are management issues in effectively managing networks. They are not simple attributes of any networked organization.

*Networks do not automatically mean that all, or most, employees are networked.* Many daily work activities and routines do not require complex cross-organizational integration or network activity.

*There are many networks.* Implicit is the existence of many overlapping networks in the firm. In general, the number of networks is tied to the complexity of work to be accomplished.

*Networks are highly sensitive to complexity.* Finally, it is important to note that if the firm's products and services are complex, then the networks supporting them are complex. Again, there is no organizational law stating that a more networked approach to the firm implies simplicity. Moreover, there may be realistic upper boundaries to network complexity for the individual manager. As the firm grows more complex, how many networks do we expect the individual manager to track effectively—five? fifty? five hundred? Conversely, what kind of complexity would the manger face without the network?

## IT'S ROLE IN ENABLING THE NETWORKED ORGANIZATION

We turn now to reviewing several of the academic literatures that discuss the impact of IT on the organization. We review how our concept of managing interdependence through IT-enabled networks expands and refocuses this earlier work, and then turn to our examples from the field. We identify five organizational contexts where IT-enabled networks have strikingly improved a company's ability to effectively manage its functional, product, or geographic subunits: in integrating across the firm's value-added chain, in within-function integration, in IT-enabled team support, in the firm's internal planning and control system, and within the IT organization itself. (These forms of integration are also discussed in Chapter 5 of this book.)

### IT's Major Impacts on the Firm: A Brief Review

We have argued earlier that a more networked organizational approach to managing interdependence is enabled by two key characteristics of IT. Vastly improved com-

munications capabilities and more cost-effective computer hardware and software
have enabled the "wiring" together of individuals and suborganizations within the
single firm, and of firms to each other. It is this multifunctional, multilevel, multior-
ganizational, coordinative aspect of current technology that provides managers with
the capability to design networks to manage interdependence. It is the technical
dimension or platform through which managers have access to the people and data
they need to direct and accomplish work.[25]

The second major characteristic is management's capacity to enable and drive
organizational innovation and business process redesign through IT. As Venkatraman points out in Chapter 5 of this book, business process redesign reflects a "con-
scious effort to create alignment between the IT infrastructure and the business process. . . . Instead of treating the existing process as a constraint in the design of the
optimum IT infrastructure, the business process itself is redesigned to maximally
exploit the IT capabilities."

Our research in IT-enabled networks and managing interdependence refocuses
and expands several earlier IT impacts perspectives in the academic and business
literatures. Although these literatures often disagree, four major classes of impact are
generally posited. First, there is the view that technology changes many facets of the
organizations's *internal structure,* affecting roles, power, and hierarchy. A second
body of literature focuses on the emergence of *team-based,* problem-focused, often-
changing work groups, supported by electronic communications, as the primary
organizational form. Third, there is the view that organizations today are *dis-integrating*—their borders punctured by the steadily decreasing costs of electronic interconnection between firms, suppliers, and customers. Companies, it is believed, will
gradually shift to more market-based organizational forms, with specialized firms
taking over many of the functions formerly performed within the hierarchial firm.
Finally, a fourth view of organizational impact arises from a technical perspective. It
is argued that today's improved communications capability and data accessibility
will lead to *systems integration* within the business. This, in turn, will lead to vastly
improved group communications and, more importantly, the integration of business
processes across function, product, or geographic lines.

### *Major Changes in Managerial Structure, Roles, and Processes*
In the first class of literature, Leavitt and Whisler argued that IT would lead to a
general restructing of the organization, ultimately eliminating middle management.[26]
In their view, IT moved middle managers out of traditional roles and allowed top
managers to take on an even larger portion of the innovating, planning, and other
"creative" functions required to run the business.

Others were quick to comment on these predictions. Some speculated that IT
would lead to greater organizational centralization, greater decentralization, reduced
layers of middle or upper management, and greater centralization of managerial
power or, alternatively, greater decentralization of managerial power.[27] Others developed contingency-based models of organizational impact.[28] Although it is clear that
IT has affected many organizations in many different ways, it is also clear that this
often conflicting literature has produced very little insight into how managers should
plan for IT-enabled role or structural changes within their firms. Three more recent
perspectives begin to address this issue.

### The Team as Hero

According to this second view, teams and other ad hoc decision-making structures will provide the basis for a permanent organizational form. Reich, for example, argues that a "collective entrepreneurship," with few middle-level managers and only modest differences between senior managers and junior employees, is evolving.[29] In short, he suggests a flat organization composed of teams.

Drucker speculates that the symphony orchestra or hospital may be models of future team-based organizations.[30] Druker sees in the emergence of teams flatter companies that will look more like an assembly of players in a symphony—each player responsible for a specific part of a larger score, with only minimal guidance from the top (the conductor). Again, the design concept is a flatter team-based organization.

The relationship between teams and technology in much of this work appears based on a technical dimension. On the one hand, this view stresses technology's role in enabling different geographically dispersed groups to better coordinate their activities through enhanced electronic communications.[31] On the other hand, some authors stress the importance of "groupware" in facilitating teamwork through better decision-making aids and project and problem management.[32]

Unfortunately, the team-based literature to date is highly speculative. As a general model of organizational structure, it leaves many questions unanswered. Primary among these are the long-term implications of organizing in such a manner that moves primary reporting relationships away from the more usual hierarchical, functional, geographic, or product structures. These structures work to immerse employees in pools of "front-line," continually renewed expertise. Team members separated too long from these bases tend to lose this expertise.[33]

### Corporate Dis-integration: More Markets and Less Hierarchy

A third perspective argues that today's hierarchical organizations are steadily dis-integrating; their borders punctured by the combined effects of electronic communication (greatly increased flows of information), electronic brokerage (technology's ability to connect many different buyers and suppliers instantaneously through a central database), and electronic integration (tighter coupling between interorganizational processes). In this view, the main effect of technology on organizations is not just in how tasks are performed (faster, better, cheaper, etc.) but rather in how firms organize the flow of goods and services through their value-added chains.

There are two major threads to this argument. Malone, Yates, and Benjamin state that new information technologies will allow closer integration of adjacent steps in the value-added chain through the development of electronic markets and electronic hierarchies.[34] They argue that advances in IT will steadily shift firms toward proportionately more forms of market coordination, since the costs therein will gradually fall beneath those of hierarchical coordination. Johnston and Lawrence argue that IT-enabled value-adding partnerships (VAPs) are rapidly emerging.[35] Typified by McKesson Corporations' Economost drug distribution service, VAPs are groups of small companies that share information freely and view the whole value-added chain—not just part of it—as one competitive unit.

These proposals, however, are very recent and have only small amounts of sample data to support them. And the exact opposite case—the cast for increased vertical integration offirms—is also being strongly propounded.[36]

*Systems Integration:   Common Systems and Data Architecture*

A fourth, more technically oriented view is that business integration is supported by systems and data integration. Here the concept of IT-enabled organizational integration is presented as a natural outgrowth of two IT properties: improved interconnection and improved shared data accessibility.[37] In this view, *integration* refers to integration of data, of organizational communications (with emphasis on groups), and of business processes across functional, geographic, or product lines.

## The Move to the Networked Firm: A Descriptive Framework and Examples

Although each of these four perspectives offers important insights, there is need for a fifth perspective that expands these views into a more active managerial framework. We have argued that technology's major impact on the firm will be in supporting a more networked approach to effectively managing interdependence within the firm. Technology, as we have stated, provides both the technical capacity for interconnection of people and resources and the management capacity for business process redesign.

Given pressures from the drivers noted earlier, our research has uncovered six organizational contexts where characteristics of a more IT-enabled networked approach has strikingly improved a company's ability to manage its functional, product, or geographic subunits. We focus here on five of the six, as illustrated in Figure 7-6. The sixth area, interorganizational integration, is covered in Part II of this book.

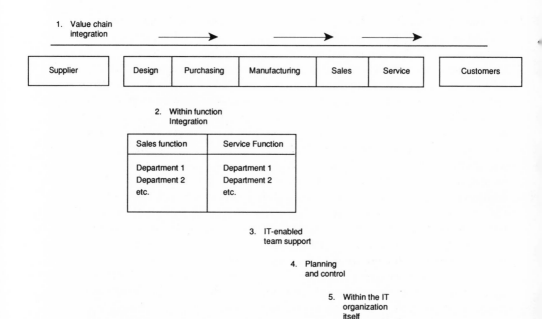

**Figure 7-6.** Examples of network approaches in five organizational contexts.

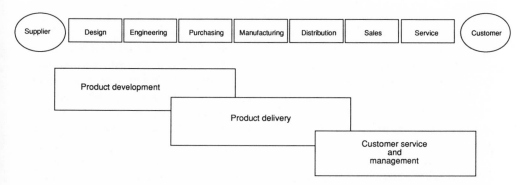

**Figure 7-7.** Product development, product delivery, and customer service and management: Collapsing the value-added chain.


### Integration across the Firm's Valued-Added Chain

Lawrence and Lorsch noted the use of "human integrators" to manage the concurrence of effort between adjacent functions in the value-added chain (e.g., among manufacturing, distribution, and sales) more than twenty years ago.[38] Today this integration is performed increasingly through an electronic interface, via communications, computers, and databases. Firms attempt between-function integration for at least one of three reasons: to increase their capacity to respond quickly and effectively to market forces (time to market); to improve the quality of conformance to customer requirements (what we have earlier termed process quality objectives); or to reduce costs.

We have found that successful between-function integration collapses the multistage value-added chain into three major segments: producing new products, delivering products to customers, and managing customer relationships (see Figure 7-7).[39] In manufacturing companies, for example, it is clear that interdependence revolves around these three macro-organizational activities. In the insurance industry, discussions with five major companies revealed that the same three segments were targets for functional integration.

Turning to the two ends of the modified value-added chain—the product design segment on the one hand and the customer service segment on the other—the effects of a more networked technology-enabled integration are clear. To speed product development, companies such as Xerox, Lockheed, and Digital are introducing CAD/CAM and other design aids that provide integrated support to product designers, product engineers, materials purchasing, and manufacturing personnel involved in the design-to-production process. This compression has resulted in joint "buy-in" on new product designs, eliminating a lengthy iterative development process (which previously occurred because the designers did not take the needs and capabilities of other departments into account). Dramatically shortened product development time—a key component in improving aggregate time to market—had been a consequence of this buy-in.

At the customer service end of the chain, Otis Elevator, Digital, Xerox, and other firms have developed new service approaches based on electronic communications networks, an integrated database of customer and service history, and fault signaling that goes directly from damaged equipment to the supplier's maintenance-monitoring computer. The advantages of Otis's centrally coordinated electronic service system have been well publicized.[40] A major advantage is senior management's ability to view the status of maintenance efforts nationwide and to direct sales and service attention where needed. In addition, it is now feasible to provide the company's design, engineering, and manufacturing personnel with direct access to fault data.

In many ways, the most interesting stage of the collapsed value chain is product delivery, which requires integrating several different information systems: order entry, purchasing, materials resources planning, and distribution management. The critical business issues are to provide customers with information about when orders will be completed and to forecast and manage outside supplier, product manufacturer, and product distribution processes.

No company has yet accomplished the fully networked, large-scale integration of functions and systems required to fully manage the product delivery process. A division of the Norton Company, however, pioneered efforts in this direction in the mid-1980s. Norton initiated a set of major IT projects, ranging from the "Norton Connection" (a computer-based telecommunications link between the company and its distributors), to a more effective order-processing system, to a series of manufacturing technologies targeted at flexible manufacturing and automated materials control.[41] More recently, Westinghouse initiated a product delivery integration process in several segments of the company. And at General Foods a series of task forces has been charged with developing a similar approach.

Most efforts, however are more limited in scope. British Petroleum Company's chemical business has developed an integrated order management process spanning thirteen divisions. Baxter Healthcare Corporation is working to enhance its well-known ASAP order entry system to provide customers with full product line visibility to their 125,000-plus products. And a host of manufacturing integration projects have been initiated at Digital Equipment Corporation, Ford Motor, IBM, General Motors, Hewlett-Packard, and Texas Instruments, to name a few.

### Within-Function Integration

Many companies are also recognizing the interdependence of multiple units within the same function. This recognition has prompted several actions to enhance a more network-oriented improvement of coordination and cooperation across subunits—for example, centralization of certain similar tasks or functions within the organization into the single group, central management of geographically separate units, and (in some firms) the development of common systems and/or standard data definitions to facilitate coordinating diverse organizational units.

At Sun Refining and Marketing company, for example, senior management identified crude oil trading as one of the most critical business activities in the company three years ago. At that point Sun's traders were dispersed worldwide, each acting relatively autonomously. Sun began developing a centralized on-line trading function supported by integrated market information from Reuters and other trade data sources. Today Sun recognized the importance of its integrated trading function in managing risk exposure and in developing effective pricing strategies for the volatile crude market.

Similarly, although OTISLINE can be viewed as an application enabling integration across stages of the value-added chain, it is also an integrating mechanism within the field maintenance function itself. Customers with difficult problems can be immediately directed to a specialist, not left to the limited resources of a remote branch office. Frequent trouble from a specific type of elevator can be observed as the pattern develops, and corrective action can be taken on a nationwide basis. In addition, the quality of telephone responsiveness to anxious customers can be closely monitored.

Eastman Kodak provides another example, its executive support system, which assists in the worldwide scheduling of manufacturing plants. Digital is installing common MRP systems throughout its worldwide manufacturing plants. DuPont has installed common financial systems in all of its European operations. The business drivers underscoring each of these efforts range from service to cost to time-to-market to global responsiveness—but they all recognize that no single unit within a major function is truly independent.

### IT-Enabled Team Support

Ken Olsen, chairman of Digital Equipment Corporation, believes that the ability to bring teams together electronically is one of the most important features of the company's IT capability. Ford Motor has claimed that the "Team Taurus" approach, much of it IT-enabled, shaved more than a year off the time needed to develop, build, and bring to market the Taurus/Sable model line. In the future, as Drucker points out, many tasks will be done primarily by teams.[42]

Teamwork, of course, is not a new way to coordinate interdependent activities among separate units and people in an organization. What *is* new is that IT—chiefly electronic mail, videoconferencing, and computer-to-computer links such as those integral to CIM and EDI—is now facilitating teamwork and steadily adding capability to teams. Today, for example, it is feasible for team members to coordinate asynchronously (across time zones) and geographically (across remote locations) more easily than ever before. Teams, as such, are one part of the increasingly networked firm.

The development and use of computer software to support teams is also moving into an explosive phase. There is a growing body of software labeled "groupware," for specialized computer aids designed to support collaborative work groups. As Bullen and Johansen point out, "Groupware is not a thing. Rather it is a perspective on computing that emphasizes collaboration—rather than individual use."[43] Several companies, including Xerox, General Motors, Digital, Eastman Kodak, IBM, and AT&T, are experimenting with state-of-the-art meeting and conferencing aids in addition to more "routine" communications systems such as electronic mail or voice mail systems.

*Planning and Control*

A fourth area where a more IT-enabled networked organizational approach is increasingly in evidence is in planning and control. It is also an area where until very recently the typical process looked much the same across most major firms.[44] Before the new fiscal year began, an intense planning process culminated with an extended presentation to senior management of the proposed activities of each strategic business unit (SBU). Agreed-upon plans were then monitored on a monthly basis. Parallel to this formal control process was an informal system of keeping in touch by which senior management assured itself that all was going well in key areas of the business in the interim between formal reports.

Volatility in the business environment, coupled with technology's ability to provide management with efficient communication and information, is radically changing this traditional planning and control scenario. The major issue is how best to use IT for coordination and control of the firm's activities.

At Xerox, chairman David Kearns and president Paul Allaire have implemented an executive support system that now makes the annual planning and control process a more on-line, team-based, networked, communication- and coordination-based process. The system requires all of Xerox's thirty-four business units to submit their plans over an electronic communications network in a particular format. This allows the staff to critique the plans more effectively and to reintegrate these plans when looking for factors such as competitive threats across all SBUs, penetration into particular industries by all SBUs, and so forth.

More important, each SBU's plans can be reviewed not only by senior executives and corporate staff but also by other top officers in the firm. Each officer receiving an SBU's plans is encouraged to send corporate headquarters an electronic message raising the issues he or she sees in the plan. The officer may also be asked to attend the review meeting. There is no "upfront" presentation at this meeting. Only the issues raised by the executives, the staff, or the other officers are discussed.

In short, Allaire's planning and control process is a computer-age process. By using a communication- and coordination-oriented network, it draws on the entire executive team for input. Understanding of the important issues facing each SBU is deeper, and its activities are therefore sometimes subtly, sometimes more precisely coordinated with the other SBUs.

A team-based networked approach to the senior executive job of managing the business is also in evidence at Philips Petroleum Company's Products and Chemicals Group. The executive vice president, Robert Wallace, is linked to his other top nine executives through an executive support system that provides on-line access not only to one another but also to varying levels of daily sales, refinery, and financial data. External news summaries relevant to the business are entered into the system three times a day. Unlike Allaire, who limits his input to planning and review meetings, Wallace has used the system to take operating command of a few critical decisions for the business. In the volatile petroleum pricing arena, Wallace believes that he and his executive team can confer with the advantage of immediate data access and can make better pricing decisions than those farther down the line. He cites increased profits in the tens of millions as a result of the system.

By far the majority of senior executives today do not use their systems in nearly as dramatic a manner as Allaire and Wallace do.[45] Yet the technology provides the capability for better coordination at the senior management level. It also provides opportunities to move decisions either up or down in the organization. Team decision making is a growing reality, as geographically separated executives can concurrently access and assess data and communicate in "real time." Vertical on-line access to lower levels of data and text, however, violates many long-established management practices. Yet informal telephone-based systems have always provided some of this information. In an era where management is seen more as a cooperative, coaching activity than an iron-fisted one, vertical as well as horizontal networking may come of age.

### Within the IT Organization Itself

Line managers and IT managers are finding themselves more mutually dependent than ever before. Today there is a small but rapidly growing number of senior line and staff executives who are taking responsibility for significant strategic projects centered on computer and communication technologies in their companies, divisions, or departments. We have described elsewhere the full extent and importance of the line taking the leadership.[46]

As the line role grows with regard to innovative systems, the role of the information systems group is becoming more complex, more demanding, and more integrated into the business. In short, the IT organization is responsibile for building the network infrastructure—the vital set of roads and highways through which the networks of shared work, expertise, decision making, and so on work. A key first step in planning and developing this infrastructure is partnership between the line businesses and their IT organizations in designing, developing, and implementing new systems.[47] This necessary degree of partnership places four major demands on the IT organization.

First, with regard to systems development, even those systems in which the line is heavily involved require greater competence and skills on the part of the IT organization. The technical design, programming, and operation of business-critical, often highly complex systems present a far greater challenge than do systems of previous eras. Today's integrated cross-functional product delivery systems require database, project management, telecommunications, and other skills not previously demanded of IT personnel. Second, today's new systems require the development and implementation of a general and eventually seamless IT infrastructure (computers, telecommunications, software, and data). The challenge to IT management is to provide leadership in defining this seamless, networked IT infrastructure. Third, there is a need for IT management to educate line management about its new responsibilities. And fourth, IT executives must educate themselves and their staffs about all significant aspects of the business. Only if this happens will IT personnel be able to knowledgeably assist line managment in creating effective strategy-enhancing systems.

The concomitant demand on line management is twofold: the need to learn enough about the technology to view it as a key factor in strategic and operational business planning, and the need to select effective IT personnel and to work closely with them.

## MANAGING INTERDEPENDENCE IN THE NETWORKED FIRM

Tomorrow's successful corporations will require increasingly effective management of interdependence to realize the performance gains made possible by a more networked organizational approach. IT-enabled changes in cross-functional integration, in the use of teams, or in within-function integration will force individual managers' agendas to change as well. In short, what managers do now and what they will do in the future are in the process of important change.

Zuboff argues that in the new "informated" organization there is considerable interdependnece among four domains of managerial activity: intellective skill development, technology development, strategy formulation, and social system development.[48] She notes that intellective skill development cannot proceed without the social system management that helps to foster roles and relationships appropriate to a new division of learning. Similarly, activity in either domain cannot proceed without technological development that supports an informating strategy.

This view of a multiplicity of dimensions that together enable a more networked approach to organizational functioning is widely established. The key problems confronting researchers, however, have been to define the operational components of these dimensions and to specify the sequence of changes in the transition from current to future organizational functioning. This presumes, of course, that we do not have some sort of "big bang" theory of organizational change, which would posit instead that no such sequence or linearity of change takes place, only the move from "before" to "after." The issues of implementation and organizational change are treated at length in Chapter 9 of this book.

### Dimensions of Change

What, then, are the dimensions of change to a more networked approach to organizational functioning? Our research has uncovered eight:

1. *Increased role complexity brought on by continuous changes in products, markets, processes and organization.* The manager's job is getting harder. The critical difficulty will be the need to manage continuous change in many dimensions of the organization. As companies seek new business opportunities by aggressively defining and executing new ways of doing things—for example, new strategies, new products and services, new customers—managers will need to define and adjust more rapidly to new situations. Similarly, companies must also respond to heightened competitive pressures by continually improving (renewing) internal processes.[49] Again, managers must initiate and respond to new situations. Frequently this will involve organizational changes.
2. *The manager's need to cope with unclear lines of authority and decision making.* As the complexity of shared work, decision making, expertise, and accountability increases, uncertainty increases. When March and Olsen, Mintzberg, and others studied decision making under uncertainty, they invariably found—not surprisingly—that good managers respond to uncertainty by defining and sorting things out for themselves.[50] Of course, as individual managers in any organization see

information, decision making, and responsibility differently in many circumstances, conflict and uncertainty about the way some decisions will go are inevitable. This will be very uncomfortable for many managers.

3. *Increased skill requirements.* Skill requirements increase markedly in the transition to a more networked organizational approach. We think of skills to include both the tools and techniques necessary for higher-order analysis and conceptualization and the intuitive capacity, experience, and interpersonal skills necessary to work effectively with others. There are a variety of theories, stemming largely from cognitive science, that define skills more in terms of cognitive complexity, conceptualization, and different problem-solving capacities.[51] Whatever the level of analysis, however, managing networks requires more coordinative skills in team-based conceptualization, problem solving, and decision making.

4. *Many Teams.* Teams are real. A vastly increased number of space- and time-spanning, problem-focused, task-oriented teams are becoming the norm. This growth in peer-to-peer as opposed to hierarchical activities requires new managerial skills and role definitions.

5. *Changing measurement systems.* Measurement systems are also changing. Measuring individual, team, or suborganizational success is difficult in an environment where cooperative work is increasingly the norm. New measurement approaches will need to be devised. We are entering a transitional period, during which people will need to adjust both to a changing work mode and to a changing measurement process. There is generally a lag in understanding and applying the correct measures of performance after a change in organization or roles. As new measurement systems evolve, therefore, they will almost surely lag behind other organizational changes. Figure 7-8 develops a preliminary list of changes in dimensions of organization and performance as firms move from their current organizational designs to the more networked approach.

6. *Changing accountability and authority.* We have trained an entire generation of managers to equate accountability with full control over the resources that affect them.[52] Increasingly, we will now require managers to share resources more freely and operate in an environment of more diffuse responsibility and accountability for many decisions. In many peer-to-peer situations within the firm, for example, there may not be a single individual in control or accountable. This will be hugely countercultural in many corporate environments.

7. *Changing the planning process.* Information technology is enabling the new planning approaches required to meet new competitive conditions. Our research underscores two major new capabilities. First, better information access and information managment allow firms to target what is most critical to the organization. Second, organizations now have the ability to conduct "real-time," stimulus-driven planning at all levels—in short, to bring key issues to the surface and react to them quickly. The technology provides both the conduit for moving critical data to all relevant decision makers and, more importantly, the capability to disseminate changes in direction to all parts of the firm.

8. *Changing the technology infrastructure.* Changes in the technology infrastructure of the organization are now a top management priority. As technology becomes more deeply embedded within the business process, changes in either will influence and respond to the other.

| Dimensions of change | Time 1 | Time 2 | Time 3 |
|---|---|---|---|
| **Performance goals** | | | |
| • MARKET LEADERSHIP/FINANCIAL RETURN<br>  -- Profitability, ROI, ROA<br>  -- Revenue Growth Rate, Investment Productivity<br>  -- Strategic Market Position<br>  -- Market Share Relative to Key Competitors<br>  -- Time to Market Key Product Line(s), New Product Introductions<br>• SERVICE<br>  -- Customer Satisfaction<br>  -- Internal Customer Partnership Orientation<br>• QUALITY<br>  -- Product, Process Quality<br>• RISK MANAGEMENT<br>• COST MANAGEMENT<br>  -- Cost Performance<br>  -- Cost/Investment Attitude<br>• PARTNERSHIP<br>  --External Partnership/Alliance Strategies, Performance | | | |
| **Actions** | | | |
| *Product/Market Strategy Changes*<br>• NUMBER OF PRODUCTS, MARKET SEGMENTS TARGETED<br>• PRODUCT LINE INTEGRATION | | | |
| *Organization Structure Changes*<br>• DIVISION, SBU, FUNCTION, GEOGRAPHIC STRUCTURE<br>• MANAGEMENT LAYERS | | | |
| *Management Process Changes*<br>• PLANNING AND CONTROL SYSTEM<br>  -- Individual Performance Measures<br>  -- Management Structure<br>  -- Accountability and Authority<br>• HUMAN RESOURCES<br>  -- Management Education<br>  -- Motivation, Guidance, Control<br>  -- Compensation and Span of Control | | | |
| *Network Infrastructure, Capacity Changes*<br>• COMMUNICATIONS INFRASTRUCTURE<br>• INFORMATION ACCESSIBILITY<br>• USE OF TASK FORCES, TEAMS, OTHER HORIZONTAL LINKAGES | | | |
| *Information Systems Changes*<br>• SYSTEM DEVELOPMENT<br>  -- Development Approach/New Technologies<br>• OPERATIONS<br>  -- Data Management<br>• MANAGEMENT PLANNING AND CONTROL<br>  -- Degree of Business/IS Integration<br>• IS ORGANIZATION STRUCTURE<br>  -- Centralization/Decentralization | | | |

**Figure 7-8.** Understanding the transition to the networked organization.

People-intensive integrative mechanisms are limited in what they can accomplish. Accessible, well-defined data and a transparent network are therefore the keys to effective integration in the coming years. Developing these resources, however, is not easy. Justifying organization-spanning networks whose benefits are uncertain and will occur in the future, and whose costs cannot be attributed clearly to any specific suborganization, is in part an act of faith. Developing common coding systems and data definitions is a herculean job. This task increases short-term costs for long-term gain—a practice not encouraged by most of today's measurement systems.

Schein has pointed out that in the complex interweaving of cultural and technological factors in the organization, cultural assumptions that favor innovation will increase the likelihood of individuals inventing and implementing those new ideas that can make the organization more adaptive.[53] In other words, if technological and cultural conditions favoring innovation and change are not present, people will simply resist the kinds of changes that may be necessary. This is to remind us that although IT may enable the technical infrastructure to connect people and information together more effectively in the networked firm, to realize the benefits we are looking for we need also to have—or to develop—a favorable cultural setting for innovation and change. See Chapter 9 of this book for an expanded discussion of this issue.

## CONCLUSIONS AND FURTHER RESEARCH

We believe that the IT-enabled networked organizational approach is the important design phenomenon of the 1990s. Firms increasingly will turn to network approaches with the goal of improving performance through the existing organization. In this chapter, we have identified several key characteristics of the more networked organizational approach and discussed specific areas where firms are attempting to increase performance in the business. We then argued that in their efforts to increase performance, firms are recognizing the need for more effective management of interdependence across subunits and people within the firm. IT-enabled networks are the most effective way for firms to manage this interdependence.

We discussed specific examples of the network approach and looked at the implications of networks for the individual manager. Further research will consider in part two key questions raised: How do specific characteristics of the networked firm contribute to improved aggregate firm performance? And what are the implications of these network characteristics for managing interdependence effectively?

## NOTES

The authors wish to acknowledge the contributions of colleagues Christine V. Bullen, J. Debra Hofman, and John C. Henderson, Center for Information Systems Research, MIT Sloan School of Management, to the research on which this chapter is based. We are also indebted to others who read and commented on the manuscript: John Carroll, Michael S. Scott Morton, Edgar Schein, and N. Venkratraman of MIT's Sloan School; Lee Morris, CIGNA; Thomas Main, Aetna Life & Casualty; and Ron Smart, Digital Equipment Corporation.

1. S. Zuboff, *In the Age of the Smart Machine* (New York: Basic Books, 1988); R. G. Eccles, and D. B. Crane, *Doing Deals: Investment Banks at Work* (Cambridge: Harvard Business School, 1988); P. F. Drucker, "The Coming of the New Organization," *Harvard Business Review* (January–February 1988): 45–53. Also see R. K. Mueller, *Corporate Networking: Building Channels for Information and Influence* (New York: Free Press, 1986), p. 2.

2. See *California Management Review* 28, no. 3 (Spring 1986), for articles by R. E. Miles and C. C. Snow, "Networked Organizations: New Concepts for New Forms" (pp. 62–73), and M. Tushman and D. Nadler, "Organizing for Innovation" (pp. 74–92.) Miles and Snow define "dynamic networks" by *who* is in them (designers, suppliers, brokers, producers, distributors) and by *how* they behave (characteristics such as vertical disaggregation, market orientation, and information access). Also see *California Management Review* 30, no. 1 (Fall 1987), for articles by J. Child, "Information Technology, Organization, and Response to Strategic Challenges" (pp. 33–50), and H. Bahrami and S. Evans, "Stratocracy in High-Technology Firms" (pp. 51–66.) Also see "A New Industrial Organization Approach" and "The Emergence of the Network Firm" in C. Antonelli, ed., *New Information Technology and Industrial Change: The Italian Case* (Dordrecht: Kluwer Academic Publishers, 1988). On organizational innovation, see J. R. Galbraith, "Designing the Innovating Organization," *Organizational Dynamics* (Winter 1982): 5–25; and T. Burns and G. M. Stalker, *The Management of Innovation* (London: Tavistock Publications, 1961).

3. P. F. Drucker, *Management* (New York: Harper & Row, 1973), p. 638.

4. See Child, "Information Technology"; and Tushman and Nadler, "Organizing for Innovation."

5. For example, in intraorganizational, small group research, "communications networks" are generally considered one of three variables, along with work task and leadership, which together establish norms for group interaction. As early as 1951, Bavelas and Barrett compared group performance, in their case problem-solving ability, across "centralized" and "decentralized" communications networks. See A. Bavelas, and D. Barrett, "An Experimental Approach to Organizational Communication," *Personnel* 27 (1951): 366–71. Other definitions of networks and network characteristics are found in research in social psychology, organizational communications, and cognitive science. For example, see "Communication Networks," in A. Paul Hare, *Handbook of Small Group Research* (New York: Free Press. 1976), pp. 260–77; L. K. Porter and K. H. Roberts, "Communication in Organizations," in M. D. Dunnette, ed., *Handbook of Industrial and Organizational Psychology* (Chicago: Rand McNally, 1976), pp. 1553–89; R. L. Burgess, "Communication Networks: An Experimental Reevaluation," in B. M. Bass, and S. D. Deep, eds., *Studies in Organizational Psychology* (Boston: Allyn and Bacon, 1972), pp. 165–79; E. P. Hollander and R. G. Hunt, eds., *Current Perspectives in Social Psychology* (New York: Oxford University Press, 1976). A more cognitive-based view is contained in T. Winograd and F. Flores, *Understanding Computers and Cognition: A New Foundation for Design* (Norwood, N.J.: Ablex Publishing, 1986).

6. R. G. Eccles and D. B. Crane, "Managing through Networks in Investment Banking," *California Management Review* 30 (Fall 1987): 176–95.

7. In this chapter, we do not address the "informal" organization as such, in which trust is a key factor. The classic reference in this area is C. Barnard, *The Functions of the Executive* (Cambridge: Harvard University Press, 1938).

8. Eccles and Crane, *Doing Deals.* pp. 119–46.

9. P. R. Lawrence and J. W. Lorsch, *Organization and Environment: Managing Differentiation and Integration* (Homewood, Ill. Richard D. Irwin, 1967), p. 13.

10. Researchers disagree about a precise definition of *interdependence.* An early influential view is contained in J. D. Thompson, *Organizations in Action: Social Science Bases of Administrative Theory* (New York: McGraw-Hill, 1967). Also see J. E. McCann and D. L. Ferry, "An Approach for Assessing and Managing Inter-Unit Interdependence—Note," *Acad-*

*emy of Management Journal* 4 (1979): 113–19; and B. Victor and R. S. Blackburn, "Interdependence: An Alternative Conceptualization," *Academy of Management Journal* 12 (1987): 486–98.

11. J. F. Rockart and J. E. Short, "IT in the 1990s: Managing Organizational Interdependence," *Sloan Management Review* 30, no. 2 (1989).

12. G. Hamel and C. K. Prahalad, "Strategic Intent," *Harvard Business Review* (May–June 1989): 63–76.

13. There are at least three key dimensions to this integration of process: shared work, shared information and expertise, and shared accountability. Getting agreement on what and how to measure joint performance across formerly independent operations is a key management issue. The dilemma is "how joint" are the measures.

14. T. J. Peters and R. H. Waterman, Jr., *In Search of Excellence* (New York: Harper & Row, 1982), p. 156.

15. See G. A. Pall, "Quality Process Management" (Thornwood, N.Y.: Quality Improvement Education Center, IBM, February 1988).

16. "The Big Loss at Merrill Lynch: Why It Was Blindsided," *Business Week,* May 18, 1987, pp. 112–13.

17. "Bankers Trust Restatement Tied to Trading Style," *New York Times,* July 22, 1988, p. D2.

18. T. W. Malone, J. Yates, and R. I. Benjamin, "Electronic Markets and Electronic Hierarchies," *Communications of the ACM* 30 (1987): 484–97.

19. R. Johnston and P. R. Lawrence, "Beyond Vertical Integration—The Rise of the Value-Adding Partnership," *Harvard Business Review* (July–August 1988): 94–104.

20. H. Mintzberg, *The Structuring of Organizations* (Englewood Cliffs, N.J.: Prentice-Hall, 1979).

21. Lawrence and Lorsch, *Organization and Environment.*

22. J. L. Galbraith, *Organization Design* (Reading, Mass.: Addison-Wesley, 1977). Galbraith also introduced the concept of the organization as information processor in this work. He distinguished computer-based, vertical information systems from lateral relations and emphasized the division of organizations into suborganizations because of the need to minimize the cost of communications.

23. Mueller, *Corporate Networking.* Note also how the *Wall Street Journal* reported GE's decision to invest in new global communications technology: "GE has of late been pushing communications as the way to build a common system of corporate values and culture. John F. Welch, Jr., the company's chairman, believes that better communications is the key to giving GE a small-company culture while becoming a global corporate giant. Mr. Welch himself insisted on having videoconferencing technology to enable him to talk to his employees in Europe." See "GE Will Give Major Contract to Phone Firms," *Wall Street Journal,* May 26, 1989, p. A6.

24. In this case, however, there are important implications for how information moves throughout the network and the potential for significant information overhead at each level in the hierarchical firm.

25. See R. I. Benjamin and M. S. Scott Morton, "Information Technology, Integration, and Organizational Change," MIT Sloan School of Management, Management in the 1990s, working paper 86-017, April 1986.

26. H. J. Leavitt and T. L. Whisler, "Management in the 1980s," *Harvard Business Review* (November–December 1958): 41–48.

27. For more on organizational centralization, see M. Anshen, "The Manager and the Black Box," *Harvard Business Review* (November–December 1960): 85–92; T. L. Whisler, *The Impact of Computers on Organizations* (New York: Praeger, 1970); I. Hoos Russakoff, "When the Computer Takes Over the Office," *Harvard Business Review* (July–August 1960):

102–12. Also see D. Robey, "Systems and Organizational Structure," *Communications of the ACM* 24 (1981): 679–87. On organizational decentralization, see J. F. Burlingame, "Information Technology and Decentralization," *Harvard Business Review* (November–December 1961): 121–26; J. L. King, "Centralized versus Decentralized Computing: Organizational Considerations and Management Options," *Computing Surveys* 15 (1963): 319–49. On reduced layers of middle or upper management, see C. A. Myers, ed., *The Impact of Computers on Management* (Cambridge: MIT Press, 1967), pp. 1–15. On greater centralization of managerial power, see A. M. Pettigrew, "Information Control as a Power Resource." *Sociology* 6 (1972): 187–204; J. Pfeffer, *Power in Organizations* (Marshfield Mass.,: Pitman, 1981); and M. L. Markus and J. Pfeffer, "Power and the Design and Implementation of Accounting and Control Systems," *Accounting, Organizations and Society* 8 (1983): 205–18. On decentralization of managerial power, see S. R. Klatsky, "Automation, Size and the Locus of Decision Making: The Cascade Effect," *Journal of Business* 43 (1970): 141–51.

28. Carroll and Perin argue that what managers and employees *expect* from technology is an important predictor of the consequences observed. See J. S. Carroll and C. Perin, "How Expectations about Microcomputers Influence Their Organizational Consequences," MIT Sloan School of Management, Management in the 1990s, working paper 88-044, September 1988.

29. R. B. Reich, "Entrepreneurship Reconsidered: The Team as Hero," *Harvard Business Reivew* (May–June 1987): 77–83.

30. Drucker, "The Coming of the New Organization."

31. M. Hammer and G. E. Mangurian, "The Changing Value of Communications Technology," *Sloan Management Review* (Winter 1987): 65–72.

32. C. V. Bullen and R. R. Johansen, "Groupware: A Key to Managing Business Teams?" MIT Sloan School of Management, Center for Information Systems Research, working paper 169, May 1988.

33. O. Hauptman and T. J. Allen, "The Influence of Communications Technologies on Organizational Structure: A Conceptual Model for Future Research," MIT Sloan School of Management, Management in the 1990s, working paper 87-038, May 1987.

34. T. W. Malone, J. Yates, and R. I. Benjamin, "Electronic Markets and Electronic Hierarchies," *Communications of the ACM* 30 (1987): 484–97.

35. Johnston and Lawrence, "Beyond Vertical Integration."

36. T. Kumpe and P. T. Bolwijn, "Manufacturing: The New Case for Vertical Integration," *Harvard Business Review* (March–April 1988): 75–81.

37. Benjamin and Scott Morton, "Information Technology."

38. Lawrence and Lorsch, *Organization and Environment.*

39. Although our three collapsed segments in the value chain are integral units, data does flow from one to another. The three segments are also interdependent but less strongly so than the functions within each segment.

40. "Otis MIS: Going Up," *InformationWEEK,* May 18, 1987, pp. 32–37; J. F. Rockart, "The Line Takes the Leadership—IS Management in a Wired Society," *Sloan Management Review* (Summer 1988): 57–64; W. F. McFarlan, "How Information Technology Is Changing Management Control Systems," Harvard Business School, Case Note no. 9-187-139, 1987.

41. Rockart, "The Line Takes the Leadership."

42. Drucker, "The Coming of the New Organization."

43. Bullen and Johansen, "Groupware."

44. R. N. Anthony, *Planning and Control Systems: A Framework for Analysis* (Cambridge: Harvard University Press, 1965).

45. J. F. Rockart and D. W. DeLong, *Executive Support Systems: The Emergence of Top Management Computer Use* (Homewood, Ill.: Dow Jones–Irwin, 1988).

46. Rockart, "The Line Takes the Leadership."

47. T. J. Main and J. E. Short, "Managing the Merger: Building Partnership Through IT Planning at the New Baxter," *Management Information Systems Quarterly* 13 (1989): 469–484.

48. Zuboff, *In the Age of the Smart Machine.*

49. R. H. Waterman, Jr., *The Renewal Factor: How the Best Get and Keep the Competitive Edge* (New York: Bantam Books, 1987).

50. J. G. March and J. P. Olsen, *Ambiguity and Choice in Organizations* (Bergen, Norway: Universitesforlaget, 1976); H. Mintzberg, D. Raisinghani, and A. Theoret, "The Structure of 'Unstructured' Decision Processes," *Administration Science Quarterly* 21 (1976): 246–75.

51. A standard reference in this area is W. A. Scott, D. W. Osgood, and C. Peterson, *Cognitive Structure: Theory and Measurement of Individual Differences* (New York: John Wiley, 1979).

52. See, for example, Jacques's discussion of "accountability hierarchies" in E. Jacques, *Requisite Organization—The CEO's Guide to Creative Structure and Leadership* (London: Cason Hall, 1988).

53. E. H. Schein, "Innovative Cultures and Organizations." MIT Sloan School of Management, Management in the 1990s, working paper 88-064, November, 1988.

# CHAPTER 8

# Impact of IT
# on Jobs and Skills

## PAUL OSTERMAN

This chapter focuses on the parts of the 1990s model highlighted in Figure 8-1. The impact of information technology on the organization is contingent upon its context. We have already seen in Part II of this book the importance of the external environment, particularly the dynamics of industry structure under the new forces of IT. Part II also discussed new strategic options available for exploitation. What is feasible for a firm to exploit and the ways it chooses to do so are very much a function of the corporate or current management philosophy and the skills already present (or absent) in the organization. Thus, even though many options are available in theory, only a small subset of these can be realized in practice within a given organization.

The key aspects of IT that affect implementation are its integrative capabilities, which affect organizational boundaries and thus people's perceptions of power and status; its speed, which affects the way work gets done and the feedback systems that are used; and the costly consequences of a faulty system in use, increasing the risk people are asked to bear.

All of these effects require people to think and work differently—to change their behavior significantly. This is something that runs counter to most people's natural caution—caution which, if poorly handled, can turn into active resistance. This resistance was very visible in a number of 1990s program research settings and led to a lack of performance of the new systems and ways of working. Evidence from both theory and practice strongly suggests that to increase the chances of success one has to involve people earlier in the implementation process than has been typical. The importance of proper phasing of investment in people and technology is discussed at length in Chapter 9.

Beyond investing in people early, through education, training in new skills, and so forth, it turns out to be helpful for the organization to develop flexible human resource policies that enable and encourage the organization to capitalize on the new IT. Employees at all levels are more inclined to experiment with new ways of working if they know their standing in the organization will not be affected by their learning process.

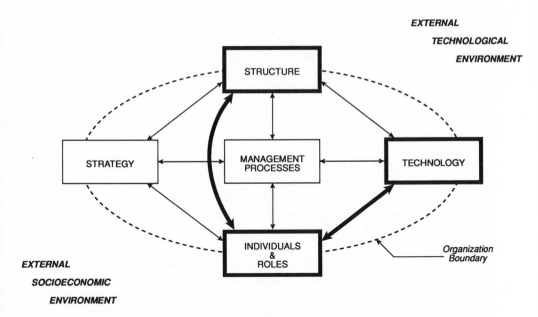

**Figure 8-1.** MIT90s framework—Chapter 8 emphasis.

As organizations begin to change the way they work and the new IT-enabled changes begin to take hold, there can be major changes in employment. Changes can occur in overall levels of employment as well as in the kinds of skills required and the rate of change of these skills. Very often the groups most threatened are low-level supervisors and operators.

There is a tendency for IT to move organizations into greater use of "high-risk" systems. These are systems that are central to the operations of the firm, and thus, if they go down or malfunction, they can bring the organization to its knees, or at the very least cost a great deal of money. These risks can be reduced with greater use of more highly skilled people. However, many organizations face a major task in developing and retaining the levels of skill required for the kind of organization we expect to see in the 1990s. The importance of education and training is central and will require a continuous and sustained effort of a kind not seen before in many organizations.

Everyone knows that IT will reshape work. Everyone also knows that this reconfiguration will have deep impacts on the distribution of workers across occupations and firms and on the skills employees will be expected to bring to work. The rub comes when we move beyond these easy generalizations. What will be the job description of the manager or production worker in the 1990s? Will their work become more or less skilled, broader or narrower? Will organizations become flatter and more decentralized, or will the power of IT concentrate decision making and control at the top? How will the organizational transformations induced by IT feed back upon careers?

There is, in fact, a debate centering upon these questions. Some believe that new technologies will have generally negative consequences for individual employees, in terms of either employment loss or degradation of skill and job quality. On the other hand, optimists believe that creative use of new technology can expand employment opportunities, expand the demand for workers with new and high skills, and open up new possibilities for creative expression and satisfaction at work. In addition to the impact on the individual, there is also great concern about how technology will affect productivity, with the optimists hoping that gains in this area will set the stage for the positive consequences of technology to win out.

This section will try to address these questions, but we will do so by demonstrating that there is no single answer or impact that can be deduced from the nature of the technology itself. Our research strongly suggests that the impact of technology is contingent. Technology interacts with other environmental factors, particularly the human resource strategy of the firm and the external economic institutions. It is the nature of these interactions that determines the trajectory and impact of new technologies.

Recognizing the contingent consequences of technology is so central to our research and findings that this chapter begins by demonstrating the point through several case studies. We then turn to the more conventional task of mapping what is known about the potential and actual impacts of technologies in different circumstances. We pay special attention here to those aspects of IT that distinguish it from previous innovations. With this research base in hand, we can then ask what determines why a similar technology has varying consequences, and we develop an explanation that emphasizes the product cycle of the firm, the enterprise's human resource strategy, and the external environment.

## THE CONTINGENT IMPACT OF TECHNOLOGY

In a society grown accustomed to scientific progress and innovation, technology is often viewed as a mysterious black box. This can be seen from a variety of perspectives:

Economists typically model technology as a variable that enters production functions in a multiplicative way and simply "shifts up" the function. A given "dose" of technology is implicitly viewed as equal in all settings and circumstances.

Senior management devotes considerable time and effort to making informed judgments about the amount, timing, and location of capital investment. These questions capture the atttention of the most able and informed decision makers in the firm. By contrast, less attention is devoted to the human resource and organizational requirements for introducing and maintaining/using the technology.

Employees, whether they are production workers or managers, view the specific characteristics of a new technology as a given. Hence, while their reaction may range from acceptance to opposition, it is typically passive. Few opportunities are perceived to interact with and shape the technology.

All of these attitudes ultimately derive from a deterministic view of technology. In this view—which has long dominated both scholarly and popular thinking—there is a single optimum way to configure a given technology. Much of the employment system surrounding the technology is therefore simply derivative of that technology. The only real challenge is to discover that optimum arrangement and move toward it as quickly as possible. Also implicit in this view is that the technology in some sense drives its users toward the optimum, and so over time if we observe firms employing the same technology we will also observe very similar employment systems and productivity.

Over time the evidence against this perspective has mounted. Numerous observers have noted that similar or identical technologies are used in dramatically different settings. This finding, if true, is important because it implies that we can influence the course of technology in several ways. Alternative modes of implementing technologies have quite different implications for the economic and social welfare of employees and firms. Furthermore, if a given technology does not automatically imply a given level of output, then there is a choice of paths aimed at maximizing the productivity of the innovation.

Several studies undertaken by the Management in the 1990s Research Program illustrate the variable impact of similar technologies and also provide clues to what determines these alternative patterns.

## THE VARIATION IN TECHNOLOGY'S IMPACT ON THE AUTO INDUSTRY

The auto industry provides a rich natural laboratory for assessing the effects of human resource systems and new technology. All U.S.-based firms have been aggressively investing in the development and use of new technologies in their manufacturing operations while at the same time working hard to introduce reforms in their traditional labor-management relations and human resource systems (Katz, 1985). With the growth of Japanese investment in the United States in the past decade, even greater variation in human resource practices and manufacturing policies has been introduced into American settings with American workers. One of the most highly visible of these new Japanese-American ventures, the subject of a great deal of debate and discussion, has been the New United Motors Manufacturing Incorporated (NUMMI) facility located in Fremont, California. This plant is a joint venture between General Motors and Toyota.

Figure 8-2 positions the NUMMI plant along with several other comparison facilities in a two-dimensional space according to the extent of innovation in human resource management systems and the amount of new technology found in each plant. In the lower left quadrant of the figure is located a General Motors low-technology plant with a traditional labor relations and human resource management system. Earlier work (Kochan, Katz, and McKersie, 1986) characterized this traditional system as one that perpetuated a high-conflict/low-trust cycle; low trust levels manifest themselves in high levels of grievances, which in turn give rise to demands for specification of more precise work rules and regulations, which in turn give rise to

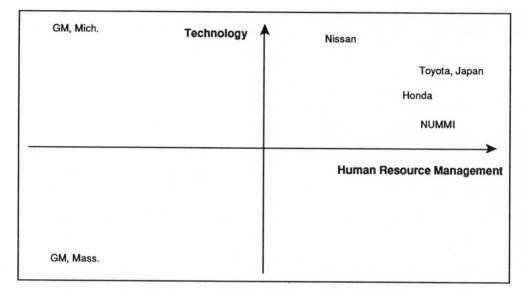

**Figure 8-2.** Technology and human resource management.

further grievances and mistrust. The analysis then showed that plants experiencing this high-conflict/low-trust cycle have significantly lower levels of quality and productivity than plants with fewer conflicts, higher trust relations, and better labor-management relations. Thus, the lower left quadrant represents the traditional human resource system operating in a low-technology environment. Clearly, we expect this to be the base or lowest performing mix of technology and human resources.

The upper left quadrant provides a comparison of a plant that invested more than $650 million in new information and manufacturing technologies without significant reforms in the human resource or labor-management relations system. The comparison of this plant with the traditional low-technology plant provides the best test of a "technology alone" strategy.

Plants located in the upper right quadrant provide different mixtures of human resource management reforms and advanced technologies. The NUMMI plant combines a very moderate technological upgrade—far from the technological frontier for high-technology auto plants—with a fundamentally reformed human resource and labor-management relationship. While the same local union (and union leadership) and approximately 80 percent of the work force were carried over into this plant from a prior traditional GM plant, NUMMI is managed by Toyota and has adopted the production and human resource policies that this company employs in its Japanese plant. The NUMMI plant therefore provides the best test of the effect of human resource management changes in the context of a moderate technological upgrade strategy.

The other plants shown in this quadrant differ from NUMMI in several respects. The Nissan plant is a new very-high-technology plant in Tennessee which introduced a number of human resource management reforms (few job classifications, flexible work organization, extensive communications) but does not go as far on this dimension as NUMMI. Likewise, the Honda plant is slightly lower on the technology scale but, like NUMMI, has implemented a broader range of human resource innovations. Unlike NUMMI, however, both Honda and Nissan plants are nonunion and therefore provide another interesting dimension on which to compare performance. Finally, the home plant of Toyota in Japan (shown in this quadrant) provides a useful benchmark for comparing the performance of these various U.S. plants.

Table 8-1 presents quality and productivity data for these plants during 1986. Quality is measured by the number of defects per 100 cars. Only defects attributable to assembly operations are included in this measure. Productivity is measured by the number of work hours required to perform a standard set of assembly tasks after controlling for differences in product size, option content, and a number of other factors (see Krafcik, 1988, for details on the methods used to develop these standard measures).

The results presented in Table 8-1 are rather astounding. Indeed, they send such a strong message that they have been widely cited and used within the auto industry and in the public press to bring home several important lessons. For our purposes, the central messages from these data appear to be the following:

1. High-technology strategies, in the absence of significant changes in human resource practices (GM low-tech/traditional versus GM high-tech/traditional), produce no significant productivity or quality improvements. It took 34 hours to produce a car with an average of 1.16 defects per car in the traditional low-tech plant. After an expenditure of $650 million on high technology, it still took almost 34 hours to produce a car with an average of 1.37 defects.

2. NUMMI, in contrast, with moderate investment in new technology but a fundamentally different human resource management and production system, took 60 percent as much time to produce a car with an equally significantly lower defect rate.

**Table 8-1.** Productivity/Quality Performance of Selected Auto Assembly Plants

|  | Productivity[a] (hrs./unit) | Quality[b] (defects/ 100 units) | Automation Level[c] (0: none) |
|---|---|---|---|
| Honda, Ohio | 19.2 | 72.0 | 77.0 |
| Nissan, Tenn. | 24.5 | 70.0 | 89.2 |
| NUMMI, Calif. | 19.0 | 69.0 | 62.8 |
| Toyota, Japan | 15.6 | 63.0 | 79.6 |
| GM, Mich. | 33.7 | 137.4 | 100.0 |
| GM, Mass. | 34.2 | 116.5 | 7.3 |

*Source*: John Krafcik, MIT International Motor Vehicle Research Program. For further discussion of these data, see Kochan, 1988.

[a] *Productivity* here is defined as the number of man-hours required to weld, paint, and assemble a vehicle. These figures have been standaridized for product size, option content, process differences, and actual work schedules (i.e., differing amounts of break time).

[b] *Quality* is based on a J. D. Powers survey of customer-cited defects in the first six months of ownership. The numbers in this column are the numbers of defects per 100 vehicles. Only defects attributable to assembly operations are included.

[c] *Level of automation* is a ratio of robotic applications in each plant divided by the production rate. These figures have been normalized with 100 indicating the highest level of automation in this group.

3. Comparing NUMMI to Nissan and Honda suggests that union-management relations need not be the barrier to improved performance that many American managers have traditionally believed. NUMMI's performance is equal to Honda's and slightly better than Nissan's, again despite the higher levels of technology found in the Nissan facility.
4. Finally, productivity and quality at Honda and NUMMI approach the levels achieved in Toyota's home plant in Japan.

These pairwise comparisons suggest that (at least in this industry) significant improvements in economic performance are achieveable in the United States, with American workers, and with American unions. To turn this potential into a reality requires a fundamental rethinking and restructuring of traditional human resource and labor-management relations practices in conjunction with a more careful and strategic use of new technologies than has often been recognized by American managers and technology specialists.

The question can legitimately be raised: Do these results generalize to a larger and more diverse sample? To answer this question, another body of productivity and quality data was collected by John Krafcik (Krafcik and MacDuffie, 1989). This research produced correlations that demonstrate that the results of the pairwise plant comparisons generalize to a larger international sample of auto assembly facilities. The correlation between the index of human resource and manufacturing practices that reflect the high-trust/high-commitment human resource system and measures of quality and productivity are nearly twice as strong as the correlations between these performance measures and the robotics index. The robotics index correlations are not significantly different from zero at this sample size. Finally, when these measures are entered into a regression equation that controls for differences in plant size, age, and product complexity, the management index remains statistically significant while the robotics index does not. Thus, we interpret these results as providing further support to the proposition that human resource policies are critical to achieving high levels of productivity and quality in manufacturing. High technology, standing alone in the absence of a corresponding set of human resource investments, does not seem capable of achieving comparable results.

## ADDITIONAL EXAMPLES OF THE VARIABILITY OF TECHNOLOGY'S IMPACT

Although the research presented above for automobiles is perhaps the most dramatic available to show that comparable technologies have different impacts in different settings, it is far from the only evidence we have.

Examples of the disparate use and impact of similar technologies can also be found in white-collar settings. Carroll and Perin (1988) examined the use of microcomputers in the accounting departments of two firms. In one site the manager responsible for introducing the equipment thought of microcomputers as "fancy adding machines," and the impact of the machines was consistent with this expectation. That is, routine tasks were automated, some time was saved, but in no fundamental way was the organization of work or people's activities reshaped by the technology. In the other firm, by contrast, the equipment was implemented with a more ambitious agenda (with senior management playing a more active role). The consequence was a broader impact of the computers upon the organization. In particular, some jobs were reconfigured, and there was a good deal more "as if" simulation.

Another striking example is provided by a study of the implementation of flexible manufacturing systems (FMs) conducted by Jaikumar (1986). He compared similar FMs in firms in the United States and in Japan. In Japan, the time it took to develop the system was half that of the United States; the number of different parts the Japanese setups produced was much higher; the labor requirements were lower; the fraction of the day the machines ran was higher; and total output was higher. Jaikumar attributed these differences to the different skill levels of the labor force and training levels provided by the firms, that is, to human resource policy.

The lesson from these studies (and many others like them) is that technology alone does not drive the outcome. Of course, this point can be exaggerated; the nature of a technology does set limits and establish patterns. For example, Piore and Sabel (1984) distinguish between flexible and mass-production technologies and show that the possibilities of each are quite different with respect to a range of issues including shop-floor relations and macroeconomic policy. This argument is similar to the long discussion in the sociology literature concerning the relationship between technology and organizational form (see, e.g., Woodward, 1965). Nonetheless, it is apparent that one cannot understand outcomes by examining only technology; a wide range of additional factors must be considered.

Much of the remainder of this chapter will be devoted to understanding the strategic contextual factors that shape the impact of technology. To set the stage for this discussion, we now turn to the large literature that has examined the impact of technology on employment. We will see that no single lesson emerges from this literature and that we are led again to a contingent view of the process.

## MAPPING THE IMPACT OF TECHNOLOGY

If a group of workers, researchers, managers, or union officials was asked to describe how IT changes work, their list would be long, diverse, and not necessarily consistent. However, in all likelihood, the discussion would focus on two questions:

1. What is the impact of IT on the level of employment, that is, on the numbers of jobs in a firm, industry, or the economy?
2. What is the impact of the technology on the content of particular occupations, such as skills and duties?

We will discuss the research record concerning these questions but will conclude that these questions are too constraining. In several respects, IT cannot be understood in a narrow context. IT has the potential for reshaping the organization and for changing production and distribution systems in fundamental ways. In settings where this potential is reached, the impacts are far broader than the traditional questions suggest. However, to make this case and to set the stage, we will first take up the more narrow concerns.

## The Volume of Employment

The most consistent concern about the impact of new technologies—and IT is no exception—is that the innovations will cost jobs. The worst case is the image of the computer composition technologies that rendered obsolete the skills of and demand for an entire profession of typesetters.

While typesetters represent one extreme, the most significant new technologies have led to economic growth and job creation at the other end of the spectrum. Communications and transportation innovations—the railroad, the automobile, the telephone, the computer—expanded the economy and led to economic growth far beyond the dreams of their inventors.

The typical case is considerably more shaded than either of these extremes. Most new technologies do in fact ease the substitution of capital for labor and hence, for a given level and quality of output, reduce employment. By the same token, however, the very efficiency induced by the technology leads to a lower price per unit. This in turn can expand overall demand for the product and increase employment. (Consider the effect of the automobile assembly line. Labor input per car fell, but demand for autos soared, resulting in a net increase in employment.) There is, of course, also a third channel of influence: some occupations that are complementary with technology grow as a direct consequence of the innovation. Obviously, the demand for computer programmers has increased as computers have diffused throughout the economy.

Several research efforts carried out by the Management in the 1990s Research Program have demonstrated the complexity of this topic. In one study we examined the impact of the spread of mainframe computers on the employment of clerks and managers (Osterman, 1986). For this project we had data on employment, wages, and output in about forty industries for the years 1972 to 1978. By combining these data with information on the number and size of mainframe computers, we estimated employment (labor demand) equations. Each 10 percent increase in computer power was associated with a 1.8 percent decrease in the employment of clerks and a 1.2 percent decrease in the employment of managers. Hence, there is a clear employment loss. It is also interesting to note that the fate of managers is linked with the fate of the clerks. This results in part from the fact that the U.S. Census classifies many individuals as managers whose job it is to supervise clerks. This must also reflect, however, the observation that one of the functions middle managers play in firms is to organize and process information for superiors; computers are capable of taking over some of this work.

Although the study does suggest that displacement occurs, there are two important qualifications. First, the study held output constant and examined the impact of computers on employment for a given level of final demand. In reality, output may grow. This suggests that we may observe not actual declines in employment but slower growth than would otherwise pertain. Whether this is true depends on the strength of the substitution effect (of computers for labor) and the relationship between output and employment. A recent study (Hunt and Hunt, 1986) concluded that clerical employment nationwide will level off but not actually fall as new technolgies diffuse through offices.

The second qualification is that in the study itself we found that after the initial impact, part of the displacement effect (although not all) was reversed as firms increased the employment of clerks and managers above the minimum point. We attributed this to the effect of computers in creating a new demand for internal organization and coordination. In effect, computers reduce the price of coordination and hence increase the demand for it.

This finding points to an important but overlooked aspect of IT: it can often create new demands which at least partially offset disemployment effects. Word processing may reduce the need for typists, but this is somewhat offset by the tendency to create more drafts of documents. Computer-aided design (CAD) may ease the task of circuit board design, but engineers therefore experiment with more designs.

A final qualification concerns the distinction between industrywide or economywide effects and the impact on particular firms or groups of occupations. In the clerical case, after all factors are considered, computers may not lead to an actual decline in employment nationally, but in specific firms the effect an be quite dramatic. Particular insurance firms might, for example, vastly streamline their back-office operations. If the labor market worked well in matching workers with openings, then the pattern of localized employment declines in the context of overall stability or growth would not be that serious. On the other hand, if experienced skilled employees have difficulty finding new work, then overall employment growth could coexist with a "residual" labor force that is displaced by technology. We will return to this question later.

A second study completed for the Management in the 1990s Research Program illustrates how the industry effect of technology can differ from the impact in particular firms (Lynch and Osterman, 1989). Information technologies are expanding the demand for and power of communications services, both voice and data, and a host of new firms are expanding in this area. Yet in the large mature telephone company we studied, these technologies reduced employment levels. Both operators and craft employees (inside and outside repair and installation) saw actual employment reductions in the face of electronic switching, automatic repair, and mechanized director assistance technologies. As a final example, consider industrial robots. In manufacturing settings robots represent the quintessential example of smart machines taking over work from humans. Much of the discussion of the factory of the future and the factory without people has centered on the use of robots. Several studies have examined the impact of robots, the most comprehensive of which is Hunt and Hunt (1983). Based on projections of robot usage and the number of jobs displaced per robot, they estimated that by 1990 robots would lead to a loss of between 100,000 and 200,000 jobs nationally, of which between 30,000 and 50,000 would be in the auto industry (this job loss would be partially offset by the creation of between 32,000 and 64,000 new manufacturing and repair jobs in the robot industry).

Are these numbers large or small? The answer depends on the base against which they are judged. Hunt and Hunt estimated that robots would displace between 1 and 2 percent of all operative and laborer employment by 1990, clearly a small number. Yet for painting jobs in the auto industry robots would displace between 27 and 37 percent of jobs. The figures for auto industry welding jobs were 15 to 20 percent. For painting jobs in all manufacturing, the displacement rates would be 9 to 15 percent, and for welding 4 to 7 percent. So the answer on the overall impact really depends on how well the labor market—and this means both the external market and the internal training and transfer policies of firms—succeeds in moving people from old to new jobs. If, for example, welders and painters can be retrained and shifted to other employment (which will, in fact, be there), little difficulty will ensue. On the other hand, labor market rigidity can lead to real problems.

What, then, can we conclude about the relationship between technology and employment volume? We need to distinguish between events at the aggregate level and at the firm level. At the aggregate level it seems clear that overall employment will increase. The fears of jobless growth are not justified. However, beneath this happy picture can be a very different reality at the firm level.

The first issue at the firm level is that some companies may experience employment decline while others are growing. The impact of this on the labor force depends crucially on the effectiveness of labor market institutions in matching workers with jobs. If the people who lose their jobs can find new ones, then all will be well. If there are substantial difficulties, then this will have consequences with respect to issues ranging from work rules to international trade.

The second question refers to the internal rules, or human resource systems, of the firms themselves. Within the firm some occupations will gain employment while others lose. How this is experienced, and its consequences, will depend on the firms' policies with respect to retraining and employment continuity. Simply put, are the new jobs made available to those who lost the old ones? Again, the answer to this question will have substantial consequences for how the impact of technology on employment is played out.

In summary, the impact of technology is not experienced at some abstract economywide level in which overall job gains and losses are computed. The impact is experienced at the job site and the firm. If a given group of workers loses employment because of an innovation, it is not relevant to them that there are compensating gains elsewhere unless they have access to those opportunities. There are good welfare reasons to be concerned with this; it is not simply a private problem of distribution. As we will argue below, firms cannot fully reap the gains from flexible work organization unless the labor force cooeprates; the labor force will not cooperate in an insecure environment.

## The Traditional Debate about Job Design

In the early twentieth century, Fredrick Taylor revolutionized the way American managers thought about work. At the core of his argument was the view that there is a single best way to accomplish any task. This best way can be discovered by management experts and then conveyed to the labor force. The role of the labor force is to carry out exactly instructions generated by management, and this in turn implies that the supervision and personnel system is aimed at enforcing this obedience through carrots and sticks.

The key assumption of this model is that the labor force has nothing to contribute to the production process. In effect, employees are simply appendages to machines. Whatever creativity is required for coaxing the highest possible productivity out of a given technology is to be generated from management.

Whereas the Taylorist position is typically advocated by management on the grounds of technical efficiency, in recent years analysts more sympathetic to labor have also argued that technology deskills the work, but for a different set of reasons. Emanating from the work of Braverman (1974), proponents of the deskilling hypothesis argue that firms follow the Tayloristic strategy not because it is technically efficient in the sense of increasing output but rather because managers seek to control the labor force and remove knowledge, and hence power, from the shop floor.

We are thus left with two separate arguments about why technology deskills work. One of these rests on technical efficiency, and the other draws on notions of managerial control.

A good illustration of how the technical efficiency/managerial control perspectives come together is the advent of electronic switching in the telephone industry. Prior to the introduction of electronic digital switching, the repair of mechanical switching equipment was a highly skilled craft job in which an individual developed a substantial feel for the equipment. Wires would break, circuits would fail, foreign matter would get into the equipment, and the craftsperson's job was to find and fix the fault. By contrast, the new system is essentially a computer. The rate of mechanical failure is low and rapairs are more straightforward in that modular boards can be removed and inserted. Software failures are more likely to be the province of programmers than craftspeople. All of this is not to argue that the new repair jobs are not skilled. However, the nature of the skill has changed considerably, and it is arguably the case that from the former craft perspective the job has been deskilled.

It is possible to argue that the move to electronic switching and the shift in job boundaries that ensued resulted from the characteristics of the technology itself in that the substitution of computers, or "boxes" as they are derisively termed by telephone people, inevitably implied a loss of skill on the part of the craftspeople. However, this proposition is open to some question since it begs the issue of whether the old craftspeople were taught the new programming skills. Whether to train blue-collar workers in white-collar skills has been a troubling issue in the telephone industry, and case studies suggest that the question turns as much on managerial ideology as on technical issues (we discuss below a specific case centering on this issue). This issue is quite similar to the often studied example of numerical controlled machining in which some firms train machinists in the programming skills necessary to control the new equipment while other firms adopt a deskilling strategy (Kelley, 1989; Thomas, 1988).

In short, then, when we do observe deskilling it is not easy to disentangle the technical from the social factors behind the outcome. At the same time, however, the more important point is that deskilling is not the only possible outcome, and, indeed, in recent years there has been a reaction against it.

## An Alternative Perspective

Although the Tayloristic view dominated American management, an alternative perspective grew up alongside it. This view has several labels, such as *sociotechnical systems* and *work redesign*. At the core is the notion that jobs should be broadened and shifted away from the narrow division of labor and tight job boundaries implied by Taylorism. However, there is some confusion in the literature about the benefits to be gained from this. In some views, the main purpose is to make work more meaningful and fulfilling for the labor force, a goal that in itself can justify change. A more general claim, found in the sociotechnical literature, holds that if work design, social needs, and technology are jointly optimized, then productivity will rise. This view, with its emphasis on work teams and loose job boundaries, directly challenges the Tayloristic presumption that workers have nothing to contribute to technology.

In short, what distinguishes these alternative positions is the question of whether the labor force has anything to contribute to improving the design and execution of production. Taylorism would argue that the answer is no, that a good employee is one who does the assigned job and nothing more. The empowerment perspective argues that an interaction between employee and technology will lead, over time, to improved production. Such interaction can only occur, however, if there is scope for employee creativity. This in turn implies relatively fluid job boundaries, the very antithesis of Taylorism.

Whereas the Tayloristic perspective held sway for many years, recently the burden of opinion has swung against it. Perhaps the most persuasive evidence comes from that most Tayloristic of industries, automobile production. The Japanese organize their production systems in a way that permits extensive worker interaction with technology, and this seems to have large payoffs. A striking way of capturing this notion is the phrase "giving wisdom to the machine," which Shimada and MacDuffie (1986) used to describe the interaction of Japanese production workers and technology. They go on to define the concept as follows:

> This refers to innovative activities carried out through the joint efforts of production workers, engineers, and supervisors in the attempt to improve the capability of machines and production systems by modifying or adding relevant function to them. . . . A second component is self-management of the work process, which contributes substantially to the self-generating innovative property of the system.
> . . . While production standards and the basic framework of work methods are given by engineering requirements, production workers have the discretion and responsibility for specifying work content . . . and [they] revise them continuously, based on their daily production experience.

There are similar examples from other industries. For example, in a study of circuit board design, Salzman (1985) examined whether CAD technology deskilled circuit board designers. His conclusion was that it did not. While it was possible to use a relatively unskilled employee and a CAD system to design a board, the outcome was not satisfactory. There was enough nonprogrammable intuition and feel required that the prevailing view was that such a board "would look like a board designed by a computer." Far better results flowed from using the new technology but making it a tool in the hands of skilled workers.

Which strategy—the Tayloristic approach or the empowerment perspective—has characterized American practice? As the examples make clear, there is evidence of both at work, but is there a central trend or tendency? It is obviously difficult to answer such a question, since data are not collected in these terms. The best that can be done is to examine a range of evidence.

One approach is to examine changes in the economywide occupational distribution and infer skill shifts. On this basis, the relative rise of white-collar and craft employment and the decline of manual labor and personal service jobs suggest net upgrading. Even in the past two decades, during which there has been much discussion of the rise in low-skill jobs and the "declining middle," the occupational distribution has in fact shifted toward more high-skill work (Osterman, 1988, Chapter 3). There are, however, several problems with this approach. Constancy in job titles may conceal substantial shifts in content. In addition, whatever changes we observe may be the result of the changing composition of output rather than technology per se.

A second strategy is to examine skill levels within occupations by employing "objective" measures based on the *Dictionary of Occupational Titles (DOT)* or other sources. The *DOT*, for example, seeks to measure several dimensions of skill for occupations. Studies for the United States, based on the *DOT*, and for Canada, based on the *Canadian Classification and Dictionary of Occupations*, suggest that a mild skill upgrading has occurred in recent decades (Spenner, 1987; Myles, n.d.).

The discussion above should not be read to imply, however, that there is a clear tendency toward upgrading of employment. Interviews with managers and observations of firms suggest that there is considerable tension and confusion about the direction work will take. Some firms are implementing technology in a manner that does deskill the labor force, while others are seeking to enhance or maintain skill levels. Our ultimate goal is to understand why these different strategies are followed and what are the costs and benefits of each. Before turning to this question, however, we first ask how new information technology has changed the terms of the debate.

## THE IMPACT OF IT ON WORK AND SKILL: A BROADER FRAMEWORK

Much of the foregoing analysis focuses on the impact of IT on specific jobs. This impact is an appropriate starting point, but to end there would underestimate the issues involved. New technology, and in particular new information technology, may reshape work in more fundamental ways. In particular, these technologies will change the very nature of skills and will alter the interrelationship among jobs and functions within the firm. It is to these phenomena that we now turn.

### The Characteristics of IT

In order to understand these effects, we need to examine how new IT differs from past innovations. There are three technical characteristics of the technology that have significant implications for understanding its impact on the organization of work:

1. Tighter integration across functions and tighter interdependencies of activities.
2. More rapid speed and real-time response.
3. More costly consequences of errors and breakdowns.

Computers and IT knit closer previously semidependent aspects of the production system. This is true for both blue- and white-collar work.

Paul Adler (1986) provides a persuasive example of this phenomenon from banking. Vastly oversimplifying Adler's description, one can speak of a transition between two states. Prior to the introduction of computers, the processing of customer requests and accounts by the "front office" resulted in a paper flow to the "back office" which was entered into account records. Each of these clusters of activities involved numerous steps. There were various checks for errors; because of the paper flow, an error made by a teller could be caught by a back-office processor. Under the new regime, computers integrated the two functions to the point where tellers could introduce data directly into the bank's account database. This led to great efficiencies but also (as discussed below) to considerable risk. The point here is that a series of separate functions were tightly linked together because of the introduction of computers.

A good blue-collar analogy is flexible manufacturing systems (FMs). These automated systems typically consist of a series of machine tools for materials cutting and moving, production planning, and inventory controlling systems. All of these are under the control of computer systems which include extensive monitoring and simulation capacities. What in the past had been a series of separate workstations is now linked; the activities of one work station are tightly interwoven with the activities of the next workstation. The integration extends beyond the simple notion of physically linking work sites, however; much tighter links evolve among different functions such as planning, control, and operations. These different functions now share a common real-time database (Graham and Rosenthal, 1986).

It should be clear from both of these examples that the speed of system performance increases as functions are linked together by computer. In one sense the production system becomes much more powerful than before. However, it is also important to realize that the consequences of errors increase sharply. A useful way of thinking about this is to borrow the language of Shimada and MacDuffie: the production systems become less robust and more "fragile."

In a robust production system, an error or delay in one part of the system does not reverberate with serious consequences elsewhere. For example, if there are quality problems with several cars in an auto assembly plant, they are taken off the line for repair, and normal production continues. Similarly, the system is protected from external shocks because a large inventory of parts is maintained on the premises. By contrast, in a fragile system, quality is maintained on-line as part of the normal flow of production (each station is responsible for repairs), and inventory is kept to a minimum through just-in-time systems.

In a number of ways, the fragile system is quicker and more efficient. It saves time because of its high attention to quality at all points; it saves money because it does not need to maintain a separate repair staff or high inventories. However, the system is much more vulnerable to problems. The system has low tolerances for failure; each step in the system is dependent on the successful operation of each other step. The adverse consequences of a problem are magnified.

Shimada and MacDuffie develop the distinction between fragile and robust production systems in the context of their discussion of automobile production, but the concepts apply just as well in other settings. For example, Adler's example of a bank, described above, demonstrates how the introduction of IT led to a more fragile production system.

## Organizational and Human Resource Implications

The technical characteristics described above—tighter integration across functions, more rapid response time, and increased fragility of the system or costliness of errors—carry with them implications for the organization of work within firms.

Even casual reflection on the technical aspects of the technology identified above raises questions about the Tayloristic strategy. In addition to the more general case for a high-skill labor force—"giving knowledge to the machine"—the characteristics of IT add additional reasons for high skill. In an environment in which activities are tightly linked and in which the costs of errors are high, it does not pay to risk a labor force that does not understand the system and cannot respond to problems.

This rationale for increased skills levels does imply, however, that the nature of skills will shift. The emphasis will move away from manual skills and toward working with data and understanding the operation of the entire system. Indeed, this aspect of IT is at the heart of Zuboff's (1988) distinction between automate and informate. She argues that IT will distance workers from the physical "feel" of production and will require, instead, that they learn the meaning of the data generated by computer-driven processes and discover how to fit these data together into a coherent understanding of the process. A very similar argument was advanced by Hirschhorn (1984).

In order for firms to take advantage of the possibilities of the technology, they must be willing to teach employees enough for them to gain this overall vision and must then permit the labor force to act on it. This requires both a new version of skill, from the labor force's perspective, and a considerably more trusting and teaching-oriented management than that which has traditionally characterized American firms. As is apparent, then, this message is very similar to the lessons derived from studies of American and Japanese auto production as well as other cases.

An important element of new skills required by information technologies will be responsibility. That is, in most instances the system may perform well on its own, but the importance of spotting and understanding malfunctions increases sharply. Some researchers argue that there is a dangerous irony associated with this issue. Although the responsibility is great and the costs of failure very serious, many monitoring jobs are boring for most of the time. The consequence is that when problems do occur, workers may be in some psychological sense unprepared (Hirschhorn, 1984).

IT will reshape work well beyond its impact on specific jobs. The way jobs link together will change, and with these changes will come new forms of work organization and career patterns. Several examples illustrate this point. On the production floor, considerable evidence suggests that work teams, in which job boundaries are quite diffuse, are more productive than more traditional arrangements (Katz, Kochan, and Keefe, 1987). A useful example along these lines, and one that harks back to our earlier discussion, is provided by MacDuffie and Maccoby (1986). They discuss AT&T's move from mechanical to electronic switching and report on an initial effort by the company to limit programming knowledge and diagnostic skills to staff at central offices. In the field, under this plan, the role of the technician was simply to carry out repair orders. This led to considerable organizational conflict, as experienced field workers sought to maintain their power, and was inefficient in that problems could be identified and repaired more rapidly via cooperation. The fact of the benefits from teams was established by the informal, and underground, efforts of the field workers to gain the knowlege and tools that the company had sought to limit to central staff. Productivity was higher when the underground worked.

The most significant development along these lines is the tendency of information technologies to break down organizational barriers. Within the firm, separate functions such as design and manufacturing are integrated more closely. Across the firm, the boundary between customers and their suppliers becomes blurred as the firms work jointly on designing products and have access to each other's databases for the purposes of ordering parts and updating inventory.

The dissipation of these traditional barriers has several implications:

*Roles change.* The traditional roles of supervisor and manager change. We have already hinted at this point. Because employees have more access to data, they will take over many of the functions associated with supervisors. For example, production planning, inventory control, and quality control will increasingly be under the control of employees. This will pose a major threat to lower-level supervisors. Just as employee roles will change, so will the skills required to be an effective manager and supervisor. As Zuboff has emphasized, teaching skills will become increasingly important. Managers will need to be willing to share their knowledge of the production process and technology with workers and, assuming they are willing, they will need to learn the skills necessary to do so.

*Managers' perception of their job change.* The stress induced by the role shifts outlined above may be exacerbated by another impact of IT. Based on a series of interviews with managers, Attewell (1985) concludes that the greater availability of data has two contradictory impacts on managers' perceptions about their jobs. On the one hand, they feel greater local control because they have more information on what is occurring in their area of responsibility. On the other hand, they feel greater global vulnerability. Because the IT links together disparate areas of the organization, a given manager is more immediately affected by actions elsewhere. This is a consequence of the shift discussed above toward a fragile system. Managers feel a loss of control over events that affect their performance.

*Career paths shift.* The breaking down of intra- and interorganizational boundaries may also have significant implications for careers, although these implications are not yet well understood. As teams become a more important organizational form within firms, individuals will need to learn new roles and skills, and promotion patterns may shift (Ancona and Caldwell, 1987). For example, whereas in the past many firms have emphasized technical abilities, in the future skills involving negotiation, persuading, and conflict management will become salient. Furthermore, difficult issues will arise regarding career tracks and compensation.

Other shifts in intraorganization boundaries can also have significant career implications. For example, Westney and Skakibara (1988) have studied the careers of engineers in Japanese and U.S. high-technology firms. They have discovered that one key to the successful Japanese coordination of product development and production, and the relatively short "time to market" patterns in Japan, lies in career movements. Japanese engineers who design products follow the product from the lab to the manufacturing facility. Knowledge is transmitted by movements of the knowledgeable individual. It may be that as American firms seek to break down the barriers between design and manufacturing, similar shifts will occur in the career patterns of American engineers. If the foregoing description of intraorganizational career shifts seems vague, there is even more uncertainty concerning the implications of the breakdown of interorganizational boundaries. For example, as producer and suppliers increasingly work together, will they also exchange staff? Will the creation of "industrial districts" based on flexible technology lead to groups of small firms who share their labor force, as Piore and Sabel predict? These and similar questions can only be posed; the answers are simply not known.

*The real world imposes limitations.* Finally, it is important to introduce a note of caution. Many expectations about the impact of IT are based on an abstract assessment of the possibilities without an appreciation of how social systems and a complicated reality place limits on change. We have already seen this in the example of the continuing importance of workers' "feel" for the production process. The same lesson holds for the changes in career patterns. For example, much is made of the new possibilities for "telecommuting" and "home work" which computers and communications technology bring. Yet the reality is more shaded. In a study for the Management in the 1990s Research Program, Bailyn and Perin examined the extent to which the ability of IT to break down spatial and temporal barriers was being realized in practice. They found that, while in a technical sense such an arrangement could work, a number of aspects of organizational life tended to limit and encapsulate such arrangements. Managers felt a loss of control and contact with employees who worked at home and were reluctant to permit workers to undertake such arrangements. As a result, the system was largely restricted to a female part-time labor force. In other words, the reality of telecommuting and home work fell far short of the potential as described by pundits who fail to appreciate how reality can intrude (Bailyn, 1987, 1988; Perin, 1988).

Despite this caution, it does seem likely that IT will reshape organizational relationships and careers. It also seems likely that, as in much else, the impacts will vary across organizations. We now turn to develop an explanation of the contingent nature of new technology.

## TOWARD A MODEL OF TECHNOLOGICAL IMPACT

We have provided a framework and given examples of the impact of IT. Nonetheless, it is crucially important to understand that comparable technologies have different impacts in different settings. One firm may use factory automation not simply to improve quality and reduce labor input per unit but also to sharply reduce actual employment levels. Another firm will use the same technology to maintain employment. In one setting operators receive training and learn how to use the data and control possibilities of technology to manage the production process; in another firm, control and planning are shifted to managers, and the labor force is deskilled. How can we explain and understand these variations?

Our goal is to develop a framework for explaining the empirical variation we observe. Even casual reflection suggests that such a framework needs to be able to encompass a range of factors. Clearly, purely economic considerations should play a role: firms for whom cost cutting is a major competitive priority will deploy technology differently from firms who can sell all they can produce at assured prices. However, this cannot be the entire story; there is also evidence that firms in the same industry behave differently. There must be a role for firm-specific philosophy and human resource systems. Finally, the pattern of cross-national variation suggests that national characteristics, such as differences in training and education systems, must play some role. Therefore, our task now is to sort out each of these three categories of explanation.

In developing a model, the following three considerations seem most important:

1. The point in the product cycle at which the firm finds itself.
2. The managerial, industrial relations, and human resource management philosophy of the firm.
3. The broader environment in which the firm operates, particularly the education and training system.

## The Product Cycle

There is substantial evidence that human resource practices vary in a systematic way with the firm's position in the product cycle (Kochan and Chalykoff, 1989; Flynn, 1988). Growing firms, or divisions of firms responsible for products that are growing, place great emphasis on product innovation and recruiting adequate numbers of employees with the appropriate skills. Cost minimization is not the most salient goal.

Because the competitive advantage of a firm early in its product cycle is the innovative quality of the product itself, there is a high premium on maintaining this advantage by continuing to innovate. As a consequence, new technology is conceived as a way of augmenting the product. Technology augments products when combined with a skilled labor force.

The skill-enhancing impact of IT that characterizes its use by firms early in the product cycle contrasts with how the same technology can be employed by mature firms or firms producing matrue products. In these circumstances, the major competitive edge firms seek is cost, not product innovation. As a result, the emphasis shifts to employing new technology to reduce employment per unit of output. It is in these settings that we observe the most negative employment consequences of IT.

The labor-cutting strategy is likely to be intensified when a large portion of labor costs is accounted for by pools of relatively homogenous employees. A firm with a very large level of clerical employment (a bank or insurance firm) or large numbers of semiskilled operatives will be especially eager to reduce employment and will feel that there are few constraints in terms of the skill or knowlege lost when employees leave.

One reasonable question is why firms cannot have it both ways. Why can they not simultaneously employ IT to shed labor and produce more efficiently while also upskilling their remaining labor force and innovating in the product market? Such a strategy is not impossible. It is relatively straightforward when the employment effect is not outright job loss but rather slower employment growth and a falling dose of labor input per product. However, the story is different when actual job loss occurs. The difficulty is that the strains induced by labor shedding may block the level of work-force cooperation required to innovate successfully. Employees will ask themselves why they should creatively engage with the technology when the consequence may simply be that they or a workmate will lose their job.

Finally, it may be important to distinguish between the product cycle and the technology cycle. In the foregoing discussion we emphasized the income and price elasticity of product demand, the product cycle. Flynn has also developed evidence that the impact of technology varies over the lifetime of the technology itself. Early in the introduction process, she argues, "uncertainty in the quantity and quality of skill requirements, coupled with unavailability of workers already trained in the newly emerging fields, encourages employers to add new tasks onto existing job—*at least* on a temporary basis" (Flynn, 1988, p. 39). Hence, subskilling is the likely outcome. Over time, as the technology itself becomes better understood, it becomes possible to routinize, and subdivide, employment, and this in turn implies deskilling. In short, Flynn argues that there is a technology life cycle as well as a product life cycle effect.

## The Firm's Human Resource Strategy

American firms are pulled in two directions regarding how to organize work. Some firms, in both the union and the nonunion sector, are adopting systems of job classification, wages, and employment continuity which are flexible and involve high levels of job security. In these systems employees agree, either explicitly or implicitly, to take on a wide range of activities and to provide a high level of effort. Narrow work rules and job classifications are not pursued. In return, the firm undertakes to make a substantial effort to maintain employment even in the face of temporary downturns. An important aspect of this may be the extensive use of temporary and other forms of contingent labor.

Other firms find this model too expensive or too much at variance with their philosophy of management. The competing model is to improve productivity through strong, and often unilateral, management actions. Rather than employment continuity, hire/fire is the rule. The natural consequence of such an approach is strong efforts by the labor force to protect themselves via clear and well-defined work rules, job boundaries, and so on.

The former approach to organizing work has been termed the "salaried model," and the latter the "industrial model" (Osterman, 1988), and it is far from clear which will emerge as the dominant way of organizing work in America. It is clear, however, that they have very different implications for understanding how technology affects the organization of work.

In order to understand the relationship between these alternative human resource strategies and technology, recall our earlier evidence on the disparate impacts of technology. The best current evidence is that effective use of information technologies implies that employees exhibit considerable flexibility on the job and that knowledge and understanding of the production process be widely diffused. It is impossible, however, to achieve such a system in isolation from the rest of the firm's employment practices. The employment relationship has to be viewed as a whole: compensation, employment security, and training systems must be internally consistent and aimed in a common direction. What this logic implies, of course, is that firms that seek to deploy new technologies in the empowerment sense will likely adopt salaried models of human resouce management. Or, switching the causal arrows, firms with a tradition of "progressive" or salaried models of work organization will be the ones in which technology is most likely to be deployed in an upskilling and job-enhancing way.

Because technologies appear to have higher payoffs when in the empowerment mode and because this implies a broader reform of human resource practices, many firms are seeking ways to provide at least a core of their labor force with a degree of job security. Many of the innovations in human resource management—work teams, quality of work life, and increased use of contingent workers (temporary and part-timers) to shield the employment security of the core labor force—can be understood as efforts to shift to the flexibility of the salaried model.

The gains derived from the salaried model can be assessed by observing the expense and effort firms are willing to incur in order to maintain or develop the system. In one of the research projects undertaken as part of the Management in the 1990s Research Program, we documented the process Digital Equipment Corporation used to maintain employment security in the face of a declining labor demand partly resulting from technical innovation (Kochan, MacDuffie, and Osterman, 1988). That the firm was willing to undergo this time-consuming, complex, and expensive undertaking is testimony to the gains attained under high-commitment salaried systems.

Although many firms are attempting to capture these gains, many others do not believe either that the benefits are worth the costs or that they are in a position to undertake the necessary investments in human resources. There is, for this reason, considerable variety in firms' human resource strategies. For this reason, the central point here is not that the labor market is shifting in one particular direction. Rather, to return to our effort to develop a model that explains the impact of technology on employment, our point is that one significant variable is the nature of the firm's internal labor market and human resource system.

**The External Environment**

Understanding the impact of product cycle and human resource strategy takes us much of the way in explaining the diverse impacts of technology on employment levels and skills. However, this cannot be the complete story, because there appears to be systematic variation across countries in the use and impact of technology. Nations such as Germany, Sweden, and Japan seem to achieve higher productivity and less employment loss than does the United States for comparable technologies.

In part, the explanation can be cast in terms of our two prior considerations. For example, Japanese firms, or at least the large ones at the core of the economy, provide lifetime employment and are organized with considerable internal flexibilty and high levels of training. Hence, these are in some sense salaried firms and should be expected to reap the benefits of that model.

At the same time, there are several characteristics of the external labor market in other nations that are relevant to this discussion. In Germany the level of vocational training provided to young workers during their high school education is very high. This is the result of the so-called dual system under which more than 70 percent of the youth cohort receive two to three years of vocational training in well-defined occupations. The consequence of this system is that firms have a highly trained labor force able, and indeed eager, to adapt to new techniques.

A strong level of public training is also characteristic of Sweden, in terms of an extensive high school vocational program and also in terms of a training system aimed at reskilling unemployed workers. In addition, in Sweden the costs of job loss to workers are quite low because of several factors: the retraining system, narrow wage differentials between firms which reduce the cost of job change, and a welfare state which undergirds family income. To recall our earlier discussion about the volume of employment, we argued that even if jobs in a specific firm were lost because of technology, the consequences of this would depend on the success of external institutions in matching those workers to new jobs. Sweden's public policy accomplishes this, and as a result Swedish workers are much like the Japanese in their willingness to provide considerable on-the-job flexibility. Hence, again the impact of new technologies is very much in the upskilling direction.

## CONCLUSION

The logic of this chapter can be conceived as follows. We identified three categories of outcome variables:

1. The productivity of the technology relative to expectations.
2. The impact of the technology on the volume of employment.
3. The impact of the technology on skills, job boundaries, and careers.

We reviewed research on each of these topics and developed the central message of the section: The impact of the technology in each area is contingent on context.

To support this claim, we provided empirical evidence that similar technologies have widely varying impacts in different circumstances.

If it is true that the impact of technology is contingent, then the issue is understanding the key factors that determine outcomes. We identified three contextual variables:

1. The firm's position in the product and technology cycle.
2. The human resource system of the firm.
3. The nature of external education and training institutions.

Taken together, these considerations provide a powerful framework for integrating the rich and varied research on technological impact.

The second core argument of the chapter is that new information technologies have several characteristics (integration, speed, and costly consequences) that shift the cost-benefit calculus in favor of a particular configuration of human resource and job design characeristics. Our evidence suggests that if this strategy is followed, then the technology will achieve its potential, and managers and employees will find work more satisfying and secure. The open question, of course, is whether this potential can be achieved. What it takes to accomplish this is the theme of the next chapter of this book.

## REFERENCES

Adler, P. 1986. "New Technologies, New Skills." *California Management Review* 29, no. 1 (Fall): 9–28.

Ancona, D., and D. Caldwell. 1987. "Management Issues in New Product Teams in High Technology Companies." In *Advances in Industrial Relations.* Greenwich, Conn. JAI Press.

Attewell, P. 1985. "The Effects of Interactive Technology on Management." Mimeo, Department of Sociology, State University of New York at Stony Brook.

Bailyn, L. 1987. "Freeing Work from the Constraints of Location and Time: An Analysis Based on Data from the United Kingdom." Management in the 1990s Working Paper 87-037, MIT, June.

———. 1988. "Toward the Perfect Workplace? The Experience of Home-Based Systems Developers." Management in the 1990s Working Paper 88-045, MIT, March.

Braverman, H. 1974. *Labor and Monopoly Capital.* New York: Monthly Review Press.

Carroll, J. S., and C. Perin. 1988. "How Expecations about Microcomputers Influence Their Organizational Consequences." Management in the 1990s Working Paper 88-044, MIT, April.

Flynn, P. 1988. *Facilitating Technological Change.* Cambridge, Mass. Ballinger.

Graham, M., and S. Rosenthal. 1986. "Flexible Manufacturing Systems Require Flexible People." *Human Systems Management* 6(1986): 211–22.

Hirschhorn, L. 1984. *Beyond Mechanization: Work and Technology in a Postindustrial Age.* Cambridge: MIT Press.

Hunt, H. A. and T. Hunt. 1983. *Human Resource Implications of Robotics.* Kalamazoo, Mich: Upjohn Institute.

———. 1986. *Clerical Employment and Technological Change.* Kalamazoo, Mich.: Upjohn Institute.

Jaikumar, R. 1986. "Postindustrial Manufacturing." *Harvard Business Review* (November–December): 69–76.

Katz, H. 1985. *Shifting Gears.* Cambridge: MIT Press.

Katz, H., T. Kochan, and J. Keefe. 1987. "Industrial Relations and Productivity in the U.S. Automobile Industry." *Brookings Papers on Economic Activity, Special Issue on Microeconomics* 3, pp. 685–728.

Kelley, M. 1989. "Unionization and Job Design under Programmable Automation." *Industrial Relations* (Spring).

Kochan, T. 1988. "On the Human Side of Technology." *ICL Technical Journal* (November): 391–400.

Kochan, T., and J. Chalykoff. 1989. "Computer-aided Monitoring: Its Influence on Employee Job Satisfaction and Turnover." Management in the 1990s Working Paper 89-065, MIT, January.

Kochan, T., H. Katz, and R. McKersie. 1986. *The Transformation of American Industrial Relations.* New York: Basic Books.

Kochan, T., J. P. MacDuffie, and P. Osterman. 1988. "Employment Security at DEC: Organizational Values and Strategic Choice." *Human Resouce Management* (Summer).

Krafcik, J. 1988. "High Performance Manufacturing: An Innternational Study of Auto Assembly Practice." Working Paper, International Motor Vehicle Program, MIT, Cambridge.

Krafcik, J., and J. P. MacDuffie. 1989. "Explaining High Performance Manufacturing: The International Automotive Assembly Plant Study." Paper presented at Third Policy Forum, International Motor Vehicle Program, MIT, May.

Lynch, L., and P. Osterman. 1989. "Whatever Became of the Wichita Lineman? Technological Change in the Telecommunicaitons Industry." *Industrial Relations* (Spring).

MacDuffie, J. P., and M. Maccoby. 1986. "The Organizational Implications of New Technologies: Remote Work Stations at AT&T Communications." Harvard University Kennedy School of Government Discussion Paper 154D, Cambridge, September.

Myles, J. n.d. "The Expanding Middle: Some Canadian Evidence on the Deskilling Debate." Carleton University.

Osterman, P. 1986. "The Impact of Computers upon the Employment of Clerks and Managers." *Industrial and Labor Relations Review* (January).

————. 1988. *Employment Futures; Reorganization, Dislocation, and Public Policy.* New York: Oxford University Press.

Perin, C. 1988. "The Moral Fabric of the Office: Organizational Habits vs. High-Tech Options for Work Schedule Flexibilities." Management in the 1990s Working Paper 88-051, MIT, June.

Perrow, C. 1986. *Complex Organizations: A Critical Essay.* New York: Random House.

Piore, M., and C. Sabel. 1984. *The Second Industrial Divide.* New York: Basic Books.

Salzman, H. 1985. "The New Merlins or Taylor's Automatons? The Impact of Computer Technologies on Skill and Workplace Organization." Center for Applied Social Science working Paper 85-5, Boston University, May.

Schneider, L., R. Howard, and F. Emspak. 1985. "Office Automation in a Manufacturing Setting." Office of Technology Assessment (OTA Contract 4330055), Washington, D.C., April.

Shimada, H., and J. P. MacDuffie. 1986. "Industrial Relations and 'Humanware': Japanese Investment in Automobile Manufacturing in the United States." Sloan School of Management Working Paper 1985–86, MIT, December.

Spenner, K. 1987. "Technological Change, Skill Requirements, and Education: The Case for Uncertainty." Mimeo, Department of Sociology, Duke University, July.

Thomas, R. 1988. "Technological Choice: Obstacles and Opportunities for Union Involvement in New Technology Design." Sloan School of Management Working Paper 1987–88, MIT, February.

Thompson, J. 1967. *Organizations in Action: Social Science Bases of Administrative Theory.* New York: McGraw-Hill.

Walton, R. 1987. *Innovating to Compete.* San Francisco: Jossey-Bass.

Westney, D. E., and K. Skakibara. 1988. "Comparative Study of the Training, Careers, and Organizations of Engineers in the Computer Industry in Japan and the United States." MIT-Japan Science and Technology Program Working Paper.

Woodward, J. 1965. *Industrial Organization: Theory and Practice.* New York: Oxford University Press.

Zuboff, S. 1988. *In the Age of the Smart Machine: The Future of Work and Power.* New York: Basic Books.

# CHAPTER 9

# Organizational Change

## ROBERT B. McKERSIE AND
## RICHARD E. WALTON

This chapter focuses on the three central forces of the 1990s model as shown in Figure 9-1. Each is individually affected by information technology changes, but they interact with each other strongly through the action of human resource policies and practices. Effective implementaiton of IT is, at its core, a task of managing change. As such, it is centrally concerned with people, structure, and process issues. To use the terminology adopted in this chapter, it is necessary to be sure that these organizational choices and the technological and strategic choices are properly aligned with one another. For example, approaches to the design and implementation of the organizational aspects of IT systems are quite different depending on whether one is attempting to automate, informate, or transform, as spelled out in Chapter 7.

Some aspects of organizational structure and style as well as specific human resources policies are particularly important to the successful use of IT. For example, an enabling culture and an adaptive organization appear to characterize successful implementations. This section lays out the key choices in the implementation process that must be understood to increase the likelihood of successful change.

Beneath all of this are the organization's underlying assumptions about the nature of its employees. Are employees thought of as cogs in a machine who have to be told precisely what to do, or are they people who can be trusted to think for themselves and the organization? Management's assumptions in this regard can encourage or kill the movement toward the organization as a learning system, a necessary move if the organization is to adapt successfully for the 1990s.

Many different groups within the organization have an essential role to play in ensuring effective implementation of IT and organizational change. First, top management vision and the presence of a "product" champion are crucial in this change process. The kinds of changes that have to take place if an organization is to successfully compete through the decade of the 1990s require a challenging degree of organizational "reengineering." The fact that these changes span the full breadth and all levels of the organization suggests that active leadership by the CEO is requisite.

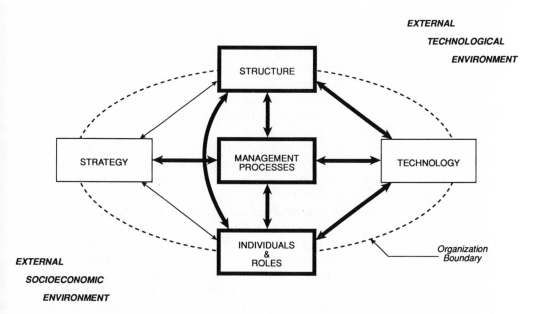

**Figure 9-1.** MIT90s framework—Chapter 9 emphasis.

Second, human resource policies play a key role in facilitating the development of a new culture and the ease and success of introducing specific IT projects. Using these policies as an active component of the change process requires a proactive stance on the part of the human resources professional and a real partnership with line management.

Third, the maximum feasible participation by users/stakeholders helps to bring about the integration/coordination of technology and organizational choices. Each of these groups can help ensure that the introduction of an IT system into an existing organization meets both immediate business and longer-term organizational objectives.

Increasingly the full potential of advanced IT can only be realized if it is associated with appropriate changes in the organization and human resource practices. Thus, implementation of IT—adoption, introduction, and diffusion of IT systems—involves both social and technology development processes.

Sponsors of the Management in the 1990s Research Program have identified implementation as the key challenge their organizations face with respect to IT.

This chapter identifies concepts and practices that appear to be associated with effective implementation—that is, adoption, introduction, and diffusion—of IT systems. We examine the experience of firms that have faced the challenge of introducing IT and identify the organizational prerequisites and human resource policy change processes that help ensure implementation success. We draw heavily on a number of core studies[1] done in conjunction with the 1990s program—two from the telephone industry, two from the Internal Revenue Service, and one each from Eastman Kodak and General Motors Corporation—as well as from a wide range of other materials, including an electronic conference between one of the authors and a dozen middle managers with extensive experience in IT.[2]

The six cases vary broadly along several dimensions. First, the work settings differ. The system in the GM case affects workers on the plant floor; the Kodak case concerns managerial decision making in a factory setting. One IRS system affects professional-status revenue agents, the other the work of clerical personnel involved in collection activities. The two telephone systems affect workers in settings that are neither classic office nor classic factory settings.

The cases also vary in purpose. Four of the core cases clearly emphasize cost reduction. The two telephone systems and IRS's collection system were introduced to mechanize the presentation and recording of information for important clerical operations. Management's primary objective was to increase the productivity of these operations. Deskilling occurred in at least one of the telephone cases; the new system incorporated as imbedded computer code much of the knowledge that formerly resided in the heads of operators.

The other cost-reduction case involved the introduction of stand-alone PCs to 14,000 IRS revenue agents. Initial implementation was aimed at giving the agents a tool that would save time. The longer-term vision was of an integrated system of PCs that would increase the effectiveness and transform the nature of the IRS work system. As it happened, many agents enjoyed mastering and using the tool and believed it enhanced their professional image with taxpayers. But these were beneficial side effects, not results sought by those who sponsored the PC diffusion project.

Two of the cases emphasized increases in both effectiveness and efficiency. A computer-integrated manufacturing (CIM) system of General Motors and MRPII system at Kodak were intended to qualitatively change how things were done. GM's highly computerized operations (which involved flexible machining stations and automatic movement of parts in process) required organizational arrangements that involved teams, flexible movement of personnel, and delegation of responsibility from management and staff groups to operating personnel. Similarly, Kodak's incorporation of an inventory and resource control system at the level of the business unit necessitated much more horizontal integration and a more creative use of financial data than had been the case with a centralized accounting system.

The six implementation cases also varied in effectiveness. Consider, for example, the criteria proposed by Goodman and Griffith (1989): on-time introduction; adherence to the acceleration schedule; acceptable utiliztion rates; and user satisfaction. In the judgment of involved parties, expected benefits of the IT were, in most cases, either not realized during implementation or realized long after the projected steady-state conditions.

Probably the most successful of the core cases was the pilot implementation of an MRPII system in Department 23 of Kodak's manufacturing organization. This system was implemented on a reasonable schedule, improved decision making and planning as promised, and had a favorable effect on the climate of the organizational unit. But while Department 23's MRPII system was successful on its own terms, it did not produce clear evidence of its relevance to other, less self-contained Kodak departments.

A survey of 1,000 revenue agents one year after they were issued PCs by the IRS showed mixed results (see Pentland, 1989). Implementation was successful in terms of use and user satisfaction. Most agents used their PCs more than twenty hours per week, and three-quarters agreed that it was an appropriate tool. But only 15 percent reported that the PCs reduced the time they spent on a case. (As mentioned earlier, some agents derived other professional benefits from the PCs.)

The three office cases that emphasized cost reduction yielded both positive and negative outcomes. In all three cases (the two telephone installations and the IRS collection centers), the IT was installed and diffused throughout the organization approximately on schedule. Implementation of the new computerized collection system involved twenty locations. Though not as many separate offices were involved for the assignment technology in the two telephone companies, the ability of these firms to diffuse the new system throughout two very large organizations must be seen as a positive result.

On the other side of the ledger, personnel turnover was extremely high for the two years following the introduction of the collection system technology. The offices involved came to be known within the IRS as "automation shops," to which neither operating personnel nor management wanted to be detailed for very long. The cutover from the labor-intensive to computer-driven operations in the telephone offices was characterized by many customers complaints. Insufficient "slack" made it impossible to take the changeover in stride, and a number of operating problems developed.

The start-up of GM's CIM implementation took approximately two years longer than anticipated (five years rather than three) and involved certain inflexibilities, specifically the inability to incorporate in the manufacturing process product variations requested by the design and marketing departments. This point was made emphatically in one of our interviews: "This new system has enabled us to manufacture an extremely high-quality product that has received high acceptance by customers, but we can only make one flavor, vanilla. With the old system, we had much more ability to incorporate small changes in specifications and customer requirements."

## HOW TO THINK ABOUT THE SUCCESSFUL INTRODUCTION OF IT

A useful way to think about the successful introduction of IT is to identify concepts and practices associated with the desired results. Figure 9-2 summarizes the elements of a framework.

IT implementation comprises three broad subtasks: designing the IT system and the organization that will operate it, developing enabling human resource policies, and managing the implementation processes. The design and development tasks involve decisions about what changes to seek. The implementation process involves choices about how the changes will be accomplished.

The design, development, and implementation choices influence three key conditions—motivation, competence, and coordination—which, in turn, strongly influence the effective integration of the technology.

The motivation level of those who can influence the successful implementation of IT can range from opposition through reluctant compliance to a high level of spontaneous commitment. The competence of those who operate and manage IT can range from narrow operating skills to comprehensive understanding and mastery of IT and its relationship to broader organization purposes. Coordination can range from strictly individual action taking (without active coordination) to tight teamwork.

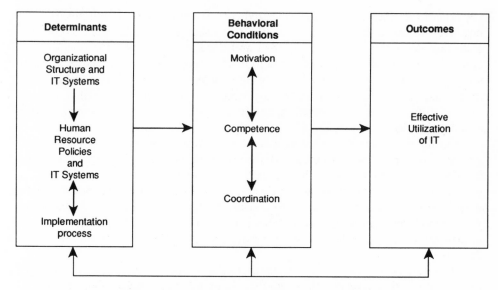

**Figure 9-2.** Framework for effective utilization of IT.

Generally, there are escalating requirements for the three conditions associated with advances in IT. Earlier forms of automation, for example, could be effective with compliant workers trained to perform highly circumscribed tasks, whose actions were coordinated by supervision or by the technology itself.

Increasingly we are finding that advanced forms of IT—CIM, for example, can only be fully utilized by highly committed operators who can engage in complex diagnostic activity and work as a team. Similarly, effective use of personal computers by professionals and managers, who often have discretion over how extensively they reply on computer-based tools, is critically dependent on their motivation level and comprehension of the technology and its performance potential.

The key roles we assign to motivation, competence, and coordination in our implementation framework are based on our own field observations and our review of a sample of the rapidly growing literature describing IT in practice. Where IT's potential has not been exploited or its implementation has been delayed, we invariably find insufficient positive motivation on the part of some stakeholder group, competence gaps, or coordination failures. Different types of IT, as suggested above, depend on a unique pattern of motivation, competence, and coordination for their effectiveness.

## ALIGNMENT OF THE ORGANIZATION AND IT

Fundamental to effective implementation of IT is the alignment of the technology and the organization that operates it. *Alignment* refers to the idea that the requirements of the particular IT system—for certain levels of motivation, types and amounts of knowledge and skill, and communication and coordination—are matched by the capabilities of the organization. Conversely, alignment also means that the requirements of the organization—for example, decentralized decision making, continuous learning, challenging jobs, or attractive career paths—are accommodated by the design of the IT system.

Many routes can lead to alignment. First, some of the enabling organizational conditions may already exist or can be developed in anticipation of the introduction of an IT system. Second, the organization, in effect, helps pull the technology into place. Organization and technology can be developed simultaneously, each adapted to the other. Third, management can focus exclusively on implementing the technology, letting the technology drive subsequent organizational adaptation. The technology is in effect pushed into the organization. This third sequence is the most common, but it presents certain obstacles to alignment.

After exploring some evidence that organizational change is a necessary condition for effective utilization of IT, we will examine each of these three patterns of orchestrating the technological and organizational changes.

## The Need for Organizational Change with IT Implementation: Some Evidence

Our key premise regarding the critical importance of aligning technical and social systems with new technology is clearly in evidence in the automobile industry. Five U.S. assembly plants (Krafick and Womack, 1986) analyzed by researchers associated with the MIT International Motor Vehicle Program were found to vary in the amount of technological and organization change they employed to become world-class competitors. Organizational reforms, where they occurred, took the form of participation mechanisms, flexible assignment patterns, multiple skilling, self-supervision, quality problem-solving groups, and similar policies designed to elicit employee commitment and promote competence.

One GM plant in Massachusetts typified plants in which neither new work practices nor new technologies were introduced. A GM plant in Michigan was infused with $650 million of advanced manufacturing technologies but did not undertake significant organizational change. Two plants—the California plant of NUMMI (the GM-Toyota venture) and the Honda plant in Ohio—effected technology upgrades coupled with very ambitious work reforms. Finally, a Nissan plant in Tennessee exhibited somewhat more technological sophistication than the NUMMI and Honda plants but slightly less ambitious work reform.

An analysis of productivity and quality in these five plants led to startling conclusions. First, the performance of the GM plant with high technology but no work reform was not significantly better than that of the low-tech plant that continued traditional organizational practices. Advanced technology by itself clearly made little difference. Second, the NUMMI and Honda plants, with their moderate investments in technology but fundamentally reformed work organizations, dramatically outperformed GM's high-tech/traditional plant. Both required approximately 45 percent less time to assemble a car and produced 45 percent fewer quality defects than the GM plant. Third, compared with the NUMMI and Honda plants, Nissan's slightly more automated and slightly less advanced organizational design achieved comparable quality but significantly lower productivity. Again, the technology advantage appeared to be more than neutralized by a lag in organizational upgrading.

The upshot is that advanced technology by itself fails to achieve performance gains. Only when innovation in work organization accompanies technological innovation do we see significant performance advantages.

A National Research Council committee, chaired by one of the authors, reached a similar conclusion (NRC, 1986). The business executives, trade union officials, and academics who comprised the membership of the committee on "Implementation Practices for Advanced Manufacturing Technology" visited installations of advanced manufacturing technology at Consolidated Diesel, Cummins Engine Company, FMC Corporation, Grumman Aerospace Corporation, Honeywell Information Systems, IBM, Ingersoll Milling Machine Company, McDonnel Douglas Corporation, and several other companies. The committee's conclusions were clear: the traditional work organization was ill fitted to realize the potential of advanced manufacturing technology. Specific liabilities of the traditional organization included hierarchy consciousness, the detailed and fixed division of labor, and supervisory emphasis on the performance of the individual worker. New tehcnology required more flexibility in assignments of workers, more continuous learning, and more spontaneous motivation than was provided by traditional work systems.

Advanced manufacturing technologies exhibited a far heavier reliance on IT than conventional manufacturing technologies. The newer systems were characterized by greater interdependence among work activities; more immediate and costly consequences of malfunction in any part of the system; and greater sensitivity of output to variations in human skills, knowledge, and attitudes and, in general, to mental rather than physical effort.

Implicit in this increased interdependence was the requirement that operators had to be able to communicate and coordinate their work activities. The immediacy and extent of the consequences of errors and their sensitivity to the human factor not only placed a premium on motivation but also underscored the importance of analytic and abstract thinking. The required work organization needed to emphasize flexibility in assignments, continuous learning, and a structure and set of policies capable of eliciting the necessary motivation and coordination.

Two important and related propositions can be deduced from these reported experiences with advanced IT. First, it is not always necessary to utilize extensive amounts of technology. Good results can often be achieved with moderate amounts of technology (average for the industry) if proper organizational arrangements are in place. And second, the high-tech approach requires carefully tailored organizational arrangements. If these are not present, overall results are often poorer than if less technology were used.

These points are amply illustrated by a study comparing energy conservation at several Boston area universities which hits close to home for the authors. Peter Cebon (1990) has examined the interplay of control technology for energy conservation, organizational arrangements, and overall performance. MIT's approach is characterized by a very advanced system of central control, and yet it performs much more poorly than Harvard, with a very decentralized organization in which each school has an energy conservation officer responsible for achieving better utilization of energy. According to the report, MIT is at least a decade ahead of Harvard in technology but far behind in terms of performance.

## Organizational Change Followed
## by IT Implementation

In a number of cases, we observed that conditions favorable to effective IT utilization were already in place when an IT system was introduced. IT is pulled into place by the users rather than pushed into place by sponsors or superiors.

The best example of the development of ownership by users of a new technology is in the core case at Kodak. We have already cited some evidence of Kodak's successful implementation of its MRPII system. Other aspects are also noteworthy. The system was up and running within a short period of time and has enabled the user manufacturing unit to perform much more effectively. It has, for example, facilitated implementation of a just-in-time system, which was untenable under the old system, given the long delays encountered in passing data to and from the central computer.

The benefits of involvement and commitment are captured in the following quote: "There is more ownership. People who are inputting inventory and parts controls have more respect for data integrity. The audit trail provides instant feedback on what is going on. People are more aware of performance" (Lewis, 1988).

The various aligned and nonaligned relationships between Kodak's organizational and MRPII options for the manufacturing functions are shown in Table 9-1. The general point is that for IT to be effective, it and the organizational structure must be aligned. The specific lesson of the Kodak example is that the earlier move to decentralize to departments set the stage for a relatively smooth introduction of the aligned IT system. People in the division understand the business much more directly and take responsibility for difficulties that are now shown "on-line." The new system enables them to pinpoint their mistakes and has facilitated the functioning of a decentralized manufacturing operation.

In two other cases we have examined, in which a new technology was pulled into place by a group of highly committed professionals, the key elements of what is,

**Table 9-1.** Relationship between Kodak's Organizational and MRPII Options

| Techology Choices | Centralized Manufacturing Organization to Coordinate and Optimize Manufacturing System | Decentralized Organization to Foster Local Accountability and Initiative |
|---|---|---|
| Central MRPII System | In the earlier approach this single, centralized MRPII system and centralized organization were mutually reinforcing in principle, although never fully implemented. | *Mismatch:* ineffective and unstable. IT would fail to provide local decision makers with the information they need, and the organization would not accept actions based on central IT. |
| Departmental MRPII Systems | *Mismatch:* ineffective and unstable. IT would fail to provide central decision makers with the information they need and to legitimize actions taken by departmental managers on the basis of information made available by the system. | IT and organization mutually reinforcing for Dept. 23 (although as a pilot it may not apply to other more interdependent departments.) |

in effect, advanced organizational design are already in place. A good illustration of this is the electronic conference's example of the use of IT in a high-tech organization:

> Our experience with electronic conferencing has been very positive, given the limitations of the current generation of software. It is not unusual to have 6 to 10 remotely located managers (many more if you count indirects) actively participate in formulating, reviewing, editing, and approving a document/plan. During my last weekend in Washington, an important issue arose late Friday that required an official written agency position Monday morning. A few phone calls locked in the key experts (five different states) for an electronic brainstorming session on Saturday. I got initial thoughts from everyone on electronic mail Friday night (ideas were iterated once or twice) as well as access to information and graphics from local databases with comments and proposed rewrites or reorganizations with appropriate rationale. Three iterations were completed by 5:00 P.M. and a draft was electronically forwarded to three senior managers at their homes for approval. After incorporating their revisions, the position paper was approved and printed for an 8:00 A.M. meeting Monday morning with the head of the agency.

The focus of the agency just described is clearly on the integration and development of shared databases. The particular electronic conference has substantially changed the nature of work, producing quite the opposite effect from deskilling. This example shows how a computer and its associated software can play a central role in communications among managers and professionals. IT can have a dramatic impact on organizational processes, up, down, and across the organization. In this case, IT-engendered communications capability has accelerated the absorption and increased the utility of information without producing the frequent result of information overload.

A third illustration comes from a report by Carroll and Perin, who discuss, in a case called "High Tech," a large engineering and manufacturing company in the computer industry. The unit of observation is a 45-person advanced engineering group that provides internal assistance on a wide range of activities related to end-user computing. The technology is "state-of-the-art." The computer professionals, being both developers and users, were highly invested in creating and tailoring software that would enhance both company profits and their professional careers. The intensive use of IT and the rich interplay between these professionals and the systems in place are clearly illustrated in this excerpt from the Carroll and Perin (1988) study:

> All of the members of the advanced engineering group we studied had networked terminals; some had more than one on their office desk and another at home. Hundreds of technical topics are available on the conferencing system, and there are recreational conferences as well (e.g., hobbies and games). Most people spend over 50 percent of their time on the computer, and most prefer electronic mail and computer conferencing to the telephone. When the main computer system goes down and it is no longer possible to use individual systems, just about all work comes to a standstill; employees report that they stand around chatting until the system gets fixed or it's time to go home.

Why does user or organizational pull of IT tend to produce favorable results? One reason is that the nature and scope of a technology that is pulled into place by users who have substantial input is mroe likely to be lined up with organizational arrangements than a technology pushed into place by vendors or staff groups.

## Simultaneous Implementation of Organizational Change and IT

In many cases management puzzles through the designs of the new technology and the operating organzation at the same time or in highly overlapping phases. Increasingly, researchers recommend this pattern of development because it allows for mutual adaptation of the technical and social subsystems of an IT installation. This pattern was illustrated in many of the CIM systems included in the NRC study.

A good illustration of how this works out in practice can be found in the appliance industry in the experience of General Electric. In 1983, GE started up in its Louisville facility an advanced CIM system for producing a newly designed dishwasher. Seven islands of automation were mechanically linked via a power-and-free conveyor and storage system. Computerized parts processing and assembly operations incorporated laser readers, robot handlers, nonsynchronous conveyor systems, and ultrasonic welding. An electronic order entry system integrated input from purchasing, cost accounting, production planning, and shop-floor control. Computers monitored old key functions such as injection molding, steel fabrication, and quality control.

The various activities were conducted in parallel: the design of the product, the design of the automated manufacturing process, the design of the new organization structure and roles, and the development of a participative culture in the plant. Each development activity was coordinated with the critical other processes. The result were (1) technology choices that were responsive to organization ideals, such as for worker self-control; (2) organizational choices that met the unique reuqirements of the CIM technology, such as for competence and coordination; and (3) a product design that took advantage of the unique features of automated manufacturing processes.

## New Technology as a Catalyst for Organizational Change and Alignment

We have thus far considered two basic patterns for alignment of social and technical systems. In the first, alignment takes place early because the desired organizational arrangements are in place and the users pull the appropriate technology into place. In the second, coordinated change occurs in both organizational and technical arrangements.

Here, we turn to a different strategy in whch a firm moves ahead with the introduction of IT, leaving existing organizational arrangements in place, and subsequently attends to organizational changes on a responsive or adaptive basis.

This strategy is viewed by some practitioners as the only realistic way to proceed, arguing that preemptive organizational change would not be feasible. As one commentator observed at one of our presentations, "If we followed the advice of changing the organization first, there would be blood all over the floor."

To be effective, this strategy, like the others already discussed, requires a firm to have a vision of what the new organization should be like in terms of structure, style, and relationships. It emphasizes getting started (perhaps even emphasizing the cost-reduction attributes of the technology) and in due course, moving toward more powerful uses of the technology (value added) made possible by organizational change.

Conceptually, the rationale for attending first to the introduction of a technology is that it serves as a catalyst, an agent for unfreezing the status quo. In several of our cases this "significant emotional event" arose from operational difficulties that developed with the new system. Management was then forced to step back and ask itself what was going wrong and what changes needed to be made in the organization to solve the implementation crisis that had developed.

Both the telephone companies and the Internal Revenue Service left classifications and work arrangements intact when the computer technology was initially put into place. For example, although some rotation across positions was instituted at the beginning by one of the telephone companies, most of the attention to work organzation issues was triggered by the experience itself (Villiger, 1988, p. 117). In the case of the collection operation at IRS, this took the form of a negative reaction on the part of operators to the "automation shop" atmosphere. Management was then forced to look at work organization and, in some locations, instituted a team structure, the teams being responsible for all aspects of following up on accounts.

By the end of 1988, teams had been inexistence for twelve months at four locations, and the results looked promising. Worker satisfaction and job comitment had increased significantly, and employees evidenced much stronger ownership of particular client cases. Further extension of the team concept has been delayed pending the installation of communiations software that will make it possible for "callbacks" to be connected efficiently to the member of the team responsible for a particular case. The point is that high employee turnover in the collection centers had led the IRS into the program of introducing teams and reorganizing work so that groups of employees could once again be responsible for an inventory of accounts. In the telephone companies, the difficulties encountered in getting it up to speed and cutting over to the new system prompted a reexamination of the usefulness of the training packages and the adequacy of the overall staffing levels.

Another occasion for letting the introduction of technology precede organizational change is when the technology being introduced is of the discretionary variety. All the examples cited earlier are required systems in the sense that users have no choice but to employ them. In contrast, the IRS left to examiners the choice of whether to use the personal computers in their work routines.

When this type of technology is involved and management decides that its use will be voluntary, alignment becomes very much a decentralized and open-ended process. The approach is essentially "Wait and see what happens." Management is then in a position to reinforce whatever organization-technology adaptations begin to emerge. If particular user groups share software and begin to use the technology in creative ways, cross-fertilization can be encouraged, enabling others to learn about the organizational processes that are involved as well as the software adaptations.

Using technology to precipitate organizational change and alignment, as was done successfully in a number of instances in the preceding discussion, entails some inherent risks. As there is a tendency for traditional organizations to exploit the cost-reduction aspects of new technologies, introducing a new technology without explicit redesign of organizational structures may only perpetuate the status quo. For example, when a major introduction of new technology requires vendor and staff group support, the new technology is pushed into place in an "in and down" fashion. The control elements associated with such an approach can be pervasive and can reinforce existing patterns rather than setting the stage for moving the firm to new organizational arrangements.

To ensure the reform potential inherent in IT, management must have a vision and consciously work to encourage the adaptations in organizational arrangements (if only on a trial-and-error basis) that become necessary as problems develop. We will have more to say about mechanisms for this type of organizational learning in a subsequent section on implementation processes.

## ENABLING HUMAN RESOURCE POLICIES AND PROGRAMS

It became clear, in examining case studies of successful implementations of IT, that human resource policies played an important—in some instances, critically important—supportive role. If, for example, stakeholders are threatened by a cost-reduction emphasis leading to fewer people, acceptance of the new technology and the upgrading potential that may be inherent in it can be helped along by some type of employment security program that assures displaced employees positions of commensurate responsibility.

At a conceptual level, human resource policies can thus be seen as supporting and facilitating integration between organizational change and the introduction of a new technology. At a more specific or behavioral level, these policies focus on developing requisite competence, eliciting motivation, and securing adequate coordination.

### Work Organization and Job Design

To introduce a new IT system into an established work organization will require a specific set of adjustments in the way work is organized and employees managed. Though it is important, in practice, to diagnose each implementation situation in its own terms, it is possible to discuss certain broad choices in general terms.

Determination of job content is one of the most critical design issues. Job content not only has direct implications for the quality of motivation elicited and for the skills and knowledge developed in practice, but it also has a decisive impact on other human resource matters, such as selection policies, measurement and reward systems, organization structure, and supervision system.

Whether the progressive infusion of new computer-based work technologies requires an upgrading or leads to the downgrading of human resources is a major strategic human resource issue (Walton and Susman, 1987). Early generations of mainframe computers, for example, tended to automate operations and deskill and routinize work. This approach minimized training investments (rendering the organization less vulnerable to turnover) and encouraged supervisors to rely on formal controls for managing performance.

More recent developments in IT have produced more varied implications for the nature of work. Some advanced IT systems, like their predecessors, deskill and routinize work. Moreover, they incorporate an enormous capability for monitoring worker behavior and performance results, essentially automating major aspects of the supervision of work. However, the net implications of other advanced IT systems are precisely the opposite. Though they may automate certain aspects of work, such as the storage, retrieval, and manipulation of data, such systems supply workers with more information and more powerful analytic tools. Informating forms of IT enlarge the scope of responsibility and latitude for decision making and increase the rate of on-the-job learning. Often, they upgrade skill requirements, fostering a need for training investments, stabilizing employment, and introducing facilitating forms of supervision.

Job design for CIM, for example, should follow a series of questions. These shoud include (1) how to design jobs sufficiently broad and flexible to allow people to understand all or large chunks of an interdependent system, (2) how to connect those who share responsibility for the system so as to facilitate the management of interdependence, (3) how to design jobs that generate high levels of internalized motivation, and (4) how to design jobs to promote learning about both the system and the business tasks it performs.

A technology's design, especially its secondary features, can be coordinated with job design to reinforce desired communication, internalized motivation, and analytic skills and task knowledge. For example, features that provide performance feedback and allow operators to control functions can promote learning and motivation. General Motors provides an example of a CIM system for manufcturing automobile components in which operators' responsibilities for production operations and equipment maintenance involved complex mental tasks such as planning and diagnostic problem solving. As mentioned earlier, characteristics of CIM technology often call for upgraded jobs and more explicit attention to the motivation of line operators. Because CIM technology increases the degree of interdependence among work activities, it makes the use of teams more appropriate. This was precisely the experience at GM's diesel engine plant.

A number of dynamics appear to be operating in the frequently observed failure of planners to develop jobs that match IT and encourage appropriate motivation and competence. Planners who observe alienated or apathetic workers in an existing work system often assume, implicitly or explicitly, that IT should seek to reduce not only the number of workers but also system dependence on the skill and attitude of remaining workers. They thus view deskilling work and increasing the capacity to monitor work electronically as advantages. But they underestimate the demotivating effects of jobs that are deskilled, paced, and devoid of discretion. Planners clearly need to approach the design of IT and the related work organization with better knowledge and more thoughtful exploration of these types of effects.

Planners who seek to develop broad, skill-intensive, and highly responsible jobs often encounter (1) departmental or jurisdictional barriers that prevent the completion of certain tasks, and (2) labor contract provisions or labor market conditions that make it difficult to select, recruit, or retain personnel with the requisite potential. To overcome such barriers to realizing appropriate work arrangements, designers need to bring the many stakeholders affected by an IT into the development process.

## Selection of Potential Users

Those who previously performed the functions for which the technology is designed are usually the primary candidates. But given the educational limitations of many existing organizations and the upskilling attributes of many forms of IT, a serious gap may exist between the abilities of the available work force and the requirements of the new technology. How can this gap be closed?

If the new technology does not require as many people, the most capable can be selected from the larger group that previously performed the function (with the objective of absorbing the remainder elsewhere in the enterprise). Even then, extensive training and retraining may be required. For example, at the General Motors plant mentioned earlier, approximately 60 percent of those screened for the new unit needed substantial help with basic literacy skills.

Intensive counseling and guidance may help members of the incumbent work force unable to handle the new skills to understand why and as a result voluntarily opt for other positions. One of the telephone companies cited earlier used a test to determine readiness for training and made the results available to incumbent workers. Only about 10 percent of those who failed the test actually applied, but ultimately they did as well as those who had passed. (It appears that such workers adopted an attitude of "I still think I can do it" and that this motivation made the difference.)

It is usually best to allow job incumbents an opportunity to qualify for a new technology. This means resisting the temptation to select junior workers or others with special educational qualifications over more senior workers who have been performing a function.

Solutions are most readily found when the challenges are approached in a problem-solving fashion. Consider the dilemma posed by a work-force reduction if senior employees who are less qualified opt to "bump" into the department that is using a new technology. Clearly, production suffers when untrained workers move into a new operation. At the same time, equities are violated if long-service workers are laid off instead of younger workers, even though the latter possess the requisite skills. One solution drawn from the auto case sudy entailed the prequalification of workers who were then placed on an availability list. At the time of a layoff, senior workers would bump into the positions held by prequalified workers, who, in turn, would bump junior persons in the operation that was using advanced technology.

Several of the preceding examples are from unionized operations in which the conflict between seniority and ability to perform is most pronounced. Generally, though, we find unions increasingly willing to help resolve selection dilemmas. Though some of the unions in our cases stood aside and let management make the tough judgments, there is a growing tendency for unions to become involved in joint selection committees and to help with the process of sorting things out. Occasionally, an upsurge in grievances may develop, and unions that have become involved in selection decisions find it necessary to back off.

Union leaders are most likely to become involved and to play a constructive role when the objective is to honor the equities of incumbent employees until it is clear that they do not qualify and to pursue the process of sorting out equities in a careful and deliberative fashion.

## Training

Everyone we interviewed underscored the importance of training for facilitating organizational change and the introduction of new technology. The resources consumed by training are substantial. Besides explicit expenses, such as are incurred for trips to vendors and other sites and for classroom instruction, there is the large cost of forgone production that occurs during "ramp-up" or while progressing along the learning curve. The size of this cost may range from 20 to 30 percent of hardware costs for large CIM-type installations to 100 percent of hardware costs for tool-type (e.g., PCs for report writing) installations.

Though only a small part of the large investment in social infrastructure occurs on a formal basis in the classroom, it is nevertheless a key part of the introduction program. Vendors are becoming more effective at delivering useful hands-on training both in the use of technology and in the organizational and job changes that need to accompany its introduction.

The most important characteristic of the formal training approach associated with successful implementation is a willingness to adjust and adapt training packages. For example, when it became clear at several of the telephone installations that the vendor-supplied training program was inadequate, implementation was stopped and new materials were developed, and the changeover subsequently progressed much better.

Clearly, the biggest component of training is what happens on the job, what some people call on-the-job learning. The heavy "unlearning" or decay factor associated with the acquisition of formal knowledge, especially knowledge of a technical nature, accounts for the limited role formal classroom training plays in IT implementation. Learning does not become integrated until a user becomes engaged with a technology and begins to incorporate its routines and assimilate the deep learning necessary for its effective operation.

Often, self-training is desirable, especially for older workers who fail to realize that they face severe computer literacy problems quite separate from actually learning a system's software. Regarding this Darwinian approach to moving personnel into high technology, one electronic conference member commented, "I guess I am not sold on the concept of formal training, as our ad hoc approach has worked; at great pain and consequence for some, but on balance an effective strategy for creating the new human capital that is so essential."

A contrasting technique for fostering informal learning is to allow (and even to encourage) users to "play" with the new technology. Zuboff (1988) reports on the start-up of a highly computerized paper machine, in which the crew initially was allowed to experiment with the technology and to engage in a number of false starts. Operators who engaged in this type of learning gained invaluable understanding of the technology and the work process. Similar results were seen at several locations where IRS examiners provided with lap-top computers were encouraged to take them home to gain familiarity with the keyboard, play games, and become conversant with the new system at a more leisurely pace.

Another attribute of successful on-the-job learning is effective supervisor coaching and guidance. A study of eight General Motors plants, many using very advanced technology, found that the most effective plants were characterized by supervisors who knew the operations thoroughly and knew how to impart their knowledge to the workers in their groups (Schwartz, 1988). Clearly, supervision is not concerned solely with the function of coaching and support, but supervisors properly trained and skillful at facilitation can precipitate a very effective "downward cascade" of knowledge.

Ultimately, the most important characteristic associated with successful on-the-job learning is an orientation on the part of all concerned that learning is a continuing process. This point was made very effectively by a Swedish team, Oscarsson et. al (1988): "The growing emphasis on high-technology production means greater demands on the competence of each individual employee. And so the element of comprehensive, life long learning for all members of the enterprise will probably turn out to be the most characteristic feature of work in the 21st century."

## Employment Security

More and more firms are recognizing both the desirability and feasibility of providing a good measure of employment security and the associated career planning and training of employees that is necessary to make such a policy work. The following report from the electronic conference speaks to the critical need for employment security in the face of destabilizing influences of new technology:

> First the good news. We have had a lot of success using IT to reduce operating costs and to respond faster to customer demand. To a large extent we were able to land some large contracts in the last few years because of our IT capability.
>
> Now the bad news. From an HRM (human resource management) standpoint we have missed the boat in many cases. Most hourly workers now see IT in their areas as a cue to polish up the resume and look at the equity in their home mortgage. So more often than not implementation is an extreme trial and it takes far too long to realize benefits because we all are not pulling together.

Given that firms are in a position to control the pace of introduction of new technology, in most cases it should be possible to handle employment consequences without resort to involuntary layoffs. Organizations committed to human resource planning on a continuing basis can usually take the employment consequences of IT introductions in stride. The dividends that accrue to such firms can be substantial. Workers who believe that the employment consequences of change are being handled in a fair and constructive fashion will be more likely to embrace a new technology and pursue its potential than workers left to assume that they will be out the door or displaced to less meaningful positions by that technology.

Some companies, such as IBM, Hewlitt Packard, and Eli Lilly, have a tradition of strong employment security, terminating employees only for cause. Though such far-reaching assurances are not feasible for most firms, it is possible to develop more qualified assurances that emphasize the adjustment process.

The implementation of employment security policy takes many forms. It can be as simple as phasing in the new technology on a gradual basis. For example, a large defense contractor introducing CAD into one of its drafting rooms allowed existing personnel to either volunteer for the new technology or remain with the "lower-tech" operation. Management reasoned that attrition, transfers, and the like would slowly take care of people who would not be needed as the full productivity potential of the CAD system was realized.

But implementing employment security policy can also be quite complicated. Consider the experience of AT&T when it installed in its long-lines operation new switching technology with the potential of reducing personnel by 20 percent. Nationally, this amounted to approximately 2,000 craftspeople. To cope with this challenge, the company entered into the very comprehensive planning exercise detailed in the following excerpt:

> First, a manpower planning committee was established to review and clarify the impacts of the new technology for all sections of the company. (This was done by region and the case study from which this information is drawn was for the long lines operation in the South.) A key step was the imposition of a hiring freeze for all nonmanagement jobs. Surplus craftsmen from the switching centers would fill openings in accounting and marketing or be transferred to sections of the country where there were openings in the craft position. A personnel coordinator with a full staff was put in place and training programs inaugurated to implement this redeployment. To give the program some "bite," departments were actually given quotas of craft personnel to be absorbed. The central personnel group ran an assessment process to provide objective information about who could make the transition. At each step the union employees were informed. Supervisors were instructed to encourage employees to volunteer for assessment.
>
> Within two years the surplus craft programs was eliminated and the company was again hiring new employees in selected areas.

In the case of assignment-of-wires technology in the telephone industry (the key technology in two of our core cases), workers who did not stay with the function after computerization were absorbed in a variety of ways. Extensive planning and an aggressive program similar to the one described for the switching technology were not needed since the number of workers rendered excessive by this technology was much smaller, and earlier changeovers had given the two operating companies substantial experience in absorbing and redeploying excess personnel.

A key facilitating arrangement in the telephone industry has been the concept of salary continuation which guarantees that workers will not suffer economically during the transition. Salary protection at one of the telephone companies ran for three years. During this time, no layoffs occurred, although some relocations were required and some workers took early retirement. In some urban areas where many alternative opportunities existed, rebalancing took place so rapidly that the newly computerized operation found itself temporarily understaffed. This was not the case in the rural areas (as we will note later), where having extra personnel available during start-up helped the company to bring the new technology on-line efficiently.

## Performance Monitoring and Employee Appraisal

IT is unique in its ability to generate data about all aspects of the work process that it affects, including inputs to the system, transactions or operations within the system, and the results of system and related actions. A number of key decisions must be made about what performance measurements to develop and to whom they should be provided.

Given the relative ease of obtaining measures, the obvious temptation is to generate more than can be utilized and certainly more than is optimum for motivation and learning on the part of those being measured. It is thus important to consider how this information will be used for appraisal purposes. No aspect of IT better illustrates the multiple potentialities of IT than the options for using performance information on a day-to-day basis.

One approach is complete delegation of ongoing appraisal. The assumption here is that employees, given additional information, including sufficient information to judge how well things are going, will be capable of managing themselves. This was reported to be the case at Kodak, and, indeed, members of the department did use the information for effective self-management. Some, however, felt scared by the transparency (i.e., the performance information was known not only to them but to all concerned): "We want ownership but we are not sure about responsibility" (Lewis, 1988, p. 96). In view of this ambivalence, many companies blend into an overall approach of delegation some managerial use of the information, specifically for performance appraisal purposes.

Another approach might be termed feedback or coaching. Here, though management meets with employees on a regular basis to reviews results, discuss any revision to "milestones," and talk about progress, it is ultimately up to the employees and the teams to make whatever changes are necessary to keep the operation on schedule. This is very close to what has been called management by objective. Focusing on outcomes affords workers the freedom to do the problem solving necessary to achieve the desired results in the time allotted by the plan.

The next approach, moving along a spectrum from autonomy to direct control, is for management to focus attention on work-related behaviors (e.g., required procedures for phone protocol and database manipulation) as a means for instructing employees in effective handling of the operation. Emphasis is on procedures and quality of inputs, with the presumption that the results will take care themselves if all of the activities of employees are up to specifications.

Of course, as management focuses on work behaviors it is in a position to be aware of all behaviors. To the extent that this includes non-work-related actions, workers may perceive monitoring as constituting an invasion of privacy.

This brings us to the core of the dilemma. In his study of performance appraisal for the IRS collection system, Chalykoff (1987) found that managers differed sharply in their relative emphasis on using performance data to develop employees or to control and subjugate them. The ease of obtaining performance information could accentuate either management predisposition.

The choice was not a function of how much time management spent collecting data and observing worker performance. In fact, Chalykoff estimated that most managers spent one-half to three-quarters of their time observing operator performance. The critical distinction was how this activity was done (whether side by side or remotely) and how the information was used once the observations had been made.

A majority of the workers Chalykoff surveyed preferred that management make its observations remotely rather than side by side. These workers felt less nervous when management was at a distance. Most did not want to know when observations were being made but desired feedback and coaching as soon as practical after the fact. Indeed, there was a very high correlation between overall work satisfaction and the immediacy of feedback.

Chalykoff noted another important relationship, specifically, that workers gave higher marks to management's handling of performance information when feedback was presented in positive and constructive terms. What is less clear is how workers react to information containing comparisons. Like so many other dimensions of this subject, reactions vary with setting. Some organizations achieve a positive result by presenting information on the performance of all operators—a type of friendly competition develops. Some organizations have found comparisons to be coercive and destructive, causing workers to spend time "fudging" results and engaging in other dysfunctional behavior in order to look good in the overall standings. How the information is perceived and used depends in part on the organizational climate and in part on the predispositions of direct supervision.

Chalykoff's research points up the need for management to achieve alignment between workers' expectations regarding the type of observation deemed appropriate and the actual execution of this function. Meeting this need requires a judicious matching of several variables, including the nature of the work, the technology, supervision, and the expectations of users.

## ROLES IN THE IMPLEMENTATION PROCESS

The implementation process must engage the energies and talents of all who have a stake in the new technology. Consequently, we consider the respective roles of top management, middle management, users and user representatives, and, where present, trade unions. We present evidence about the mechanisms that appear to be effective in bringing these stakeholders into the implementation for IT.

### Role of Top Management

The appropriate role for top management is a blend of providing central guidance and encouraging local initiative. Top management should provide a clear vision of the organization it wants and delineate the steps to the realization of that vision. The electronic conference agreed on the following specific guidelines for the role of top management:

> Set policy regarding where to introduce information technology and how to establish priorities for competing projects,
>
> Develop understanding of the capabilities and limitations of IT,
>
> Establish reasonable goals for IT systems,
>
> Exhibit a strong commitment to the successful introduction of IT,
>
> Communicate the corporate IT strategy to all employees.

The importance of reasonable expectations was confirmed in many of our studies. Consider, for example, the experience of a large construction firm represented at the electronic conference:

> Our firm has had many bad experiences in our search for an appropriate CAD system for our business. We have tried several times to develop a CAD system (begin-

ning as far back as 1975) only to find that vendors couldn't do anything close to what we had hoped they would. This had led us to be very gun-shy and hesitant to try new systems. I believe that if our senior management had "reasonable" expectations from the outset we would be much farther ahead than we are today.

## The Role of Middle Management

At the middle of the organization, we find the stakeholder group that is probably most crucial and, at the same time, most at risk of any group in today's organizations. Middle management is at the crossroads of the forces for change: the drive and leadership that come from the top of the organization and the involvement and initiative that must come from the bottom.

Middle management typically plays a key role in guiding an IT project from beginning to end. The entire project sequence is within its purvue and responsibility. Yet the impact of organizational change and technology can be to eliminate many levels of middle management. Some of the knowledge held at the middle levels of an organization can be "put into code." Moreover, smaller work forces require smaller supervisory structures.

For middle managers who survive, the requirement for technical know-how is substantially increased. "While we don't require an executive in the loop," observed one of our collaborators, "nevertheless we need middle management that is knowledgeable about the technical side of the operation." However, middle management often has a seriously deficient comprehension of IT. A kind of generation gap exists in many organizations, with younger professionals, often in the information systems departments, in possession of substantial background knowledge about IT to which older managers have had little or no exposure. Without special catch-up programs, middle managers, especially older ones, will be unable to participate in the interplay of important technical, business, and organizational decision making.

Several themes emerge from the experiences of different firms in dealing with the generation gap. First is top-management commitment and insistence on managers' IT proficiency. Special sessions for equivalent-level managers need to be supported by a small user group that can supplement more formal sessions with personal instruction. Sessions providing nonthreatening, hands-on experience can be most effective, and emphasis on developing a supportive organizational culture can reduce the psychological costs of IT inadequacies.

Another theme is introductory instruction focused on real problems—introduction that addresses situations of interest to managers and deals with material of relevance rather than abstract techniques. Training as a means to solve meaningful problems appears to be essential to quick acceptance.

Another approach to solving generation gap problems is to designate a proxy for the manager charged with passing IT information in both directions. This might be someone at the level of administrative assistant.

Generation gap problems are resolvable in most organizations. The widespread availability and organizational use of IT, coupled with management's own use and long-term commitment to it, can overcome most early problems. Some senior people may retire early, but such casualties are rare.

Generation gap problems were deemed sufficiently important during the electronic conference to spur participants to reach consensus on the following guidelines:

1. Encourage the HRM organization to develop a management information package to present the issue in a constructive way.
2. Develop self-taught packages that enable managers to become acclimated to the keyboard and PC in the privacy of their offices or homes.
3. Make available at quarterly executive sessions information modules that stress the ease of using IT.
4. Prepare management reviews of projects that facilitate the use of and stress the simplicity of IT (e.g., programmed situations providing hands-on opportunities that do not highlight managers' typing and PC skills).
5. Encourage employees who have a close relationship with managers to support their use of IT.
6. Include in senior executive, executive, and middle-management training courses electives participants can take to become familiar with IT without embarrassment. (No one likes to admit being unable to do something in the presence of peers who appear to be experts.)
7. Get key managers (who are not proficient with IT) involved in the testing and implementation of new technologies such as voice recognition.

## User Involvement

As the implementation of IT almost invariably requires customizing a system—what Shimada and MacDuffie (1986) refer to as "workers bringing wisdom to the machine—user participation can be a key facilitator. The first of two examples drawn from the electronic conference illustrates the difficulties associated with problem solving and the lack of requisite innovation that results when users are not involved in IT implementation.

The management information systems department of a large oil company had some very specific ideas about what hardware and software were appropriate for specific applications in the geology department. In "ramrodding" this new equipment and technology into the geology department, the MIS department reasoned that it was best equipped to decide what was needed to ensure standardization. The equipment that arrived, not surprisingly, went unused. The user group, knowing what it wanted, went through the back door and equipped itself with systems of its own choosing.

The installation of an MRP system in a large factory in a non-English-speaking country provides a more positive example of the importance of user participation. Middle management and vendor representatives proposed a rather straightforward application of a total manufacturing system for which software, albeit in an English-only form, was available. Strong worker resistance quickly brought the project to a stop. About ten years later, when native-language software had been developed for this application, the project again went forward, but this time with much better planning. The factory manager got involved by becoming familiar with the proposed technology, and workers this time were involved from the start. The result was a smoothly executed installation.

We take as a basic premise that users and other stakeholders should be involved to the maximum extent feasible in the design and implementation of IT. The question is not whether to have user involvement, but when and under what circumstances to have it and for what purposes.

The word *feasible* is significant. What makes sense in practice may be a different kind of participation from what is commonly advocated. When we presented the rationale for stakeholder involvement at a briefing session for sponsor representatives, an executive of a large company that had had considerable experience with IT remarked, in effect, "We have found that extensive participation leads to better implementation, but overall we suffer from a kind of incrementalism." His point was that involving all of the vested interests impeded the implementation of big changes; it infused projects with a series of compromises. User involvement may also be limited when a new system's design must be highly specified to make it interdependent with other systems. By contrast, more adaptation and customizing may be possible with newer, increasingly software-intensive technology.

Another negative aspect of user involvement brought to light by several of our case studies is the potential for incorporating too many bells and whistles. Allowing users to specify equipment features without realistic guidelines can set them up for raised expectations that are subsequently dashed when decision makers find it necessary to eliminate some of the desired options. Management can avoid this difficulty by establishing parameters for outcome specifications and boundaries for overall project cost and timetable.

Involving all eventual users is particularly difficult when implementation is to occur across multiple sites. The presence of a union that can represent its members in the early stages of design and testing can mitigate this difficulty. So can a task force or a working party that comprises representative users from all potential sites. We consider mechanisms for resolving these dilemmas below. But first we review some guidelines for user involvement developed by the electronic conference:

Senior management should initiate the IT implementation process.

Functional management should become involved immediately after senior management.

IT professionals should become involved when it is appropriate to begin technical discussions or when management education is needed.

Users should become involved early enough to build trust among themselves and to provide useful input to system design, but not as early as to make it appear that management does not know what it is doing. (This is highly organization-dependent.)

Before users are brought in, management should ask itself the following questions:

Are we ready to expand the group?

Are we clear on project objectives?

Do we have the right technological perspectives?

Have we considered possible organizational impacts?

## Enlisting Support from the Union

Where unions represent users, as they did in five of our six core cases (Kodak was the exception), technology cannot be introduced successfully without the support and cooperation of union leadership. Generally speaking, unions today do not oppose new technology. This is in contrast to earlier periods, when limitations were imposed by some craft unions. But neither do unions automatically support IT implementation. Their support, if forthcoming, derives from active involvement in the inception and implementation of the technology project.

The UAW, which was involved in our GM case, has historically been very supportive of new technology, seeing it as the driving force for improving productivity and thereby enabling wage increases. The union in the diesel engine plant study, for example, was very supportive of the introduction of advanced IT on the new engine line. In fact, hourly workers joined the design teams and visited engineers in the vendor organization to discuss modifications in the technology that would produce a better manufacturing system.

But even in this case, the introduction of IT did not proceed entirely without incident. For example, local union leadership found itself in a bind when a screening committee (composed of supervisors and union members) selecting the members for the new line found it necessary to bypass some senior workers. Most of the workers who were not deemed suitable decided not to press their cases, despite their seniority. But when six did file grievances, claiming that their seniority gave them the right to try out for the new positions, the union found it necessary to withdraw from the screening committee in order to represent them.

Throughout the 1980s, telephone industry management worked with the two major industry unions, the CWA and the IBEW, to develop a range of constructive approaches to facilitate the introduction of new technology. In many of the operating companies, and especially in AT&T, joint union-management training committees and funds were established to support programs designed to help workers fashion responses to new technology. AT&T, under a 1986 agreement, committed $7 million annually to the Alliance for Employee Growth and Development, a partnership with the CWA. But, although supportive at the policy and program level, unions have taken a more qualified stance toward specific projects. Villiger's (1988) study of new assignment technology at a telephone company noted, for example, that union response to the technology's downgrading of the plant assigner position was noninvolvement in early planning for the introduction of this technology. This response is not atypical. When new technology reduces numbers of workers and/or skill levels, unions often choose to stand aside (as the local UAW did at the diesel engine plant) to remain free to criticize and represent workers who want to challenge these consequences.

Creative approaches are needed that allow unions to become involved with new technology early on without forsaking their freedom to contest its consequences. Unions and companies need to understand the dilemmas inherent in this mixed-motive situation, and learn to differentiate their roles in order to reach an effective resolution.

The NTEU (National Treasury Employee Union), which represents workers involved with the IRS collection and examination systems, engages the subject of new technology primarily in terms of its consequences. For example, the union was successful in gaining assurances from management that for a certain period the use of personal computers by revenue agents would be strictly voluntary and that no reference to this technology could be made for purposes of performance appraisal.

## Initiating a Constructive Climate

We have found that companies that have been successful with new technology usually adopted an approach to union management relations and the design of human resource policies that aligns considerations at three levels: strategic planning, personnel policy, and work group relationships.

There exists at the strategic level an important opportunity for unions to become involved early with new technology. Boeing's relationship with the International Association of Machinists (IAM) is a good illustration of this. The union mounted a national campaign to establish a technology bill of rights in its dealings with major companies. In response, Boeing and the IAM local developed an approach to new technology that provides for regular union briefings on new developments in CAD/CAM, robotics, computer-integrated manufacturing, and composite materials. This periodic assessment, in turn, drives a joint union-management training committee that sponsors programs designed to help workers prepare for planned new technology.

In the telephone industry, this strategic-level meeting of the minds is occurring via common-interest forums (CIFs). The Pacific Bell CIF has been a major vehicle for jointly addressing employment security issues and for fostering a new "business partnership" between the parties (Kanter, 1988). Local CIFs have been established throughout the industry to deal with other matters, including the introduction of new technology.

At the level of policymaking that shapes employment relationships, unions may choose to become a party, qua partner, in all the areas we discussed earlier in the section on human resource policies. Attracting, deploying, and retaining a skilled work force are key subjects for union-management relations. Moreover, a range of policies and programs is necessary to create a climate generally favorable to the introduction of new technology. Employment security may relieve some of the anxiety associated with technological change, but many employees are just as anxious about their ability to operate in a new computer-based environment. This sets the stage for the development of training programs, for which the union is ideally situated to play a key role.

At the operating level, we come to the programs that many companies and unions are pursuing to improve relationships on a day-to-day basis. Some of the most powerful initiatives for creating a social context favorable to new technology are those that involve employees directly in problem-solving activities designed to improve the working environment and performance. Encouraged under such umbrella concepts as quality of work life (QWL), employee involvement (EI), participative management, and quality circles, these activities help develop the increased social and cognitive skills and the attitudes of self-confidence and self-reliance that will contribute to effective use of the new technology. Naturally, positive effects occur only when such activities reflect the genuine commitment of management to the spirit of participation and are sponsored by the union and accompanied by other supportive changes such as training. The value of establishing a pattern of employee participation as a prelude to the effective introduction of new technology was confirmed by the NRC study and has been demonstrated by the experiences of GM, Ford, AT&T, and Cummins Engine.

Our research has confirmed the importance of consistency and alignment across these three levels. The most effective change programs occur when parties on both sides think comprehensively and coherently about strategy, policies, and operating practices. A good illustration of this is contained in a case study of Allen-Bradley (Goldstein and Klein, 1987). Allen-Bradley wanted to manage a CIM facility inaugurated in April 1985 to manufacture contactors and relays, with innovative organizational and human resource practices. To encourage the company to place new technology in established unionized locations rather than at greenfield sites, UE officials agreed to give management carte blanche in designing the CIM work organization during the pilot stage of the project.

Decisions on such matters as job classifications and selection procedures were deferred until the system was moved from the development unit to the production department, where it was covered by the union contract. This arrangement illustrates another condition that is helpful to the introduction of new technology, namely, a willingness to give planners room to experiment and learn. In this instance, both management and the union could withhold judgment on what departures from conventional working arrangements—such as job classifications, flexibility of assignments, pay systems, and selection criteria and procedures—would be operationally desirable and politically acceptable. They could learn from experience the operational advantages of certain practices and workers' reactions to them before deciding which to institutionalize for the CIM system.

## Mechanisms for Make the Implementation Process Work

Our discussion of the implementation process thus far has underscored a series of tension points between leadership and local initiative, and between structure and participation. In this section we consider mechanisms for resolving these dilemmas and issues on a continuing basis. In terms of the framework set out at the beginning of this chapter, the emphasis here is on developing arrangements that achieve coordination throughout the implementation experience.

We first examine the roles of key individuals, such as project champions and coordinators. Subsequently, we consider organizational arrangements and processes, including task forces and user conferences.

## Project Leadership

In all of the case studies in which IT implementation met with some degree of success, a person or group of people performed the crucial function of leadership and facilitation. Different words are used to describe the role: champion, change agent, coach, coordinator, mediator.

In terms of the concepts we have been using to understand the implementation journey, this function combines elements of both direction and facilitation. The role is not authoritarian, though there is a need to mobilize many interests, but one that provides considerable energy and leadership.

What characterizes the individuals who perform this important function? Most often, they are a triple threat, being conversant in business and organizational matters as well as with technical information. Keen (1895) calls them "hybrids":

> People who are fluent about technology and at least literate about the business and organizational context, or vice versa. While many technical staffs may never be fully comfortable with the less structured context of the technology, there are very few IT managers who do not now accept that implementation must be a joint venture between technicians and "users." Many now reject the term "user" and substitute the term "client" or "customer." (p. 46)

To understand both the business and organizational sides of a project, a coordinator needs to be familiar with the installation that is taking place. In the telephone industry, for example, where new technology typically comes "in and down" from the laboratories and vendors, there needs to be a project champion who is conversant with the particular features of the region or division installing the application.

One might reasonably ask, given the key role played by these "Renaissance" types, where people with such skills are to be found in a typical company. It is indeed hard to find in one person the triple orientation described above. Consequently, many organizations employ a steering committee approach, assembling the various talents of the project champion in one forum. This is especially appropriate for systems that are complicated or where a team of middle managers is needed to cover all bases (as was the case with the Kodak and IRS installations).

Significantly, there appears to be a trend toward project leaders emerging from line organizations. Between the system specialist who has acquired some business and organizational acumen and the general manager who has become knowledgeable about IT, the latter profile is more often being selected for the leadership role as IT becomes more available and better understood. For example, in Polaroid, in the installation of a new data system in its purchasing department, the project champion was a former buyer who had also been part of the System Development Group.

In some cases, the leader is positioned quite high in the organization. Project advocates for the new assignment equipment in one of the telephone companies and for the "paperless factory" of a large defense contractor were at the vice-presidential level. These individuals not only grasped all three dimensions of implementation but also possessed substantial authority to move these very large, complicated projects through the transition experience.

## Task Forces

Another mechanism for facilitating the implementation process is the cross-function task force, a notion we have referred to several times already. Our electronic conference representative from the railroad industry observed that "if there are few people in management who understand IT, few functional managers who understand IT, and few IT 'pros' who understand the process, then it is probably efficient to establish teams to draw the best from everyone." In the Polaroid case study, a cross-cutting group called the Procurement Task Force met regularly to perform this function.

The notion of a "start-up team" that embodies cross-functional skills and provides the energy to move the operation ahead is similarly quite attractive. A start-up team developed by the IRS, on the basis of a good track record, was moved around to introduce the Service's new collection system in various offices throughout the country.

### The Stakeholder Conference

There is a special version of the task-force approach involving users and other stakeholders that appears to be especially effective in achieving the coordination and problem solving that are so essential to successful IT implementation. Kodak has developed such a workshop technique, which it applied to a dozen projects throughout 1987 and 1988. When a project is proposed to deal with a business problem, a facilitator works with the information systems project director and primary client to identify the "user set." This includes both direct users and other stakeholders, groups whose support is needed for the system's success. The sponsor then convenes a workshop in which users and stakeholders are asked to list all elements of the business problem the proposed system is supposed to solve. Participants brainstorm the task, sorting specific problems into four types:

1. Problems that can be solved by a good information system.
2. Problems that need to be solved to make an information system work, including organizational and administrative issues.
3. Other problems that must be solved in order to solve the business problems.
4. Related business problems.

Thus, before the IT system is further defined, members of the user set have agreed on the strategic importance of the business problem it is to resolve, carefully delineated the way improved information can contribute to the solution of the business problem, and identified the noninformation system changes that will be entailed. The sponsor then asks participants to develop plans for tackling all of the problems.

This procedure fosters a problem-centered rather than system-centered project emphasis. Kodak's Rick Herbert, who developed the technique, finds potential sponsors increasingly receptive to the workshop idea, which typically improves system design, moves consideration of organizational issues forward in the development cycle, and generates broad and informed support.

## PHASES IN THE INTRODUCTION OF IT

In this final section, we touch on several themes that are better presented in terms of the time sequence that begins with the adoption and continues through the system introduction, to the diffusion of a technology across an entire organization.

## The Adoption Phase

Normally, the decision to move forward with a specific installation of IT is made at the top of an organization. Being on the receiving end of so many proposals that float upward in the organization, top management may not fully understand the essence or the organizational requirements of a particular technology. In each of the following instances, management did not possess the competence to make intelligent decisions about proposed IT.

The management in one oil company, unless absolutely convinced that a technology would provide a clear competitive advantage, generally preferred the status quo. To promote a sophisticated system for doing geological analysis for likely sources of energy, the staff and functional groups involved adopted a Madison Avenue approach of trying to dazzle management with the exotics of the new technology:

> An overwhelming proportion of our output is high-technology solutions to old problems (where to drill for oil). Senior management tends to be comfortable with old ways of doing things. But to stay ahead of our competition, we had to adopt expensive and advanced IT systems. These were 3-D seismic processing and interpretation systems, which are very useful in obtaining competitive edge. Senior management accepts these systems in principle and indeed has approved capital funding for them. How could we use this stuff to beat our competition? This may all seem so obvious now, but it sure didn't seem obvious back then. We assumed high technology was all that was needed, but that is only half the battle. The output of our system is very dramatic and colorful and can easily be compared with the more cumbersome old way of doing things. It may seem cynical to use this "Madison Avenue" approach to get people on board, but senior management tends to be more interested in concepts and areas where we can seize competitive edge and not on the intricate details of how we actually do it. We truly had to "sell" them on the idea with a dramatic presentation.

Based on field investigations, Thomas (1988) has identified interesting dynamics of decisions to adopt IT by large corporations. He found that sponsors spend considerable time figuring out how to package proposals that are in line with what management wants to hear. For example, in one instance management had indicated a commitment to move ahead with robotics. Accordingly, various groups prepared proposals that exaggerated likely benefits in order to gain acceptance and allocation of funds for robotic installations.

The solution requires top management to avoid a fixation on the financial dimensions of proposals and to acquire sufficient understanding of a technology before moving ahead with it. In survey work on the outlook of CEOs with respect to IT, Schein (1989) found that less than half were conversant with the potential of IT.

The frequent exhortation for top management to become more sophisticated in the management of technology is very much to the point of how better decisions will be made at the adoption stage.

## The Introduction Phase

Our research indicates that successful start-ups usually have extra personnel on hand. We present several examples:

1. Kodak's Department 23 was experiencing a slack period and consequently had adequate time to devote to the introduction of a new MRP system.
2. One of the locations that performed very well in the start-up of the IRS collection system was Nashville, which had extra time available as a result of the default of the assigned vendor. While waiting for the new vendor to arrive with appropriate software and training packages, key Nashville personnel spent considerable time working through the design and plan for the system. As a result, the start-up proceeded much more smoothly than at other locations. An IRS evaluation report concluded that in those sites predominately staffed with new employees, district management should consider overstaffing. This will ease the transition through the learning curve. Optimum staffing levels can be achieved through attrition during the first year of operation.
3. Villiger (1988, pp. 2, 96) noted that the telephone company's start-up proceeded much more expeditiously in some of the rural areas than in urban areas. In urban areas, employees who were not going to continue with the assignment function immediately transferred to other work, and the selection of new staff proceeded slowly, overwhelming the new personnel, who "simply stopped learning and just tried to survive in a mess of backlog transactions, undebugged programs, and angry customers." In contrast, new staffing occurred more quickly in rural areas, and some of the former staff remained on hand during a transition period.

Many firms end up with overly lean staffing because so many proposals for new technology are justified on the basis of reduced head count. Also, many managers believe that extra personnel assigned to an operation will be difficult to remove when the operation is up to speed. Overstaffing, in contrast, recognizes start-up as a very complex and difficult experience that requires extra personnel. If the broader framework of human resource policies, such as employment security and retraining provisions, are supportive, management's actions can be based on the premise that it will not be difficult to shift workers to other operations at an appropriate time.

## Continuous Learning

A big challenge in any implementation is to keep moving up the acceleration or learning curve and to avoid a premature plateau. The basic notion is of a rolling agenda of problem solving and adaptation.

In the case of the IRS, a number of very important adaptations were made that helped move the process along. For example, in several locations the software was altered so that incoming calls would not go to the operator at the console but would be channeled into the research department. Another important modification was allowing operators to make notes on paper rather than requiring complete adherence to a paperless system and immediate entry of data (obtained over the phone) into the computer. This latter modification represented reincorporation of some of the procedures of the old system into the new system. Another change involved segregating cases by complexity, thereby enabling cases to be called up according to the experience level of the operators who were on-line.

A crisis developed in another of our core studies that halted progress until management did some serious reevaluation and instituted a basic change in approach. Villiger (1988) summarizes the essence of this crisis:

> The conversion started in 1985 and for the first several months 400,000 lines were shifted over to the computer system. We were using a conversion team and considerable support from the central office. In early 1986 the conversion group requested of top management a slower schedule and top management said to maintain the schedule. Within about another 6 months a crisis developed: learning curves had slowed and the improvement that should have taken 3 months was now taking 9 months. Finally management recognized the seriousness of the situation and stopped further conversion. During the next 6 months the software was changed and a new training vendor was recruited. All of the clerks had to be retrained for the altered software. An active communication program was started with a news bulletin and a hot-line system. Thus by mid-1987 the company was ready to move again with the conversion of the remaining lines over to the new computer system. Progress was much more forthcoming as a result of the changes that had been made.

## The Diffusion Phase

Firms vary considerably in terms of their ability to successfully diffuse IT. Buzzard (1988) reports that "one recurrent complaint from most companies was their inability to easily leverage successes across the corporation." Lewis (1988, p. 146), for example, found in other departments substantial fear and resistance to the introduction of a system similar to the one that had been introduced so successfully in Kodak's Department 23. Some employees in these departments feared job loss. Others expressed a fear of failure in undertaking something as ambitious as changing over the entire accounting system for their manufacturing center.

The limited diffusion of the MRPII model at Kodak was caused not just by fear of change but also by some bona fide issues of alignment, specifically the advantages of a separate database versus requirements for being able to transmit data via a network and common accounting framework to other parts of Kodak. Department 23, which has used the MRPII system so successfully, does not play a key role in the vertical integration of the company. Thus, a major debate continues within Kodak about the relative merits of a microsystem like that installed in Department 23 versus minicomputers that would enable databases to be combined and shared across major parts of the organization. Diffusion of IT clearly requires an analysis of the total picture, including business objectives and organizational arrangements.

The pilot approach, which can be a powerful methodology for diffusion, can encounter serious difficulties when the time arrives to roll out the tested installation to the remainder of an organization. The test can have the significant disadvantage of freezing the model, which the rest of the organization must then accept. To the extent that a pilot approach defines benefits for subsequent users (in effect objectifying knowledge—not just solutions to technical problems but also social arrangements), those who follow are on the receiving end of predetermined solutions. As a result, the innovative aspects of the pilot experience may become encapsulated—with the rest of the organization continuing to follow traditional methods.

Many firms have experienced these unanticipated difficulties when a particular program idea has been perfected and is about to be diffused to other locations. What happens is that the "deep learning" that occurred at the early sites becomes codified and buried in the system protocol. A number of companies that have put on a second shift, for example, found that the new workers do not understand the operation in the same way as the first-shift workers, who did the problem solving and had to learn as the operation climbed the acceleration curve.

Another disadvantage of having some locations go first is that it can create a permanent pattern of leaders and followers. The following quote makes this point at the level of individuals, but the phenomenon applies as much to organizational units:

> Initially users were selected at random to do geophysical interpretations on a very powerful Cray system. Soon they were using new jargon and accomplishing things that an ordinary interpreter was incapable of. When this group of people finished one project, we naturally selected them for additional projects because they were so far up the learning curve. We didn't have the time to get someone new up to speed. What happened was that different groups in this population became self-selecting, and now a wide gulf separates them. This problem is very current. My dilemma is how to fulfill organization objectives (get maximum product out in the shortest period of time) with the desirable goal of getting everyone trained on the new system.

Many organizations consequently minimize use of the pilot methodology, preferring to expose all potential users to the new technology as early as possible. Starting all locations down the implementation track as soon as possible encourages each to innovate in its own right and challenges the organization to find ways to diffuse these improvements through the remainder of the organization. This creates a learning system in which all parts of the organization contribute on an ongoing basis.

In any organization, the network through which diffusion takes place is the management structure. It is not surprising that in our best examples of large organizations embarked upon "wall-to-wall" implementations—specifically the IRS and the telephone companies—the success of the initial implementations and, more importantly, the effectiveness of diffusion were explained by the quality of management.

## SUMMARY AND CONCLUSIONS

Our cases illustrate how motivation, competence, and coordination among users are key conditions for ensuring full utilization of IT potential.

The motivation of users and support of other stakeholders such as their managers and union officials have always been necessary to avoid resistance to either the IT itself or the organizational changes required to fully utilize the new technology. But increasingly advanced IT, such as CIM systems, require higher levels of positive motivation on the part of operating personnel than the technologies they replace. For advanced IT systems that are made available to professionals (but whose use is not made mandatory), motivation is a key determinant in whether the IT tool is used and how sensibly it is employed.

User skills in operating IT tools and their knowledge about the basic tasks to which the tools are applied directly influence whether IT is appropriately applied and fully utilized. And the competence requirements are rising with many forms of advanced IT, especially informating technologies that augment rather than replace user judgment.

IT invariably alters the coordination requirements of the organization. Sometimes it integrates previously separate functions, relieving the need for special staff or middle management to provide coordination. But it often creates the need for tighter coordination among individuals within a unit or between units. For example, CIM systems create new coordination requirements, which in turn make team structures more appropriate.

The design of human systems and their management of the process of change will determine whether the newly required levels of motivation, competence, and coordination are achieved.

Top management can create a vision that helps planners coordinate the design of organizational structures and IT systems. They can create a motivational context—even before the IT system is adopted—in which planners can rely on users to pull the system into place. They can ensure that the company's human resource practices also are supportive for an IT-intensive workplace. Employment assurances and practices that complement such assurance—such as phased introduction of IT, redeployment of personnel, and retaining—often play a crucial role in creating the requisite motivation and competence for IT to work.

IT systems that upgrade the skill requirements usually have a positive motivational effect, but they also call for more rigorous selection criteria. Where seniority principles are observed, management and unions must be especially imaginative in generating the necessary competence while respecting the values of the social system. We observed several examples which showed that union and management can work together to integrate or balance these needs, for example, by providing candidates for the new positions with information and counseling.

Despite widespread recognition among IT planners that most systems are underutilized because of inadequate training, the deficiency is repeated in system implementation after implementation. In addition to providing adequate classroom and on-the-job training, management can promote the acquisition of skills by creating a climate supporting continuous learning in general and by encouraging experimentation with IT tools in particular.

Many other aspects of the way a system is managed once it is implemented can affect the levels of motivation and rates of learning of users. A particularly powerful factor is how supervisors use the extraordinary capability of IT systems to monitor the results and actions of their subordinates—whether supervisors use it primarily to control, to coach, or to encourage self-supervision.

The desirable organization designs and management patterns described above are more likely to occur when the implementation process itself is a good one. We have suggested many conditions that tend to make the process constructive—top management has realistic expectations; approval decisions are based on valid information and the sponsor's real rationale; middle management's concerns about becoming technically obsolete or displaced are addressed; users are involved in developing, selecting, introducing, and assessing the systems; union support is elicited and the union is informed, consulted, or engaged in joint decision making, depending on what is both desirable and politically feasible; and other groups that are stakeholders or possess special business, technical, or organizational expertise are tapped for their perspectives. Finally, of course, a key role is played by the leadership of the process. The other required conditions can only be ensured if the leadership grasps the interplay of the technical and social aspects of the IT system and their relationship to the business priorities the system is intended to serve.

## NOTES

1. We have relied heavily on the following theses and working papers: telephones, Morley (1987) and Villiger (1988); Internal Revenue Service, Chalykoff (1987) and Pentland (1989); Kodak, Lewis (1988); GM, Schwartz (1988).

2. Members of the electronic conference included Stephen Buzzard, Carolyn Corvi, Bruce Ellis, Jerry Heavin, John Hennessy Michael Henshaw, John McCarthy, James Strassen, K. P. Tang, and Carl Willis.

## REFERENCES

Buzzard, S. H. 1988. "An Analysis of the Factors That Influence Management of Information Technology in Multidivisional Companies." Master's Thesis, MIT Sloan School of Management.

Carroll, J., and C. Perin. 1988. "How Expectations about Microcomputers Influence Their Organizational Consequences." Management in the 1990s Working Paper 88-044.

Cebon, P. 1990. "This Missing Link: Organizational Behavior as a Key Element in Energy/ Environment Regulation, and University Energy Management." Master's Thesis in Technology and Policy, MIT.

Chalykoff, J. 1987. "Computer-Aided Performance of Employees in Large Volume Office Operations." Doctoral Dissertation, MIT Sloan School of Management.

Goldstein, S., and J. Klein. 1987. "Allen-Bradley." Harvard Business School case study.

Goodman, P., and T. Griffith. 1989. "Implementation of New Technology." Carnegie-Mellon working paper.

Goodman, P., and S. Miller. 1988. "Designing Effective Vendor Training through the Technological Lifecycle." Carnegie-Mellon working paper.

Kanter, R. M. 1988. "The New Alliance: How Strategic Partnerships Are Reshaping American Businesses." In Herbert Sawyer, ed., Business in the Contemporary World. Lanham, Md., University Press of America.

Keen, P.G.W. 1985. "Computers and Managerial Choice." Organization Dynamics 14, no. 2.

Krafick, J., and J. Womack. 1986. "Learning from NUMMI." MIT International Motor Vehicle Project, working paper.

Lewis, B. 1988. "Eastman Kodak's Implementation of Micro-Based Manufacturing Software in Decentralized Organizations: A Human Perspective." Master's Thesis, MIT Sloan School of Management.

Morley, M. P. 1987. "A Review of the Introduction and Implementation of an Automated Process." Master's Thesis, MIT Sloan School of Management.

National Research Council. 1986. Human Resource Practices for Implementing Advanced Manufacturing Technology. Washington, D.C.: National Academy Press.

Oscarsson, B., et al. 1988. "A New World of Work." Development Program, Stockholm.

Pentland, B. 1989. "Implementation of End User Computing in the Internal Revenue Service." Management in the 1990s Working Paper 89-069.

Schein, E. H. 1989. "The Role of the CEO in the Management of Change." Management in the 1990s Working Paper 89-075.

Schwartz, R. J. 1988. "Teamwork and Participation Management: Elements of Successful Implementation." Master's Thesis, MIT Sloan School of Management.

Shimada, H., and J. P. MacDuffie. 1986. "Industrial Relations and 'Humanware.'" MIT Sloan School of Management working paper.

Thomas, R. J. 1989. "The Politics of Technological Change: An Empirical Study." MIT Sloan School of Management working paper.

Villiger, D. 1988. "Information Technology, Human Resource Management, and Organizational Learning: A Case Study in Telecommunications." Management in the 1990s Working Paper 88-063.

Walton, R. E., and G. I. Susman. 1987. "People Policies for the New Machines." *Harvard Business Review* 2 (March–April): 98–106.

Walton, R. E. 1989. *Up and Running: Integrating Information Technology and the Organization.* Boston: Harvard Business School Press.

Zuboff, S. 1985. "Automated/Informate: The Two Faces of Intelligent Technology." *Organization Dynamics* (Autumn): 4–18.

Zuboff, S. 1988. *In the Age of the Smart Machine.* New York: Basic Books.

# Research Projects

## PROJECTS BEGUN IN PROGRAM YEAR 1984–85[1]

### The Strategic Use of Nonpermanent Employment Relationships (1)[2]

*Katherine G. Abraham, Formerly Assistant Professor of Management[3]*
This study was designed to examine the developing pattern of temporary, free-lance, and subcontract employment among white-collar workers. The initial goal was to perform a small number of case studies of software development and maintenance environments.

### Impact of Information Techologies on Communication in a High-Technology Organization (5)

*Thomas J. Allen, Gordon Y Billard Fund Professor of Management; Oscar Hauptman, Assistant Professor, Graduate School of Business Administration, Harvard University*
This study was designed to measure the impact of new ITs on communication patterns among technical professionals. Results also provided an understanding and allowed an assessment of the importance of communication for productivity in a software development environment.

### Negotiating Transactions in the Service Sector (1)

*Max H. Bazerman, Formerly Assistant Professor of Management*
This project was aimed at understanding the nature of the contracting process in the consulting industry. The working hypothesis was that negotiations involving service sector transactions are significantly more complex than the corresponding negotiations involving physical products.

### Information Technology and Strategic Opportunity (5)

*Robert I. Benjamin, Visiting Scientist; Michael S. Scott Morton, Jay W. Forrester Professor of Management; Diane D. Wilson, Principal Research Associate*
The working hypothesis of this project was that IT impacts the strategic options open to a firm. More IT allows more and better interconnection, facilitating integration

and structural change, resulting in higher productivity and better response to market needs. A small number of firms that have achieved payoff from the aggressive use of IT were examined.

## Group Decision Making (2)

*John S. Carroll, Professor of Behavioral and Policy Sciences;*
*Thomas W. Malone, Patrick J. McGovern Professor of*
*Information Systems*
The goal of this project was to establish a laboratory to study group decision making, focusing on fundamental issues of organization and management, later extending to groups in field settings. Such a laboratory would have offered a computer environment for group decision making allowing control over the group tasks, roles and incentives, communication within and between groups, and feedback. The small group analogue would have enabled the controlled study of IT's impact on communication availability, modality, and costs, and therefore on communication and group (organizational) structure.

## Expectations and the Impact of Microcomputers (4)

*John S. Carroll, Professor of Behavioral and Policy Sciences;*
*Constance Perin, Formerly Principal Research Associate*
This project studied the effects of microcomputers in large organizations, focusing on how expectations held by implementers, users, and managers shape workplace changes, communication patterns, and productivity. Initial research sites included two large corporations that introduced PCs into accounting functions. The project was extended using interviews, questionnaires, and on-site observation, to study the expectations of end users, their managers, and DP/IS managers.

## The Impact of Decision Support Technology on Organizations (1)

*John C. Henderson, Associate Professor of Management Science*
This research focused on how individuals and work groups use the decision support system technology to improve the effectiveness and efficiency of critical decisions. The first phase of the project was to develop a comparative productivity assessment model using the Data Envelopment Analysis approach.

## Managing Human Resources in an Environment of Changing Technology (5)

*Thomas A. Kochan, Professor of Industrial Relations;*
*Robert B. McKersie, Professor of Industrial Relations; Paul Osterman,*
*Associate Professor of Management; Lisa Lynch, Associate Professor*
*of Industrial Relations*
This study developed and tested models of the effects of introducing new ITs and changing human resource management practices under different environmental con-

ditions in relation to firm goals, employees, and society. The following issues were studied:

Changing organization structure and career path.

How productivity benefits vary by the character of the introduction process and managerial style.

Employment security.

Changes in work rules as a result of new technology.

## The Management of the Implementation of Multiple Technologies (1)

*Eliot Levinson, Formerly Visiting Scholar*
The introduction of multiple technologies intensifies the problems of management because (1) the technologies interact, and the manager is usually unfamiliar with them; and (2) once implemented, the technologies often demand that managerial practices be changed. Using case studies, this project sought to identify the key issues facing managers.

## Organizational Structures and Information Technology (5)

*Thomas W. Malone, Patrick J. McGovern Professor of Information Systems; Robert I. Benjamin, Visiting Scientist*
Dramatic improvements in the power and cost of IT in recent years have changed the constraints on how communication and coordination in organizations can occur. These changes may soon lead us across a threshold where new ways of organizing human activities become possible. This project involved developing theoretical models and performing empirical studies that help understand current organizational change and future possibilities.

## The Future of the Telecommunications System (5)

*W. Russell Neuman, Associate Professor of Political Science; Charles Jonscher, Vice President, Booz Allen & Hamilton, Formerly Lecturer; Marvin A. Sirbu, Jr., Associate Professor of Engineering and Public Policy, Carnegie-Mellon University*
This project focused on the network aspects of IT. In the days of the Bell monopoly, issues of data communications standards, interoffice and intercompany communications were fairly straightforward. The United States is, however, in the throes of a critical transition from a regulated to a partially regulated and partially competitive interconnected system. Decisions made now about the technical architecture and tariff structure of the network will have a critical influence on the dominant patterns of communications for the 1990s and beyond. Issues studied in this project included broadband ISDN, new video-based telecoms services, open network architecture, and the impacts of deregulation on the U.S. telecoms network.

## Technology and Organizational Structure (5)

*Michael J. Piore, Mitsui Professor in the Problems of Contemporary Technology; Michael S. Scott Morton, Jay W. Forrester Professor of Management*

This study examined the hypothesis that new technologies are improving the ability to gain economies of scale and shorten product life cycles, leading to looser, less hierarchical structures, more participative labor relationships, and more collaborative relationships between inside organizational units and outside subcontractors, customers, and competitors.

## The Adaptive Culture and the Adaptive Manager (2)

*Edgar H. Schein, Sloan Fellows Professor of Management*

This study investigated the adaptive system characterized at the macro level by the concept of "organizational culture" and at the micro level by the "established manager," the individual who has achieved success by learning one set of ways but must now or in the future switch to new ways. The research methodology was intensive interviewing and observation.

## Measuring the Impact of Information Systems on the Corporate Office (2)

*Michael E. Treacy, Formerly Assistant Professor of Management Science*

This project was the continuation of three projects already in progress, seeking to develop:

1. A causal model and reliable measures of users' satisfaction with information systems.
2. A typology of PC impacts on productivity.
3. Understanding of how and when end-user computing impacts firms' strategic objectives.

## Managing the Single Source (2)

*Gordon Walker, Associate Professor of Management, Wharton School Formerly Assistant Professor of Management, MIT*

This research focused on effective and efficient management of single-source relationships. A single source is a dedicated supplier with whom the buyer shares technological knowledge and capabilities. Although the research began with a study of single-source relationships in cross-section, studies of buyer and single-source contracting over time were sought for understanding the dynamics of relational effectiveness.

## Global Competitor Scanning in the Multinational Firm (5)

*D. Eleanor Westney, Mitsubishi Career Development Associate*
*Professor of International Management; Sumantra Ghoshal, Associate*
*Professor of Business Policy, INSEAD*
This project analyzed how multinational corporations use information technologies
and organizational design changes to enhance the competitive advantages derived
from internally processing and distributing—or adding value to—the external information they gather in their many environments. The project also explored how
enhanced scanning abilities can contribute to corporations' capacities for learning
across national boundaries.

## PROJECTS BEGUN IN PROGRAM YEAR 1985–86

## Managerial Innovation in the Context of
## Large-Scale Organizational Change (1)

*David G. Anderson, Formerly Assistant Professor of Management*
This research examined sources and diffusion patterns of manufacturing process
innovations in two large technology-based companies. A significant proportion of
these innovations involved advanced information systems and technologies. By
exploring the histories of many process innovations, this study sought to identify
individual, organizational, and technological factors affecting their initiation, implementation, and diffusion. In particular, the research aimed to identify how changes
in top-management goals and values affect process innovation at lower levels of the
organization.

## Working with Information Technology at Both Office and Home:
## Organizational and Individual Benefits and Concerns (4)

*Lotte L. Bailyn, Professor of Organizational Psychology and*
*Management; Constance Perin, Formerly Principal Research Associate*
This project explored the issues involved in an office-home pattern of work, where
professional, managerial, and technical employees work at home for some part of the
regular work week but remain accessible via IT. The project focused on two issues:
(1) the reasons why the office-home pattern is not more widespread, and (2) the relationships between IT and the design, supervision, and coordination of work processes
and their implications for organizational innovation and individual productivity.

## Managerial Assumptions, Perceptions of Uncertainty,
## and Their Organizational and Information Systems
## Consequences (3)

*John C. Henderson, Associate Professor of Management Science;*
*Constance Perin, Formerly Principal Research Associate*
This study examined managerial resourcing for patterns of operational and world-
view assumptions in order to analyze their relationship to the ways in which man-

agers interpret, make sense of, and act to cope with the ambiguities and complexities of their environments.

## Managing Cooperating Experts: Effective IS Design (4)

*John C. Henderson, Associate Professor of Management Science*
This project examined impacts of IT on key processes used to build information systems and on structural relations among experts involved in design and problem-solving activities. Results help explain how computer-aided design technology affects the performance of a design team. In addition, the research provides a basis to assess the potential for developing group decision support systems technology.

## Pricing Residence Local Telecommunications Service (1)

*Charles Jonscher, Vice President, Booz Allen & Hamilton, Formerly Lecturer; Franck Scibilia, Formerly Research Assistant*
This project involved determining switching costs in the telecom local exchange. The study attempted to develop an economic model with fixed per line, per call, and per minute components, providing a basis for an economically efficient cost-based pricing structure.

## The Productivity of Information Technology Capital (4)

*Gary W. Loveman, Assistant Professor of Management, Harvard Business School, Formerly Research Assistant, MIT Department of Economics; Ernst R. Berndt, Professor of Applied Economics*
This project used data on a large sample of firms over several years to estimate econometrically the productivity of IT capital. Production functions were estimated in which IT capital entered explicitly as an input, and the results suggest how IT's contribution to sales compares with competing inputs and whether IT's current performance stems form under- or overinvestment. Moreover, results from stratified samples indicate how the productivity of IT capital varies according to various firm criteria, such as relative intensity of IT investment, industry, profitability, and so on. These unique empirical findings were also used to evaluate the existing organization theory and MIS literature. Finally, the study included a survey of 1990s sponsor organizations to learn how they make and evaluate IT investments.

## Intelligent Information Sharing Systems (4)

*Thomas W. Malone, Patrick J. McGovern Professor of Information Systems*
This project involved developing and studying the use of an intelligent system called the Information Lens, for supporting organizational information sharing and coordination. The project explored the power of expert systems for helping exploit semi-structured, qualitative information (electronic mail, reports, and forms) in organi-

zations. For example, Lens will help users find useful or interesting electronic mail messages in a large pool of less important messages. Possible system applications include helping top managers and staff discover patterns in field intelligence reports, helping different project team members coordinate work, and helping to find quickly the people in a large organization who have answers to specialized questions. Later work involved pilot implementation in two user organizations.

## The Timing of Standardization (1)

*Garth Saloner, Professor of Management and Economics*
This two-part project studied standardization from an economic perspective. The first part examined the optimal timing of standardization and investigated what market structures are likely to make the best decisions regarding standardization timing. The second part investigated the role of dominant firms in the process and explored whether the strategic interactions between rival firms can result in the use of standardization as a strategic weapon.

## Managing the Locus of Innovation (2)

*Eric von Hippel, Professor of Management; Diane D. Wilson, Principal Research Associate*
Evidence from some industries suggests that users, material suppliers, government agencies, universities, and others often are the sources of innovation and that this "functional" source of innovation can often be predicted in terms of innovators' relative expectations of economic benefit. These findings have opened the way for examining how innovation can be managed as a process distributed across these organizational units. The research focused on improving understanding of how firms manage this distributed innovation process and the relationships by which they shift loci of innovation. Managing such a process requires that the traditional views about the organizational boundaries of such relationships be revised.

## PROJECTS BEGUN IN PROGRAM YEAR 1986–87

## A Preliminary Exploration of Measures of Information Technology Capital in U.S. Two-Digit Manufacturing Industries, 1949–1983 (1)

*Ernst R. Berndt, Professor of Applied Economics*
This study explored the procedures used by the U.S. Department of Commerce, Bureau of Economic Analysis, in constructing captial stocks for IT and then used alternative estimates to begin addressing such questions as (1) What has been the growth rate of IT capital, and how has this compared with growth in other types of capital? (2) How has this growth of IT capital correlated with growth in labor and multifactor productivity? (3) Can these data be used to construct a model of diffusion?

## The Multinational Enterprise in the Information Age: Three Perspectives (2)

*Donald R. Lessard, Professor of International Management; Thomas A. Poynter, Formerly Visiting Associate Professor of International Management; D. Eleanor Westney, Mitsubishi Career Development Associate Professor of International Management*

This project examined strategies, structures, and processes for enhancing linkages among geographically dispersed activities within the multinational firm, increasing responsiveness to a turbulent economy, and surmounting long-standing intrafirm contradictions in effectively implementing competitive strategies. These issues were addressed in three contexts: (1) an activity that cuts across functional and geographic boundaries (managing exchange rate volatility), (2) the organizational linkage between parent firm and subsidiaries given a particular multinational strategy, and (3) a geographic context of strategic importance to the multinational firm (managing R&D subsidiaries in Japan).

## The Research Program on Communications Policy (2)

*W. Russell Neuman, Associate Professor of Political Science*

The Research Program on Communications Policy coordinates research and teaching in telecommunications at MIT. The emphasis is on the interaction of evolving information and telecommunications technologies with the regulatory environment. This program produces a separate series of working papers and a number of research seminars each year.

## Executive Managements' Implicit and Explicit Assumptions About Information Technology and Its Role in Their Organizations (3)

*Edgar H. Schein, Sloan Fellows Professor of Management; Diane D. Wilson, Principal Research Associate*

During the year, eighty chief executive officers were interviewed in depth to determine their implicit assumptions about IT as it may impact their own organizations and their own lives. The next step was to discover the antecedents and consequences of each CEO's assumptions. In particular, are the executive's assumptions congruent with his or her goals and strategies? Are these assumptions widely shared? And does such consensus (or lack thereof) impact the implementation of IT?

## Competitive Advantage Through Information Technology (3)

*N. Venkatraman, Richard S. Leghorn Career Development Associate Professor of Management*

This study consisted of two closely related subprojects. The first sought to answer the question of whether there is a superior level of strategic advantage (reduced cost of operations, increased market share, enhanced profits, etc.) available through IT that cannot be realized through alternative means. This question was addressed in the context of insurance agents. The second subproject sought to understand the shifts in strategic capabilities necessary to compete in markets altered by a technological discontinuity. The setting for the second subproject was the market for individual income tax preparation services.

## PROJECTS BEGUN IN PROGRAM YEAR 1987–88

### Computer-Mediated Communication in Small Organizations (2)

*Emanuele Invernizzi and Gaetano Luberto, University of Calabria, Italy, Visiting Scholars*
Most studies of computer-mediated communication (CMC) have examined large geographically dispersed organizations. This project addressed two questions: (1) Are the same advantages and disadvantages of CMC seen in small and large organizations? (2) Do small organizations require a different implementation strategy for CMC? The answers to these questions were being pursued through two case studies.

### The Effects of Organizational Structure on Strategic Alliance Success (2)

*Diane D. Wilson, Principal Research Associate*
A major factor in the growth and structure of the IT industry is expected to be the success of the strategic alliances being formed today between manufacturers, suppliers, and users of software, computers, and telecommunications equipment. A database of information industry alliances formed over the past five years has been created. Work was done to develop histories of alliances in two companies. The central question being asked was: How does a strategic alliance solve the structural problem of innovation?

## NOTES

1. Program years were September through the following August.

2. The number appearing in parentheses at the end of the project title indicates the number of years the project was worked. When a project title or description changed during its lifetime, the most recent title and abstract are listed.

3. Unless otherwise noted, all researchers are affiliated with the MIT Sloan School of Management.

# APPENDIX B

# Working Papers

| No. | Title | Author(s) | Date |
|---|---|---|---|
| 85-001 | Management in the 1990s Mission Statement | — | 7/85 |
| 85-002 | Sponsors' Vision | — | 5/85 (rev. 1/86) |
| 85-003 | Management in the 1990s Program Research Themes and Request for Proposals, Fall 1985 | — | 8/85 |
| 85-004 | A Survey of Current Trends in the Use of Executive Support Systems | DeLong, Rockart | 11/84 |
| 85-005 | Expert Systems and Expert Support Systems: The Next Challenge for Management | Luconi, Malone, Scott Morton | 9/85 |
| 85-006 | Future Directions in DSS Technology | Treacy | 1/85 |
| 85-007 | Information Technology and Corporate Strategy: A Research Perspective | Bakos, Treacy | 3/85 (rev. 3/86) |
| 85-008 | Supporting Senior Executives' Models for Planning and Control | Treacy | 6/85 |
| 85-009 | Designing Organizational Interfaces | Malone | 9/85 |
| 85-010 | Out of print; superseded by 86-025 | — | — |

| *No.* | *Title* | *Author(s)* | *Date* |
|---|---|---|---|
| 85-011 | Organizational Structure and Technology: Elements of a Formal Theory | Malone | 8/85 |
| 85-012 | Computer Support for Organizations: Toward an Organizational Science | Malone | 9/85 |
| 85-013 | Influence of Task Type on the Relation between Communication and Performance | Hauptman | 5/85 |
| 85-014 | Implications of Changes in Information Technology for Corporate Strategy | Scott Morton, Rockart | 1/83 (rev. 3/84) |
| 86-015 | Indentifying the Attributes of a Successful Executive Support System Implementation | DeLong, Rockart | 2/86 |
| 86-016 | Out of print; superseded by 86-025 | — | — |
| 86-017 | Information Technology, Integration, and Organizational Change | Benjamin, Scott Morton | 4/86 |
| 86-018 | Electronic Markets and Electronic Hierarchies: Effects of Information Technology on Market Structure and Corporate Strategy | Benjamin, Malone, Yates | 4/86 |
| 86-019 | Toward a Cumulative Tradition of Research on Information Technology as a Strategic Business Factor | Treacy | 4/86 |
| 86-020 | Executive Support Systems and the Nature of Executive Work | Rockart, DeLong | 4/86 |

| No. | Title | Author(s) | Date |
|-----|-------|-----------|------|
| 86-021 | Electronic Organization and Expert Networks: Beyond Electronic Mail and Computer Conferencing | Stevens | 5/86 |
| 86-022 | Out of print; superseded by 87-032 | — | — |
| 86-023 | Economic Issues in Standardization | Farrell, Saloner | 10/85 |
| 86-024 | Floor Lay-out Design for Effective Software Production: Applying the Implications from the Optimal Communication Pattern of a Software Project Team | Hauptman | 6/86 |
| 86-025 | Intelligent Information Sharing Systems | Malone, Grant, Turbak, Brobst, Cohen | 11/86 |
| 86-026 | Semi-Structured Messages Are Surprisingly Useful for Computer-Supported Coordination | Malone, Grant, Lai, Rao, Rosenblitt | 11/86 |
| 86-027 | Cognitive Science and Organizational Design: A Case Study of Computer Conferencing | Crowston, Malone, Lin | 10/86 |
| 86-028 | Stategy Formulation Methodologies | Scott Morton | 11/86 |
| 86-029 | Some Thoughts on the Information Technology Revolution in Standard Oil | Horton | 11/86 |
| 86-030 | The Value-Added of Strategic IS Planning: Understanding Consistency, Validity, and IS Markets | Henderson, Sifonis | 11/86 |

| No. | Title | Author(s) | Date |
|---|---|---|---|
| 86-031 | A Common Agenda for an Uncommon Future: Address to the Sloan School of Management | Whitmore | 11/86 |
| 87-032 | Managing the Data Resource: A Contingency Perspective | Goodhue, Quillard, Rockart | 2/87 |
| 87-033 | Information Technology in Marketing | Little | 2/87 |
| 87-034 | Finding Synergy between Decision Support Systems and Expert Systems Research | Henderson | 3/87 |
| 87-035 | Data Envelopment Analysis for Managerial Control and Diagnosis | Epstein, Henderson | 5/87 |
| 87-036 | Managing the IS Design Environment: A Research Framework | Henderson | 5/87 |
| 87-037 | Freeing Work from the Constraints of Location and Time: An Analysis Based on Data from the United Kingdom | Bailyn | 6/87 |
| 87-038 | The Influence of Communication Technologies on Organizational Structure: A Conceptual Model for Future Research | Hauptman, Allen | 5/87 |
| 87-039 | The Line Takes the Leadership | Rockart | 8/87 |
| 87-040 | Information Technology and Work Organization | Crowston, Malone | 10/87 |
| 88-041 | Out of print; superseded by 88-055. | — | — |

| No. | Title | Author(s) | Date |
|---|---|---|---|
| 88-042 | The Realities of Electronic Data Interchange: How Much Competitive Advantage? | Benjamin DeLong, Scott Morton | 1/88 |
| 88-043 | Determinants of Employees' Affective Response to the Use of Information Technology in Monitoring Performance | Chalykoff | 2/88 |
| 88-044 | How Expectations about Microcomputers Influence Their Organizational Consequences | Carroll, Perin | 4/88 |
| 88-045 | Toward the Perfect Workplace? The Experience of Home-Based Systems Developers | Bailyn | 3/88 |
| 88-046 | The Impact of Technological Change on Employment Structure in Telecommunications: Whatever Happened to the Wichita Lineman? | Lynch, Osterman | 4/88 (rev. 9/88) |
| 88-047 | The Competitor Intelligence Function in the Very Large-Scale Organization: Assessments and Uses | Westney, Ghoshal | 5/88 |
| 88-048 | Adding Value in an Information Function | Westney, Ghoshal | 5/88 |
| 88-049 | Compatibility Standards and the Market for Telecommunications Services | Besen, Saloner | 5/88 |
| 88-050 | Assessing IT Performance: What the Experts Say | Wilson | 6/88 |

| No. | Title | Author(s) | Date |
|---|---|---|---|
| 88-051 | The Moral Fabric of the Office: Organizational Habits vs. High-Tech Options for Work Schedule Flexibilities | Perin | 6/88 |
| 88-052 | Employment Security at DEC: Sustaining Values amid Environmental Change | Kockan, MacDuffie, Osterman | 6/88 |
| 88-053 | An Economic Study of the Information Technology Revolution | Jonscher | 6/88 |
| 88-054 | An Assessment of the Productivity Impact of Information Technologies | Loveman | 8/88 |
| 88-055 | Involvement as a Predictor of Performance in I/S Planning and Design | Henderson | 8/88 |
| 88-056 | Planning and Managing Change | Schein | 8/88 (rev. 10/88) |
| 88-057 | Information Technology: From Impact on to Support for Organizational Design | Invernizzi | 9/88 |
| 88-058 | Information Technology and the New Organization: Towards More Effective Management of Interdependence | Rockart, Short | 9/88 |
| 88-059 | Dimensions of I/S Planning and Design Technology | Henderson, Cooprider | 9/88 |
| 88-060 | Issues of Gender in Technical Work | Bailyn | 10/88 |
| 88-061 | More Than Just a Communication System: Diversity in the Use of Electronic Mail | Mackay | 10/88 |

| No. | Title | Author(s) | Date |
|-----|-------|-----------|------|
| 88-062 | Managing New Technology and Labor Relations: An Opportunity for Mutual Influence | McKersie, Walton | 10/88 |
| 88-063 | Information Technology, Human Resource Management, and Organizational Learning: A Case Study in Telecommunications | Villiger | 10/88 |
| 88-064 | Innovative Cultures and Organizations | Schein | 11/88 |
| 89-065 | Computer-Aided Monitoring: Its Influence on Employee Job Satisfaction and Turnover | Chalykoff, Kochan | 1/89 |
| 89-066 | Partially Shared Views: A Scheme for Communicating among Groups That Use Different Type Hierarchies | Lee, Malone | 3/88 |
| 89-067 | What Is Coordination Theory? | Malone | 2/88 |
| 89-068 | Joint Ventures in the Information Technology Sector: An Assessment of Strategies and Effectiveness | Koh, Venkatraman | 12/88 |
| 89-069 | Implementation of End User Computing in the Internal Revenue Service | Pentland | 3/89 |
| 89-070 | A Process Model of Strategic Alliance Formation in Firms in the Information Technology Industry | Wilson | 3/89 |
| 89-071 | Object Lens: A Spreadsheet for Cooperative Work | Lai, Malone, Yu | 9/88 |

| No. | Title | Author(s) | Date |
|---|---|---|---|
| 89-072 | Electronic Integration and Strategic Advantage: A Quasi-Experimental Study in the Insurance Industry | Venkatraman, Zaheer | 4/89 |
| 89-073 | Electronic Mail and Organizational Cooperation: A Case Study | Invernizzi, Luberto | 6/89 |
| 89-074 | Cotechnology for the Global 90s | Stevens | 7/89 |
| 89-075 | The Role of the CEO in the Management of Change: The Case of Information Technology | Schein | 8/89 |
| 89-076 | Strategic Alignment: A Framework for Strategic Information Technology Management | Henderson, Venkatraman | 8/89 |
| 89-077 | Strategic Alignment: A Process Model for Integrating Information Technology and Business Strategies | Henderson, Venkatraman | 10/89 |
| 89-078 | Building and Sustaining Partnership between Line and I/S Managers | Henderson | 9/89 |
| 90-079 | Corporate Reform in American Manufacturing and the Challenge to Economic Theory | Piore | 1/89 |
| 90-080 | Strategies for Electronic Integration: Lessons from Electronic Filing of Tax-Returns | Venkatraman, Kambil | 3/90 |

# Application Process for Exploitability and Interrelatedness

## K. HUGH MACDONALD

In our experience we have found the Interrelatedness/Exploitability Framework to be helpful in understanding the business environment and the trends applying within the business environment. In addition, the various versions of the framework provide checklists of the generic strategies that an organization should be considering and the threats that need to be understood and monitored. The framework can be applied at an industry level, at the level of the individual organization, and as a useful benchmark for comparisons with competitors. In some cases, it may also be appropriate to use the framework to understand the behavior, strategies, and threats faced by suppliers and customers. A simple three-phase approach is useful.

## PHASE 1. INFORMATION COLLECTION

The level of detail required depends on the the complexity of the situation and the degree to which a deep understanding of the position of the organization and its competitors within an industry is helpful for the review of strategies and threats. The information to be collected is essentially the same as that required for any strategy review. The following is an abbreviated checklist:

1. Environment and industry information
   Industry structure and market shares
   Historical and projected changes in industry structure
   Industry IT initiatives
   Industry standards initiatives
2. Customer and supplier information
   Customer and supplier rivalry assessment
   Assessment of customer and supplier power
   Customer and supplier uses of IT and maturity of application
   Customer standards initiatives

Customer and supplier associations and interests

New pressures on customers or suppliers from new market entrants or alternative/substitute products

3. Competitive information

Competitive investment strategies

Organization structure scale and history

Resource assignments

Participation in standards activities and "industry clubs"

Cost/focus/differentiation issues

Main strengths and vulnerabilities

4. Organization information historical and future current investments

Structure and resourcing

Relationships with competitors

Prime business strategies

Cost/focus/differentiation assessment

Perceived strengths, vulnerabilities, and risks

We have found it generally preferable to establish, for each of the information sections, a series of two or three pages of "bullet points," rather than a mass of text. If "bullets" need further discussion, then backup information of finer granularity should be available.

## PHASE 2.  POSITIONING PROCESS

In this phase the attributes of the industry, the organization, the competitors, and key customers (if these are a sufficiently homogeneous group) need to be reviewed. Using the Attributes Framework (Figure 6-2), the exploitability and interrelatedness positioning (i.e., the quadrant occupied) should be established "today." The current positioning is the most important and must be determined first.

Having determined current positioning, a historical review should be undertaken to determine whether the position has changed over, say, the last five or ten years (or even shorter periods). The purpose is to establish whether the organization is changing its position in the framework and whether these changes are established or have recently occurred.

An attempt should then be made to predict the "drift" of the industry, and customers and major competitors, with a view to spotting trends.

## PHASE 3.  STRATEGIES, THREATS, AND ANALYSIS

The Strategies and Threats Frameworks (Figures 6-3 and 6-4) provide a series of clues about the generic strategies that should be pursued and the threats to which the organization is vulnerable. This analysis should be completed for the organization itself, competitors, and significant customer groupings.

At this stage it may be necessary to revisit the question of future positioning in the framework, since it may be determined that certain strategies that are "required" are unachievable or unaffordable. Consequently, some alternative positioning may be needed. In particular, the impacts and feasibility of position protection and desired changes must be clinically addressed. A typical review window might be three to five years.

We have found the most valuable part of this stage derives from an exploration of the reasons for differences between the positioning and the movements of the organization itself, compared with the industry as a whole and key competitors. This analysis serves to focus on options that an organization may have to foster interrelatedness, or the need to build associations among competitors to improve market coherence, or the requirement to erect barriers to the disadvantage of particular competitors.

By comparing strategies and positioning within the framework of different players within an industry, we have found that a more realistic assessment of threats can be derived and the "signals" identified that indicate the emergence of significant threats. By an exploration of the pressures facing customers and the attitudes and likely strategies pursued by major competitors, a general view of projected customer and market changes can be derived.

Our experience suggests that the results of such an exploration will yield the strategies and threats that will become inputs to the Strategic Alignment Process described in Appendix E.

# APPENDIX D

# The Value Process Model

## K. HUGH MACDONALD

This appendix presents our extension of the value chain concept. We have found this to be a particularly useful tool in the assessment of IT-induced business process redesign, as discussed in Chapter 5 and Chapter 6.

## VALUE CHAINS, VALUE SYSTEMS, AND VALUE PROCESSES

The basic concepts of value chains and value systems are well known (Porter, 1985). Value chains provide a representation of the internal operations and costs of an organization, and a value system is a representation of the movement of goods and services from the sources of raw materials through to the "final" consumer. Frequently the intention is to represent the progressive addition of value as goods and services flow between and through organizations.

Value chain (and value system) diagrams are frequently used to illustrate the transformations that have taken place in organizations. But many practical problems arise when attempting to develop value chains for an organization and then using the value chains as the basis for strategic review and business process redesign. The concept is simple, but the application is difficult, not because the concept is weak but because the available information seldom exists in the required format, and business processes are often poorly documented, or not explicit, or so entrenched that complexity is hidden in the heads of the workers and managers.

As a generalization, processes that operate at an organization's boundary or relate to costs (or cost control) are usually well documented, and this formalization has been assisted by the use of IT systems. Processes that are concerned with balancing the organization, shifting focus or changing direction, and generally associated with innovation in the broadest sense, tend to be "softer." Even where these processes are apparently well established, it is often the case that they legitimize decisions taken less formally.

The traditional value chain approach, described in Porter's *Competitive Advantage,* focuses on costs. These can be very illuminating, but the accumulation of costs in the various boxes in the value chain diagram may reflect presuppositions regarding the structuring of activities and hence the processes the organization uses. Having accumulated costs in an assumed (process) structure, it is extremely difficult to decompose the value chain to show higher activity granularity, as may be necessary if any major restructuring is to be considered, particularly of business processes.

We have found a "Value Process Model" to be useful. This provides a picture of what is actually going on within an organization. This is a marriage of a value chain and an O&M (organization and methods) flow diagram that some mature readers may remember. Such a representation combines business and operations processes, supported by costs. This can be constructively examined against the background of changed circumstances that may now (or in the future) apply and be contrasted with equivalent Value Process Models for competitors, with a greenfield view that might apply if the organization were a new business, with the "ideal situation that could apply after a fire," and other alternatives. When compared with equivalent diagrams for suppliers and customers, it can highlight opportunities for interorganizational functional integration and provide for informed exploration of the changes that might apply inside the organization and in customers/suppliers if this integration were to occur. Noncompetitive Value Process Models provide very informative benchmarks.

In order to consider business process redesign (level 3), an organization's own internal Value Process Model is necessary. To consider business network redesign (level 4) requires an understanding of the external value process, the value system, as a minimum. This analysis can be much more productive if Value Process Models can be constructed for suppliers and customers. These will allow the potential for off-loading or absorbing of activities or functions to or from suppliers or customers. This may provide cost-avoidance opportunities, or service enhancement, or improved binding or biasing of decisions. The infiltration of supplier or customer value processes can be part of a strategy aimed at the development of binding between the organization and other members of the value system of which it is a member.

It is difficult to develop Value Process Models for customers and suppliers at anything like the same level of detail and accuracy as is possible for the organization itself. However, as information about suppliers and customers is obtained such that Value Process Models can be developed, the organization has acquired critical knowledge of the value system and hence is in a better position to identify the opportunities that derive from integration and infiltration.

Knowledge of the value system of competitors is useful:

1. To provide part of the basis for benchmarking the performance of competitors against the organization's performance and understanding some of the differences that appear.
2. To provide a simple assessment of the threats of changes by competitors of their value systems, or the probable impact that the organization's strategies may have on competitors' value systems.

Understanding a competitor's Value Process Models can help with a constructive comparison between the two organizations. It also allows an assessment of the potential for change of a Value Process Model possessed by the competitor and the recognition of threats to which the organization is susceptible because of strengths that are recognized in the competitor's organization and processes. It is *not* suggested that imitation be attempted—this may be worth considering, but processes are dependent on culture, and, although a competitor's processes may appear to be worth imitating, the organization's culture may make this infeasible.

A knowledge of the Value Process Models for some similar but noncompetitive organizations is particularly useful for benchmarking purposes. The comments on imitation above apply equally here.

## DEVELOPING THE ORGANIZATION'S VALUE PROCESS MODEL

The objective is to produce a simple model (a diagrammatic representation, supported by some essential explanatory test, definitions, and some numbers) that reflects the flow of activities involved in the business of the organization. The purpose of this model is to record what goes on and the costs of this, rather than just reflect the consequences of what is going on. The model be activity-oriented. The eventual intention is to develop a new model that reflects what *should* go on.

The approach suggested by Porter for developing a value chain does represent a starting point. The basic "powerhouse" of the organization needs to be identified and decomposed, at least to the levels of inbound logistics, operations, outbound logistics, sales and marketing, and service. In practice, some types of industries, particularly government and service industries, do not easily relate to these headings, but with imagination the principles can be applied. Supporting process elements should at least include human resource management, technology development, and firm infrastructure. All these headings represent only a starting point and no more—as the development of the Value Process Model proceeds, it may be more appropriate to consider different headings, which should reflect the terminology with which the organization is familiar.

The Value Process Model must be a true reflection of the process flows that occur within an organization, with process including both operations (such as design, manufacturing, assembly, etc.) and administration (such as purchasing, invoicing, investment planning, etc.), with supporting information. The model must reflect an appropriate level of granularity such that the major process elements are all visible.

The minimum size of a process element depends on the organization, the nature of the business, and the scale of operation. Experience suggests that the level of required detail resolves itself, although inevitably too much detail is developed at first. The fact that production depends on feeder plants, or that major subassemblies are produced as a discrete activity in one plant before being sent to another plant or to another part of a main plant, are relevant process facts.

The first level of detail can be satisfied by imagining the problem of explaining to a stranger how the organization operates—but it is stressed that what is needed is an explanation of how the organization works and not how it is structured or organized or what the costs are perceived or imagined to be. The model should support the structure, but it is still useful if it does not.

The best practical approach is a top-down (hierarchical) one. Start with a high-level picture, with fifteen to thirty operation boxes, and build up more detail as this is evidently necessary to provide a sound explanation.

There is no point in prematurely developing the granularity of the Value Process

Model to a point that it cannot be subject to further decomposition since this will inevitably generate information overload and take far too long anyway. Initially, all the main process elements should be identified and supported by some understanding of what the decomposition of each element may imply. The interrelationship and interdependencies between the elements must be understood and reflected in the model.

As the Value Process Model is used, it may become necessary to develop finer granularity in parts. If changes are proposed (including process content, decentralization, structure, integration, repositioning, distribution, termination, etc.), then the next level of granularity should be developed and the implications of the changes checked to ensure that the integrity of the overall Value Process Model is not compromised.

Having constructed a Value Process Model, probably in the form of a flow-chart, an attempt should be made to compress it into a linear format. The ideal situation is a series of overlapping and interconnected bar charts showing the primary powerhouse operations and processes, development, administration and control activities, and so on. The fact that the first-level Value Process Model cannot readily be reflected in such a picture should be no cause for concern. It is more important to construct a Value Process Model than to construct one according to some rigorous format rules.

## VALUE PROCESS COSTS

Having created the process elements, some numerical information is needed to (1) identify fruitful areas for attack, and (2) allow for measurement of the effects of change. Basically, the numbers needed are costs, but it cannot be overemphasized that what is needed is information that illustrates what is happening, rather than "perfect" (incomprehensible?) numbers that satisfy tax requirements or professional accounting or reporting standards. The numbers are those that should be used for making critical decisions about how to run the business—they are not numbers that will necessarily be visible to the shareholders or any other external group.

There appear to be five main areas of costs that should be identified for process elements. It may be desirable to have the cost in each area subdivided, as indicated in the comments below.

### Investments

This covers both real and virtual capital. Real capital expenditures are those that are typically regarded as capital, such as plant and equipment—some recoverable value is implied. Assuming that the process element is likely to survive, the capital cost of supporting the process needs to be known. If it is possible that the process could be abandoned, or significantly changed, then the net write-off cost must be known.

In some organizations, temporary capital is provided through loans of equipment from manufacturing work in process or marketing finished stock. The equivalent capital cost needs to be known, including possible refurbishment provisions.

Virtual capital covers such expenses as research and development—these are items normally treated as "sunk costs." It is *not* intended to suggest that these costs be capitalized (if this is not already permissible). However, major expenditures may have been made against expectations of result. Changes that result in the abandonment of work not only imply abandoning the sunk costs (with no recoverable value) but also abandoning capability (skills) that may not be redeployable or may imply cost of recreating capability.

Investment costs can become particularly important if process changes are considered that discontinue activities or merge activities, particularly across budgeting boundaries.

## Input Costs

These are typically material costs that flow through the value process. In a sense these are uncontrollable costs except at the purchasing policy level. It is useful to know both annual costs and the flow of these. When process steps are separated, these costs will be repeated and can give a distorted view of the costs of the value process.

These costs can often be affected by both internal process structure changes and business network redesign. Large batches may imply inventory costs and better prices; small batches may imply administrative costs and higher prices. Just-in-time systems may be related to "program buying."

## Process/Operation Costs

These are usually labor and services and local labor-related overheads. These are the local costs that are incurred in connection with a process element, whether the element is an operational or an administrative process.

## Preincurred and Postincurred Costs

Usually difficult to identify initially, provision for such costs should be made, since the failure to identify them can lead to major distortions.

An example of preincurred cost arises where additional costs are associated with bought-in materials in anticipation of later reductions in quality costs (such as rework) and servicing. By increasing the specification of a bought-in product, requiring the supplier to undertake higher levels of testing, or give higher standards of warranty, an organization may incur higher procurement costs in the form of higher prices. These can subsequently be offset against savings in quality inspection of inbound logistics, in rework deriving from quality inspection in outbound logistics or in field service costs.

Postincurred costs are generally rework costs, repairs, warranty costs, and so on, and are often the consequence of "cheapest source," or some process nonconformance, where the cost of correcting the nonconformance is avoided, such as eliminating or postponing retraining costs.

## Overheads

Some understanding of the process for derivation and allocation of overheads is required. Sufficient information is necessary so that if some process stage is eliminated, relevant overhead absorption at that stage is recognized, so that all overhead allocations can be changed.

The comments made earlier about the granularity of the Value Process Model apply equally to costs. Sufficient information is required for an outsider to be able to understand what is going on at the level of process detail currently being examined. As the granularity of the Value Process Model is increased in certain sections of the model, so the granularity of the costs will need to be increased as well. However, too much detail too early is unhelpful and a waste of time.

A simple cost processing application running on a personal computer can prove enormously helpful when the process redesign activity is under way.

## LOOKING FOR OPPORTUNITIES FOR BUSINESS PROCESS TRANSFORMATION

Three issues need to be resolved before starting:

1. Understanding and defining criteria that justify change—including the difference between efficiency (saving money) and effectiveness (making money).
2. Getting the right players involved and committed to giving up the time required.
3. Ensuring that the necessary information is available, appropriate information is distributed, and time is given by the players to understanding what has been distributed.

## Change Criteria

An understanding of change metrics needs to be established at an early stage covering both efficiency and effectiveness. There should be no doubt that some measurable results should derive from change, and where it is "cause" that is measured, the relationship to "effect" must be agreed upon.

Quantification of benefits may be very difficult if process redesign is involved. Some nicely calculated ROI or other performance index may be impossible to calculate and may be a futile exercise in spurious precision. It is likely that the major factors that require change will be so fundamental that ROI is not a helpful measurement—issues as simple as the organization's survival may be involved. However, it is useful to have some quantification of both the consequences and the implications for change and to have the discussion recorded. If it is believed that a change is better, the reasons why it is better need to be agreed on and measurements established.

Generally, the quantification of benefits of changes will be in four areas:

1. *Lower costs:* essentially improved efficiency in the operation of the fundamental business process.

2. *Improved process effectiveness:* may be expressed in terms of a measurable improvement in cash utilization, and hence lower cost, but can equally be expressed in terms of the time taken for processes, the accuracy of the processes, and other quality issues.
3. *Output quality:* related to customer satisfaction and most usefully measured in terms of the reduced cost of nonconformance against specifications or requirements.
4. *Business expansion or change:* reflecting access to otherwise unavailable business opportunities or shifting the area of business opportunities addressed to reduce dependency on reducing opportunities or to focus activities on more productive or profitable opportunities.

In looking at all these change criteria, it is important to recognize that true cost is the total of directly attributed costs and nonconformance costs. The latter may be present in the attributed costs but hidden in the overheads as write-offs and various support costs. Changes in business processes can be justified on the basis of reducing or eliminating nonconformance costs and not just on the basis of reducing directly attributed costs.

## Getting the Right Players

Our experience suggests that appropriate "process stage experts"—who may or may not be members of the senior management team—need to be involved to ensure that debate about changing processes or process elements is well informed. These experts may be strong protagonists of change or provide strong resistance to change. A particularly strong reason for senior management involvement is to provide moderation and stimulus for change.

One "expert" that must be involved is in the domain of information technology and information systems. It is particularly important that progressive thinking about the potential use of IT be contributed, but it is equally important that balanced views of IS implementation (taking advantage of the best available tools) be available to reflect feasibility, costs, time scales, and implications.

It has been argued elsewhere that senior management involvement is essential, and involvement means participation in the thinking and not just passive endorsement of the results.

Top-management leadership enables the group to accept that they must spend time thinking about the unthinkable. It may also appear unthinkable that "obvious" change may be unacceptable because it is not actually critical and implementation is costly and difficult. A compelling reason for top-management involvement is that, by association and participation in the development of change concepts, senior management will not only achieve consensus and buy into the changes but will also be sensitized to the implementation consequences.

The process is an iterative one and can involve long periods of acute mental effort with no apparent result. Top management's involvement during these "low periods" can help maintain focus and momentum and can contribute useful experience and knowledge.

## Other Information Required

Since changes of business processes may have important impacts on customers and suppliers, their interests need to be reflected in the working group. Key facts about major organizations and groups; about critical terms of trade, conditions, and practices; about channel and supply chains; and so forth are most useful.

General environmental information is also an important but less easily justified information subject. The bare minimum probably includes a knowledge of the major government and other agencies with which the organization must deal, involvement in industry associations (and any norms established by those industry associations), and an appreciation of the power and influence of external noncustomer or nonsupplier organizations.

Competitor information is particularly important, particularly if it can be presented in the form of Value Process Models for the competitors. Competitor information is required both for benchmarking and for SWOT (strengths, weaknesses, opportunities, and threats) analysis.

Value Process Models and cost analyses (and cost aggregation programs) should exist before the redesign process begins. This information needs to be supported by other information about the organization whose business processes are under review. Examples include SWOT analysis, major factors perceived to contribute to the successes and failures of the organization, customer and supplier opinion surveys (whether or not they confirm the previous perceptions), human resource management policies, and internal operation policies (for example, interdepartmental trading arrangements).

This can be an overwhelming mass of material, and presentation, particularly for participant preparation before the meetings, must be carefully considered. However, collecting and working through the key facts seems to contribute to the quality of the final product.

## THE REDESIGN PROCESS

Naturally, the specific issues faced by an organization will affect its redesign process. There is no substitute for blinding flashes of inspiration, but these can rarely be summoned on demand. Therefore, a "process consultant" and skilled facilitator will be enormously helpful. As excessive "proceduralization" is normally unproductive, the aim must be to create an environment that will draw from the experience and imagination of all the participants.

The following is a checklist of some process steps that have been found to be helpful:

1. All participants must be familiar with the information that is available. This implies that they must both understand it and agree to its correctness. At this stage relevance is not an important criterion.
2. The Value Process Model of the organization needs to be thoroughly understood.
3. As a first stage, a comparison of the organization's Value Process Model with equivalent models for competitor organizations (or other comparable organiza-

tions) should be made and the differences identified. Perceived advantages, and whether or not they are being exploited by either organization, and perceived disadvantages, and how they are being overcome, should also be identified.

4. Setting aside the Value Process Model, the essential core of the business should be agreed upon, that is, what it is that the organization does that contributes to its wealth and success, and not how it does it. The core performance of the business should then be compared with competitors, both from the viewpoint of the organization itself and also in terms of how outsiders (primarily customers and suppliers) will judge this core performance.

5. An important question to be addressed is what changes should be made to the core business that would improve external perceptions and provide access to more or larger opportunities. The basic issue here is: What would really change the fortunes of the organization?

6. Taking as an assumption that the organization is to maintain its core business, then the question should be explored of how this business would be undertaken if the organization was starting up in a greenfield situation. Alternatively, and possibly a separate question, is: Would the existing business be rebuilt if it was destroyed in a fire?

7. If the organization was starting up in a greenfield situation, how would the core of the business be changed, and how would the new business be implemented? What would be the difference between the existing business and this unconstrained new business?

8. What opportunities can be identified for integration, in terms of either functions, processes, or information? Are there any interfaces between process elements that are particularly difficult and require considerable (regular) management intervention? Are these problems caused by organization and cultural factors, nonharmonized objectives, administrative issues (such as inadequate accounting systems or information availability), or inherent conflicts that arise because the objectives and tasks of the individual process elements are orthogonal?

9. If a new way of running the business could be achieved: (a) What would be the Value Process Model? (b) What would be the cost profile of the new Value Process Model? (c) What are the major transformations that must be achieved? (d) What do these transformations imply, and what are they likely to cost? (e) What are the risks? (f) What are the benefits?

All suggestions, even apparently wild ones, should be explored, including changes that improve internal efficiency and minor (nonradical) ideas. Recording of issues and the essence of arguments is helpful, if only to prevent repetition of debates.

The implications of and for IT can be addressed in several ways. Obvious opportunities for extending the application of IT, sharing common databases, and so on, should be exposed. However, as a more radical transformation of the Value Process Model emerges, the IT implications can either be addressed at the same time or, subject to a minimal feasibility check, set aside to be addressed as a separate subject. In either case, what is implied is the Strategic Alignment Process described in Appendix E. The choice is between incorporating this in the exploration of business process redesign and treating it as a separate activity. The issues cannot be avoided.

## SOME SUGGESTIONS

The following are some additional stimulating issues that experience suggests can be used to provoke thinking:

1. Examine and compare trends in comparative performance of the organization and its competitors—understand the reasons and probable causes of differences.
2. Test the capability of the current Value Process Model to respond to a range of changes in the environment, customers, suppliers, and competitors, covering both numerical factors (increased volumes, reduced volumes, increased prices, reduced prices, etc.), as well as qualitative issues, such as changes in legislation, arrival of new competitors, and significant changes in customer expectations. The purpose here is to test the organization's capability to absorb changes, not just in terms of changes that are recognized and consistent with experience, but also some radical ideas.
3. Consider the existing Value Process Model initially independent of any IT implications. Then rethink the Value Process Model in terms of the wider use of IT and the exploitation of IT capability. This needs to be covered in terms of (a) improving the efficiency of current processes; (b) considering new process options that are enabled by IT; and (c) improving the effectiveness of processes by using IT to improve time and quality issues. The intention here is to introduce some of the concepts of the Strategic Alignment Process, in a simplified or abbreviated form, as a means of stimulating consideration of the interplay of operational and business processes with IT and the implications of close integration of IT with the new processes.
4. Consider both implications of change and the implications of not making changes. Is the maintenance of the status quo sustainable?
5. Identify what changes are going to have to happen anyway, such as moving to new materials, adopting new technologies, introducing new machinery to achieve lower operation costs, and so on.

It may very well emerge that some major changes are going to have to happen in any event, as part of general progress, so that the absorption of other business process changes may be represented as considerably less traumatic than is apparent at first sight. The fact that change is inevitable does not actually make implementation any easier, but it may make the "selling" easier.

## MEASUREMENT

Having developed a new Value Process Model, it is essential to measure the implications. Even if these have to be based on qualitative judgments, there must be a view about the consequences, covering the costs and also addressing external effects such as volume or market share. The costs of implementation must also be estimated. These numbers may be guesses, but it is essential that the rationale is shared. It is here that some simple IT tools can be helpful to reconfigure costs and permit evaluation of alternatives.

Having estimated implications for the proposed new Value Process Model, these can then be contrasted with the current model and a view taken on the trade-off of benefits and implementation costs. Sensitivity analysis is essential, covering not only possible errors in the data but also errors in the assumptions about the environment, time scales, forecasts, and so on. IT tools in the field of decision theory are particularly helpful here. Only after this evaluation of implications can a decision, in principle, be taken to pursue the changes.

## REFERENCE

Porter, M. 1985. *Competitive Advantage.* New York: Free Press.

# APPENDIX E

# The Strategic Alignment Process

## K. HUGH MACDONALD

Considerable efforts have been directed toward the linking of an organization's business strategies and information systems strategies, and a number of processes and techniques have been created to satisfy this requirement. In practice, the requirement is actually rather more complex: strategy, a capable organization (structure, resources and processes), the organization's selection of IT capability must be associated to create the "informated" organization rather than just the "automated" one.

### THE STRATEGIC ALIGNMENT MODEL (SAM)

The Strategic Alignment Model (SAM), introduced in Chapter 5, reflects this view—business success does not depend simply on the harmonization of business strategy and information systems. Rather, it depends on a more complex coalignment of strategy, organization and management processes, IT strategy (the adopted IT platform) and the information systems architecture reflected in terms of the infrastructure and the processes supported by IT. Readers seeking a more detailed description should consult Henderson and Venkatraman (1989a and 1989b).

The model implies the alignment of (1) the organization's strategic positioning in the product/market arena and (2) the particular IT capability adopted by the organization (both of which are "external" issues) with (1) considerations that relate to the choices of organizational arrangements and their implementation, both for the organization as a whole and for the information systems component of the organization, and (2) the processes that are supported by the organization, and in particular those that are supported by information systems (both of which are "internal" issues).

It is not sufficient to harmonize business strategy and information systems applications, although achieving this is both a significant achievement and a valuable one. The real objective must be to build an organizational structure (appropriately resourced and skilled) and internal processes (appropriately focused) that reflect both the organization's strategy and the IT capability the organization has chosen to develop. This IT capability covers both the adoption from the external available technical platform of that IT capability which the organization can afford and support and its exploitation at the level of both infrastructure and applications.

All the outline processes described in Chapter 6 contribute business strategies that are candidates for the strategy portfolio to be adopted by the organization. There are other sources of strategies that derive from the business goals of the organization. Some of the process elements mentioned previously contribute to these as well:

1. The development of a strategy portfolio must include a conventional competitive study and SWOT analysis.
2. This, combined with industry information and other technical information, can help with a consideration of exploitability and interrelatedness, from which can be derived a number of generic strategies that would be expected in the organization's strategy portfolio, as well as the strategies or issues that the organization needs to consider in respect to the positioning the organization may wish to obtain in the Interrelatedness/Exploitability Framework.
3. Changes in strategies can generate needs for the redesign of internal processes, and changes in processes may open up the organization's potential and imply changes that have important effects on strategy.
4. The redesign of business networks has a direct effect on strategies and also affects internal processes and their redesign, which in turn affects strategy.
5. The derived strategies may expand or shift the business domain.
6. The analysis to support previous strategy studies will expose the organization's capacity, skills, and potential reach that can contribute to either expanding or shifting the business domain.

This sequence of activities eventually contributes, with other conventional strategy processes, to the creation of a "draft" business strategy for the organization.

Each component of the Strategic Alignment Model is supported by other processes and concepts. Thus, the three other components are the results of supporting activities, as follows:

1. The IT strategy is derived from a global technology platform which represents the potential capability available to the organization and the key technical issues and trends to be taken into account. The initial draft IT strategy represents the choices the organization has made from the total available potential capability, including those capabilities the organization wishes to acquire and have in-house, as opposed to those that will be obtained in the form of services from other organizations.
2. The organizational infrastructure and processes reflect not only the organizational arrangements of the enterprise but also the processes the organization operates. In part, these may have been derived from or transformed by level 3 and level 4 reviews, business process and business network redesign (as described in Chapter 5). However, neither the organizational infrastructure nor the processes are immutable, and supporting skills and processes are needed to change the processes themselves, in terms of work design, process documentation, and so on, and to address the variety of human resource issues that arise from these changes.
3. The development of IS infrastructures and IS processes is supported by IS implementation processes, tools, and skills.

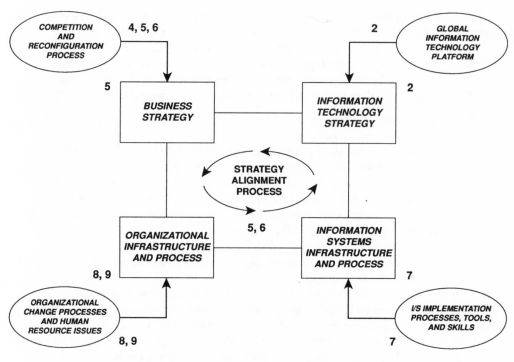

**Figure E-1.** The Strategic Alignment Process (SAP).

SAM and processes intended to build the alignment of the SAM components represent the kernel of a larger process model shown in Figure E-1. Each box and bubble is addressed in this book, and the numbers show the chapters of the book where consideration of these issues is included.

## THE STRATEGIC ALIGNMENT PROCESS (SAP)

The process of achieving alignment, like any other business process, is made up of a number of process stages. There is some feedback between various stages, and consequently the process will exhibit loops and iterations. To be useful, the process must be convergent (fairly rapidly) in the sense that it produces a unique solution that is acceptable and it is evident that continuation of the process will not generate sufficient improvement to justify further execution of the process. In order to achieve convergence, external inputs to process stages must stabilize, and the process needs to be consistent, because it is based on the consistent use of information and application of decision criteria across process stages, particularly iterative stages.

Convergence also implies that the process must have some "forward impulsion" and that feedback must weaken as the process proceeds. If the feedback strengthens, or matches the input, then the process will not converge. This instability is similar to the oscillations encountered in some numerical methods and must be recognized and eliminated.

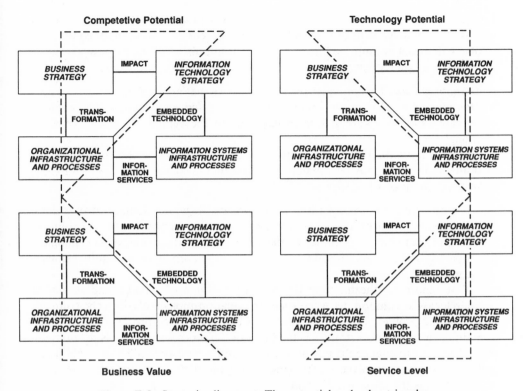

**Figure E-2.** Strategic alignment: The potential and value triangles.

The Strategic Alignment Model implies a balancing act between internal and external factors and between the business domain and the IT domain. The strategic position of the organization in the product/market arena must be supported internally by an appropriate choice of organizational arrangements, reflected by the organizational infrastructure and processes. The organization's structure, infrastructure, and processes must be supported by an appropriate information systems infrastructure and processes that reflect a series of choices about IS organizational arrangements and implementation methods. These must be supported by an appropriate IT strategy, derived from selections made in the IT marketplace, which in turn supports the business strategy with required business products and services. Establishing perfect stability and harmony among these four components is not a simple matter and cannot be resolved by decree.

The essence of SAP depends on the use of the value and potential triangles shown in Figure E-2. The process is decomposed into the progressive stabilization of each of these triangles. This implies the sequential alignment of the elements of each triangle, while assuming that the fourth element in SAM remains stable (and will look after itself in due course). The balancing act for each triangle requires a priority system applied consistently to each triangle.

A rotational process is required, in which each triangle is aligned in turn. By consistent cycling, better alignment of all components will be progressively achieved.

To achieve convergence and consistency requires both a constant direction of rotation and the management of feedback in the alignment of each triangle, so that the feedback does not swamp the forward rotational impulsion of the process stages.

Each triangle represents a problem domain with three components:

1. *Domain anchor.* This provides the change forces that are applied to the domain.
2. *Domain pivot.* This is the problem area being addressed within the problem domain (and in Figure E-2 it corresponds to the right-angle corner of each triangle).
3. *Impacted domain.* This is the component that is affected by any changes to the domain pivot and may be a major constraint on the changes that can be adopted in the domain pivot.

The domain anchor is the input to the process stage; the domain pivot is confirmed and improved by the input; there are some constraints on the freedom of change to the domain pivot implied by the initial status and the prospects of changing the impacted domain; and the adopted changes of the domain pivot require changes in the impacted domain.

If we ignore for the moment the issue of direction of rotation and assume a counterclockwise rotation, let us consider the relationships involved in the competitive potential problem domain. IT strategy is the input to the process stage; it is the domain anchor. Business strategy is the focus of the process stage and is the domain pivot. Freedom to change the business strategy will be constrained by the viability of and the time scales involved in changing the organizational infrastructure and processes, which is the impacted domain.

The primary requirement of the process stage is to consider changes to the business strategy in the light of contributions from the IT strategy, confirm the business strategy, and determine the change requirements (impacts) on the organizational infrastructure and processes.

In a generalized form, the process is taking account of the constraints and contributions of the domain anchor on the domain pivot; noting any unacceptable constraints or unneeded contributions from the domain anchor; and, after taking account of limitations on the freedom to change the impacted domain, resolving and confirming the content of the domain pivot and determining the changes to be considered in the impacted domain.

This can be expressed as a simple linear model, as shown in Figure E-3. There is strong input from the domain anchor on the domain pivot and weak feedback from the domain pivot to the domain anchor. There is weak input to the domain pivot from the impacted domain, with the primary output of the process stage being the revision and confirmation of the domain pivot, together with strong requirements for changes on the impacted domain implied by the refined domain pivot.

SAP is a series of applications of this linear model to each triangle in turn. By cycling around the model, an iterative process will be executed that will progressively improve the alignment of the four components on each cycle. The key questions are:

1. Where to start?
2. Which direction to follow—clockwise or counterclockwise?

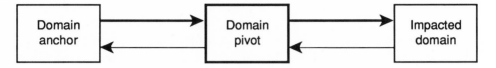

**Figure E-3.** Inputs and feedbacks in each problem domain triangle.

3. How many times to cycle?
4. Where to stop a cycle if an incomplete cycle is required in finishing the process?

Based on our experience to date, the following suggestions are put forth.

## Where to start

The starting point should contain a domain pivot that is external; that is, the issues to be addressed in the first process stage are those that affect the organization and are outside the organization, since this is where the opportunities lie and where less control probably exists. Changing the organization, its management infrastructure and processes, and the uses made of information systems may present major problems, but they are entirely internal.

Thus, the first domain pivot should be either business strategy or IT strategy. In most cases, what is available from the global technology platform and can be adopted as an IT strategy is more constrained by the capability of the organization to exploit the technology than by the capabilities of IT itself. (In certain extreme cases, this assumption may not be correct, but these are exceptions.) Hence, business strategy should be adopted as the first domain pivot.

## Direction of Rotation

If business strategy is the first domain pivot, then the choices are between the organizational infrastructure and processes and the IT strategy as domain anchor, with respectively IT strategy and the organizational infrastructure and processes as the impacted domain. In practice, IT should serve the organization, and changing the organization and its processes to satisfy strategy requirements is a far more significant task than changing the IT strategy. Thus, it is clear that the direction of the process rotation should be counterclockwise.

## How Many Times to Go Around the Cycle

Iterating to perfection at infinity is unproductive. A more useful goal is to seek significant constructive improvement from each process stage and to stop when it is clear that the effort involved in another cycle is not justified by the anticipated improvement or refinement. Because of provision for feedback in the full process, a minimum of two cycles is required to allow every feedback loop to be closed. In practice, the most difficult cycle is the first one, since new information is involved and must be absorbed by those persons engaged in SAP. The second cycle will be quicker.

The minimum number of cycles—two—should be sufficient to obtain adequate convergence and significant alignment among the four components of SAM. If it is clear that there is still considerable scope for improvement of alignment, with a significant number of unresolved issues outstanding, then a further full cycle may be justified. It is suggested that some measurement of fit should be determined, related to the goals of the organization, and it must be demonstrable that a completed cycle has not met this requirement, and that a further cycle will probably do so, before a third cycle is undertaken.

## Where to Stop

When a process stage yields no practical change in a forward direction (in the sense that implementation cannot be achieved within the limitations of the planning horizons), then it would seem that further progress around SAP is unproductive. Provided a minimum of two complete cycles have been completed, and there are no major unclosed feedback issues, the process can be stopped. In practice, it seems sensible to complete a cycle.

## PREPARATION FOR THE STRATEGIC ALIGNMENT PROCESS

Most of the issues regarding participation and information preparation that have been addressed in Chapter 6 apply to SAP.

At each process stage, the key players, besides top management, are those managers and their top advisers who "own" the main issues in the domain pivot. During the competitive potential stage, for example, business managers responsible for strategies that have derived from business process redesign and business network redesign need to be involved. In addition, effective representation from all the other components of SAP need to be involved. A balance between involvement, leading to commitment, and large, potentially unproductive meetings is needed.

Simple documentation is required to support individual process stages. This should ideally be presented in "bullet form," covering each SAM component, and with a separate "pack" assembled from "modules" covering each of the four SAP process stages. (Duplication of information for those participating in multiple stages should be avoided.) Supporting documentation—that is, evidence and argument—should exist and be available if needed and should not be included in the basic process stage pack. As before, prereading must be assumed, and each session should start with an information understanding and resolution session, to ensure common assumptions and understanding.

## Business Strategy

This should identify the business scope of the organization, the key organization capabilities and weaknesses or vulnerabilities, and the governance policies that influence or change the business strategy, that is, integrated, centralized, decentralized, collaborative, regulatory effects, and so on.

Since SAP applies as much to strategies with a significant IT component as to those without such a component, all strategies should be included. IT relevance may be exposed. Existing strategies should thus be enhanced by new strategies derived from the supporting processes discussed earlier, as well as strategies derived from all other processes employed by the organization.

Strategies should be supported, in bullet form, by statements of the critical assumptions, critical decision points, "triggers" and "signals" (evidence that will confirm the effectiveness or relevance of strategies or indicate their failure or inappropriateness), and the critical success factors for the organization.

In the case of all strategies, organization capabilities, and weaknesses, the "owners" should be identified—that is, those organizations and organizational positions that are accountable for the implementation of strategies, development and maintenance of capabilities, and the correction of weaknesses.

## Organizational Infrastructure and Processes

The basic requirement is the organizational structure and the operational assumptions about the structure. Key processes need to be identified, together with their relationship to strategies. All processes must have identified process owners.

The status of structure and processes should be noted—how well established, plans for change, and so on. Each process should be supported by a clinical assessment covering user views and management views of the effectiveness of the process, limitations, competitive significance, and so on.

Available skills should be identified, with respect to both the operation of the organization and the operation of the processes. The capabilities for modifying both organization and processes should also be addressed.

It is particularly important that the status and assessments of processes and skills reflect, as accurately as possible, the true nature of those processes and skills. It is better to underestimate the skills of the organization and overestimate the weaknesses than to produce too optimistic an assessment of the organization's capability.

## IT Strategy

This should describe the adopted IT platform, those elements from the global platform that have been adopted by the organization.

This covers products (both hardware and software), services and skills, policies, adopted tools, standards, and so on, together with an expression of the capabilities possessed by the organization to exploit the adopted technology.

What is identified is the technology scope that has been absorbed by the organization, the governance to be applied (centralized/decentralized purchasing authority, policy control, etc.), and the distinctive capabilities possessed by the organization in the exploitation of the technology.

## The IT Infrastructure and Processes

This should describe the applications infrastructure (e.g., the databases that are being maintained, network capability available), the IT processes (both operational and implementation processes), their owners and internal customers, and the status and a judgment of the value of the processes.

## General Supporting Information

Information that has been developed for the supporting strategy processes, such as industry information, customer information, competitor documentation, and benchmarks, should be available to support discussion during the process stages.

## SAP CYCLE, TIMING, AND CONTEXT

The overall process involves a series of process stages, each concerned with one potential/value triangle, and progressively cycling around the Strategic Alignment Model. The first circuit will be relatively slow as those involved need to understand the overall process, the individual process stage, and the language used, and to become familiar with the information that is available.

The meetings addressing each process stage in the first circuit may take a day or more, depending on the number of innovations, the experience the organization has with formalized planning processes, the quality of the information preparation, and so on. The meetings will speed up as familiarity with the processes develops. There is a great deal of learning in the first circuit, which includes learning about the organization itself and the assumptions about the organization, its business and capability, and the strategies being followed and proposed.

One approach we have found useful is to start with an orientation session in the form of a general discussion of SAP, and a presentation and debate covering general environmental information relating to the industry or industries within which the organization operates. The environmental information (economic, government, etc.) is often taken for granted, and such a session can generate an awareness of external changes that can otherwise be easily lost.

Subsequent cycles will be quicker. A second cycle may be completed in one to two days, and a third cycle, if needed, could take less than half a day. The intention is that each cycle should progressively solidify the content of the domain pivot for each of the problem domain triangles. After two cycles, the incremental improvement gained from a third cycle will be relatively small, and implementation can probably commence after the second cycle.

In the brief comments on the SAP process stages that follow, it is assumed that convergence after two cycles can be achieved. The third cycle is really a further, and hopefully final, repetition of the second cycle.

Strategic alignment is *not* achieved if the issues raised in SAP process stage meetings are only addressed in further process stage meetings. It is assumed that strategy and problem owners will take away from each process stage meeting the obligation to address the challenges exposed by the meeting and to ensure, outside the meetings, that feedback and requirements are reviewed and constructive responses prepared for later relevant process stage meetings. It is not sufficient to pass on the problems to others—those attending the process stage meetings are expected to bring solutions to the next meeting, and not just a report that they have "passed the parcel."

This clearly implies that, besides the involvement of a process consultant and facilitator, excellent secretarial support is needed to record issues and provide some "chasing" outside the meetings. Top management must make it clear that this is an important task and that thoughtful and thorough action is required outside meetings.

Strategy alignment should precede budgeting and should not be confused by budgeting constraints. This must be tempered by common sense—broad investment and budgeting parameters need to be known, and each process stage needs to be checked for general consistency within the overall investment and budgeting parameters of the organization.

## CYCLE 1, STAGE 1: COMPETITIVE POTENTIAL

In the first process triangle, IT strategy provides the domain anchor, business is the domain pivot, and the organizational infrastructure and processes represent the impacted domain.

The primary objective is to develop a general confirmation (provisional endorsement) of the business strategies, take account of IT opportunities as provided of the domain anchor, and identify any obvious IT strategy shortfalls or unwanted capabilities.

The secondary objective is to assess the fit of the organizational structure, processes, and skills to support the strategies and to identify needs for change.

If the discussion of these issues suggests that certain strategies should be subject to major change or should be rejected, then the processes that generated those strategies should be reactivated to either confirm the relevance of the strategies or reassess the strategies in the light of the constraints that have emerged during the competitive potential strategy domain review.

## CYCLE 1, STAGE 2: BUSINESS VALUE

Business strategy has now become the domain anchor, and the organizational infrastructure and processes is the domain pivot. The impacted domain is the IS infrastructure and processes.

The primary purpose of this process stage is to fit the requirements from the competitive potential process stage to the organizational infrastructure and processes. This involves considering the business transformations implied by the strategies, assessing the changes (feasibility, implications, impact elsewhere, etc.), and noting problems in implementation as they will affect strategy effectiveness, for review in the competitive potential process stage in the second cycle.

As changes to the organizational infrastructure and processes are identified, the supporting change processes need to be activated to assess the implications, both for change in the organization and its processes and for setting up the necessary human resource management processes that will need to be undertaken. These supporting processes are required to report back at the next visit to the business value process stage in cycle 2.

The second objective is to assess the fit of the information systems infrastructure and processes, and their support of the organization process, and to identify need for changes. What is being identified here are the new information products and services that are required to support the new organizational infrastructure and processes.

## CYCLE 1, STAGE 3:  SERVICE LEVEL

Organizational infrastructure and processes have now become the domain anchor, and the IS infrastructure and processes have become the domain pivot. IT strategy is the impacted domain.

The primary purpose of this stage is to establish the fit between the improved organizational infrastructure and processes and the existing IS infrastructure and processes, and to assess the implications of the change requirements in terms of new IS products and services. This will involve activating appropriate supporting processes to develop plans for the changing of infrastructure and IS processes. Problems that may result in the failure to satisfy business value requirements must be identified for review when the business value process stage is revisited during the second cycle.

The second objective is to identify the changes to the IT strategy that will be needed to support the technology transformation required for the enhanced IS infrastructure and processes.

## CYCLE 1, STAGE 4:  TECHNOLOGY POTENTIAL

Finally, in the first SAP circuit, the IS infrastructure and processes has become the domain anchor, the IT strategy is the domain pivot, and the impacted domain is the business strategy, thus completing the loop.

The primary purpose of this process stage is to establish the fit between the required IS infrastructure and processes and the IT strategy, moderated by the changes derived from the service level process stage. At the same time, feedback from the competitive potential process stage in the first cycle must be assessed. As part of this, searches of the global technology platform may need to be initiated to establish the new IT products and services required to support the strategic alignment. (These should have occurred after the first competitive potential process stage, and should have been completed by the time the technology potential process stage meeting is held.)

The secondary purpose of this process stage is to establish the unresolved constraints applicable to competitive potential to be addressed during the second cycle. These would derive from the likely nonavailability of the required IT capability reflected in the IT strategy.

## CYCLE 2, STAGE 1:  COMPETITIVE POTENTIAL REVIEW

This is a replay of the first competitive potential process stage. It aims to review the modified business strategy from cycle 1 against new inputs from the technology potential process stage, and to review the outputs from the strategy reviews in supporting processes initiated in the cycle 1 competitive potential process stage.

The objective is to resolve the strategies and confirm the required changes to organizational infrastructure and processes. In addition, it is necessary to agree to the strategy triggers and signals that will indicate success or failure and set up the necessary monitoring activities. The aim should be to achieve a sufficient level of resolution that this process stage does not need repeating. Repetitive "mini-cycling" of support processes must also be avoided, if necessary by making hard decisions to exclude strategies, even though they are attractive, if implementation cannot be achieved. There is little point in retaining strategies that are no more than dreams, even if happy dreams.

## CYCLE 2, STAGE 2:  BUSINESS VALUE REVIEW

This is intended to review the implementation of proposed changes from the first competitive potential process stage, resolve any (hopefully) minor issues from the second competitive potential review, update the organizational infrastructure and processes, and confirm that these changes can be implemented. Feedback from the change processes and other reviews initiated at the last business value process stage is essential.

The main risks should be identified and correction and monitoring processes established, impacts on the IS infrastructure and processes agreed upon, and various change processes and revised HRM policies committed.

Value system and value process models that reflect the new process goals need to be finalized. Process review triggers and signals must also be established, with appropriate monitoring/control mechanisms.

## CYCLE 2, STAGE 3:  SERVICE LEVEL REVIEW

In this process stage, the proposed changes to the IS infrastructure and processes from the previous cycle are reviewed against the reports from the supporting processes. Final plans for the improved IS infrastructure and IS processes must be documented. Risks from the previous technology potential process stage need to be cleared, and intercept plans developed for new IT strategic capability. Final agreed impacts on the adopted IT platform, expressed as the IT strategy, need to be recorded. Planning of implementations must be initiated.

## CYCLE 2, STAGE 4:  TECHNOLOGY POTENTIAL REVIEW

This process stage closes the second cycle, and should close the SAP as sufficient alignment has been established. Proposed changes from previous service level process stages need to be resolved and matched to the outcome of searches of the global technology platform. The final adopted IT platform is now consistent with the organization's IT strategy.

Projects to absorb the changes and acquire the new products, services, and skills need to be initiated. Any unexploited potential needs to be noted as an input to a further cycle if this is required, or the next strategic review cycle needs to be implemented by the organization.

## CONCLUSION

The achievement of strategic alignment is a valuable precursor to budgeting. It equally contributes to the development and commitment of new HRM policies, new skill acquisition or development programs, IS planning, and many other processes. It has been discussed here in the context of IT and its impact on strategy and organization structure and processes. The process, with some changes, can be applied to other technologies.

Alignment is precious: because it is hard to achieve and is done in the context of major transformations of the organization arising from business process and business network redesign, its implementation deserves care and attention. Just reaching useful agreements may be motivational, and this will help change to come about. Having recorded new strategies, processes, organization structures, IS plans, and so on, will not make them happen.

## REFERENCES

Henderson, John C., and N. Venkatraman, 1989a. "Strategic Alignment: A Framework for Strategic Information Technology Management." Management in the 1990s Working Paper 89-076.
————. 1989b. "Strategic Alignment: A Process Model for Integrating Information Technology and Business Strategies." Management in the 1990s Working Paper 89-077.

# Index

relationship to other capital equipment, 9,
10, 70
trends in, 31
Crane, D. B., 192, 213
CRSs. *See* Computer reservation systems

Databases
distributed, 31; capability of 40–42; shared
access, 34, 35, 38
knowledge-based, 35
as link between company functions, 80
as link between product and service markets,
84–85
Data processing, 11, 56–57
DBMS. *See* Database Management Systems
DECNET, 49, 99
DeLong, D. W., 73
Diebold, J., 124
Digital Equipment Corp.
DECNET, 49, 99
engineering network, 18
process for maintaining employment
security, 240
worldwide installation of MRP system, 209
XCON, 77
Distance, IT ability to compress, 10, 12
cost, 72
by increasing bandwidths, 73–74
by integrating IT functions, 74–75
Drucker, P. F., 193, 209
DuPont
common financial system in Europe, 209
systematic management techniques, 89–90

Eastman Kodak Company
executive support system, 209
IT system implementation, 245; workshops
for, 270
MRPII system: implementation, 246, 272;
limited diffusion of, 273; options, 251; and
employee self-management, 261
Eccles, R. G., 192, 213
Economies of scale, impact of IT on, 18, 63
in across the firm activities, 198
in production, 103–4
Economy, impact of IT on, 63, 124, 228
EDI. *See* Electronic data interchange
Electronic conferencing, 34, 252
Electronic data interchange (EDI), 13, 34,
in business networks, 171, 172
described, 140–1
potential increase in, 40
standards for, 51
Electronic mail, 34
Employment
IT impact on level of, 87, 221; firm
differences in, 229–30, 237–38; from
displacement, 228; reversal of, 229
IT impact on nature of, 88–89, 221–22
need to provide security in, 259–60
robots impact on, 229–30
Ethernet network, 48, 49
Expert systems technologies, 42–43

Exploitability of markets or products, 95
computer reservation systems and, 107–8
dynamics in, 116
and firm profitability, 104
high: and high interrelatedness, 104–9; and
low interrelatedness, 111–16
low: and high interrelatedness, 109–12; and
low interrelatedness, 112–14

Facsimile machines
cost and functionality, 71, 73
as example of low exploitability and
interrelatedness, 113
and interrelatedness, 165
Japanese role in expanding use of, 71, 113,
115
market shares of U.S. vendors, 114, 115
number of, 113
price, 114
Flexibility, IT
human adaptability and, 78
to increase flexibility of manufacturing
processes, 78, 91
Flexible manufacturing systems (FMS), 227,
234
Flynn, P., 238, 239
Ford Motor Company
strategic partnership with Ryder Truck, 14,
199
time needed for product development, 197,
209

Galbraith, J. R., 193
on management of integration, 200, 217 *n*22
General Electric Company
computer-integration management system,
253
investment in global communications
technology, 217 *n*23
General Motors Corp.
computer-integrated management system,
245; implementation, 246; job design for,
247; start-up, 247; union involvement in,
266
manufacturing automation protocols, 99
technological and human resources
management, 224–25, 249
training of employees for new technology,
258–59
Germany, vocational training, 241
Goldstein, S., 268
Goodman, P., 246
Graham, M., 234
Griffith, T., 246

Hamel, G., 196
Hardware, 4
general advances in, 38–39
"open system" for, 105, 118
trends in, 31
Hauptman, Oscar, 279
Henderson, John C., 7, 185, 210, 280, 283,
284, 310

Walker, Gordon, 282
Wallace, Robert, 210, 211
Walton, Richard E., 8, 89, 244, 255
WANs. *See* Wide-area networks
Western Union, network of public money
    transfer outlets, 97
Westlaw legal knowledge base, 76
Westney, D. Eleanor, 236, 283, 286
Whisler, T. L., 217
Wide-area networks (WANs), 36, 48
Williamson, O. E., 84
Wilson, Diane D., 7, 279, 285, 286, 287
Womack, J., 249
Woodward, J., 227
WordPerfect, sales, 112
Word processing programs
    as example of high interrelatedness and low
        exploitability, 110
    impact on employment, 229
    proliferation of, 111–12
Workstations
    as enablers and inhibitors of *1990s* IT, 42–43
    functions, 189

increased connectivity from, 31, 34–35
potential progress in, 27–28
specialized, 37
trends in, 31–32

Xerox
    planning and control process for strategic
        business unit, 210
    storage of legal knowledge, 76
    time for bringing products to market, 197
    worldwide document management network,
        73
X-OPEN Group
    alliance with IBM for open environment
        software, 106
    efforts to establish open standards around
        UNIX system, 105

Yates, JoAnne, 8, 61, 80, 82, 83, 84, 87,
    205

Zuboff, Shoshana, 16, 62–63, 76, 77, 212, 235,
    236, 258